JOURNEY TO MY MASTER TEACHER

Dedication

This book is dedicated to Ramtha, JZ Knight, the students of Ramtha's School of Enlightenment and one student in particular - my daughter, Tiara Nia Jane Webb for her patience and love. She is indeed "a great woman of the future."

TABLE OF CONTENTS

Acknowledgements

Compiling these stories has been a journey of love. I am grateful to all of the story-writers and thank you profoundly. I honour all those who assisted with their guidance and words of encouragement. I would like to give special thanks to the master students of RSE who assisted in making this book happen: Mitja Kadow for championing the project and helping to get people writing; Greg Simmons for his sterling advice and wisdom; Jaime Leal-Anaya for transcribing Ramtha's teaching and for his editorial advice; Paulina Amador of Holo-Graphics, for the creative book cover and assistance; and my editor Heidi Smith, whose wisdom in editing is second to none, and for her kind intellectual and emotional support.

I would like with much gratitude and love to thank JZ Knight for the sacrifice and love that she gives in presenting Ramtha to us. To our Master Teacher Ramtha the Enlightened One, there are no words.

Author's Note

Ramtha's School of Enlightenment has thousands of students from forty-nine countries. Some have left their countries of origin to move closer to the school, while others fly to Yelm, Washington, for periodic visits to pursue knowledge, then return home and continue to apply it. The ways in which we found Ramtha's school and the reasons we pursued it are as individual as we are. However, all of us share an appreciation for the powerful, magical being who is our beloved teacher, Ramtha.

The contributors to this book have lived rich and diverse lives. We range in age from 21 to 70+ and span a wide variety of cultures, countries and experiences. Many of us have found the process of writing our stories to be at once a healing and an opportunity to reflect on who we are, where we've been, where we are, and where we're going. We hope that this book serves as an explanation to those who have wondered what drew us here and an inspiration for others who are considering doing the same. The words that follow are in our individual styles of writing and language.

THE INITIATE'S JOURNEY TO THE MASTER TEACHER

Excerpt adapted from: Ramtha, *Evening with Ramtha on the Field.*
Yelm, May 10, 2005. Ramtha's School of Enlightenment.

I have set up this school from elder times in which the initiates were either selected by a master teacher, their fathers sent them, or the initiates started the journey from a different part of the world to find the teacher and the school, a super school set apart from the madness of the marketplace. They had to live through the journey, the desert, and hostile tribes of robbers, highwaymen, and merchants to find it. We could take all of that and put it in modern-day terms: deceivers, the marketplace, the highway, and people surviving on a day-to-day basis. Imagine trekking across some forbidden, arid continent and having to spend your night under the stars or by some limpid pool. In the hopes of keeping your mind on finding your master so that destiny and that silver cord of want and desire will not be broken by anything that harms you, along the way you learn to be clever and outwit any danger. You learn to then pass from one land into another land, from one principality into a land that is forested with all of its creatures, predators, its indigenous people, and its tribes.

So many great initiates in antiquity walked those paths that went through the jungles and forests which led to the highest peaks in Turkey, the highest peaks of the roof of the world, those meadows with ferocious beasts, with indigenous tribes people and cannibalistic monkeys on the scent. If you are endeavoring to have no scent, eat no meat and you will not smell like it. Initiates had to learn to keep their silver cord connection unbroken to reach the door of the master's abode. This is all a true story. This has all happened.

If you survived the journey to get there, it allowed you to already own the world of highwaymen, robbers, deceivers, social consciousness, and fear. To be absolutely caught up in the imagination of your fear, thinking that the shadows that lurk under the moon are all treacherous, would nearly cause your heart to break in one night. Living through the treachery of shadows cures it in the mind as well.

The long journey to the high places of knowledge, which supersedes common human beings, is born, and the fire lives in a few. If they are lost along the way, it will be reflected in another life. In today's civilization all of these horrors and terrors are now confined within a city block, on a freeway, or the Internet, so nothing changes. It changes form but it doesn't really change. The students who walk through all of these landscapes to find their teacher are the ones who are going to make it out of here, and they live in the future. They live elsewhere.

In coming to school, your life is like the journey and romance of students leaving their homeland, their father's house, their mother's house, looking for greater knowledge — a desire of destiny that is a future place that lives in the mountains somewhere — and finding it. That is where they are going. They are finding that silver thread, their lifeline, that unfolds them into the future and their destiny and takes them through all of this morass.

You only had to move here from Illinois, New Jersey, terrible jungle, Los Angeles — lost angels, literally — and you are here at school. Coming to the great school and knocking on your master's door is about finding that silver cord and remembering why you came here. In this modern-day romance novel where teachers are very rare to find — a lot of wannabe people out there are stopped along the way — the true journey of becoming extraordinary is what you have come here to find.
As I said in the old days in your time, the Antichrist, the saboteur, is the personality.

The structure of the personality is a very dangerous place. It might as well be the jungles of India, the arid places and the forests of Turkey, the highwaymen, the robbers, the treacherous people, and the unsafe shadows. It might as well be all of that, because it is. The personality is all the knowledge you know in your father's house and your mother's house. When you walk right outside that door, all of the world will be based upon what you learned in your father's house and your mother's house. It will be in your genes. It will be in your culture. It will be in your neighborhood. The entire world is contained on the doorstep of your father's house, your mother's house. Isn't it interesting that the whole world, the whole future, is framed by the experiences, those things that happened to you right outside of your father's house before you even started the journey to the master in the Far North. Your whole world and your opinions are based upon what you learned in your father's house and your mother's house. Just imagine the whole world, billions of planets, the journey from here to the top of the mountain where the great school is, all of it can be assumed by the people who live in that house. They base their whole interpretation on where they have lived. That is their world-view.

People speak with absolute certitude about something they know nothing about. They say, "You are never going to make it. You are going to go there to India or to that great mountain. You are never going to make it." Their world-view is based upon that house. The moment they take a hundred steps away from their father's house, their world-view is about to change.

Great students who came into this life took the journey to find their teacher. They had to make the journey and traverse continents, cross raging rivers, be a part of villages, indigenous peoples, highwaymen, robbers, deceivers, and be afraid of shadows at night. What allowed them their connection to find their master teacher in the great school hidden in the mountains at the roof of the world was abiding that silver cord that kept their mind arriving at their master's house at the end of the journey. When they were afraid at night, all they thought about was that door opening and entering to begin the work of the higher order, the Great Work, to understand themselves in a deeper, more meaningful way. They are initiates of the Great Work. When their minds went to that imaginative door — not knowing what it looks like but knowing that it opens and they get to come in — they were able to have a world-view that transcended the campfire in Turkey outside the forests and being robbed, or indigenous people asking where you are going and saying you will never make it across the river, across that desert, and that landscape. The world-view of those people ends there but the initiate's doesn't.

This is not an allegory. It is a true story. It has always happened to a select being, a select few, whether initiated by their parents to study under a teacher in a school far away or by the students themselves who have elected to come here to this school. The one thing they are clear and know is that there is knowledge they have come here to find, and they are going to find it. They make their way here, which means that the silver cord has connected them as destiny to the master's house. In the mind of the master, the master picks up that cord and knows they are coming. Then the initiation is happening to the student who is going through all these perils and overcoming the fears of their mind, their world-view, and their thoughts. How they thought things were isn't necessarily the way they are at all. Their father's house has now disappeared.

By the time the student arrives, the student's greatest celebration is that he has found his master teacher and the master teacher accepts him into the class. A whole different work can now begin because the student is already here and the deconstructing of his world-view or his personality was overcome, which started a hundred yards from his father's house or the hovel he left behind to make the solitary journey to find the Great Work and the school.

The greatest of our students then would be those who really have worked on deconstructing and mastering the concepts of who they thought they were and changing in their mind to become who they are. Their ideas don't have to go through the personality anymore. They are simply ideas that are taken, initiated upon, the body then experiences them in life, and now we have a whole different perception. We are two hundred yards outside of our father's house, and we will make it. We will make it to Turkey. We will make it to the mountains, from the mountains across the river, and from the river into the long desert. From that we will exist through those tribes. We will not be eaten by wild animals. We will not be hunted down. We will not be drowned by raging waters, by the torrents of life. We will have a world-view that will change all the way to where we rap on the door of our master's house. By the time we arrive there, we will have already conquered everything that our personality was — everything.

— Ramtha

RENEE WEBB
Bermuda

YOU REALLY DO KNOW EVERYTHING…

From out of nowhere the darkness fell. It became pitch black in an instant. I instinctively turned and ran for the dune buggy which I could hear but not see. The engine was still running in case I needed a fast get away from the male nomads crossing the desert. A lunar eclipse, I thought, my mind racing ahead. I had been to Saudi Arabia often enough to know that night does not fall at two o'clock in the afternoon, and never as suddenly as this darkness.

My thought had not finished before the wind and the desert sand began to swirl. It raged, engulfing me. I kept moving in the direction my mind told me to head for. Every orifice was filling up with sand. My nostrils, my ears, my hair, and every inch of my body and clothing were thrashed with the red-hot desert sand. Luckily, I had recently returned from skiing in the Swiss Alps and was sporting my new ski shades which adequately protected my eyes. My eyes avoided the blinding desert sand which was a blessing, although the darkness prevented me from seeing anything.

I continued to bounce over the dunes, without any understanding of what was going on. The words "sand storm" never entered my mind; I had no point of reference for what was happening. Although the wind was forcing sand and darkness upon me, I had no fear. I certainly did not fear the wind for I always loved the havoc that it caused in the storms and hurricanes of my childhood.

The desert had been calm; the skies a clear radiant blue as I bounced on the rich red sand in my matching sand-coloured dune buggy. I had no particular destination; I wanted to explore what I had not seen. The ability to drive freely as a woman on Saudi soil was a relief. I found a new freedom of womanhood as I drove over the private estate which covers thousands of acres. I drove for miles, and what seemed like hours. I stopped now and then to gaze at the vast desert, the stillness reminding me of the ocean.

I had suddenly come upon the nomads and their camels as they moved along under the hot desert sun. They looked quite startled to see me; all stood still. I came close to them wanting to capture the moment in photographs. I dismounted from my jeep, but kept the engine running. I was not familiar with the temperament of desert nomads and I wanted to ensure a quick escape if I needed it.

I was clearly a mystery to them; they looked at me as if they had seen a UFO. They were in fact gawking at a western woman dressed, not in the normal Saudi attire, which I wore outside of this private ranch, but in blue jeans, a red sleeveless top, and ski shades; riding in a bright red dune buggy in the middle of the desert! They stared at me with curiosity, amazement and caution. I was clearly not something they were used to looking at. They did not utter a word but continued to stare at me and not move an inch. I was indifferent, although the sound of the camels, which grew loud the nearer I approached, was disconcerting.

Now I found myself racing across the desert with the stinging force of nature being driven by a raging wind hitting me from all sides. I drove for what seemed like an inordinate amount of time. In the distance, near what turned out to be our encampment, there were fifty or so cars, trucks, and dune buggies lined up around the desert's edge to guide me back all of their lights blazing. My Saudi hosts, who were members of the Saudi royal family, were relieved to see me return for they knew the treachery of desert storms and the potential of being buried alive when the sand shifts in an instant.

After I had washed myself from head to toe, we had a feast in one of the huge tents. There I heard of the dangers of sand storms. Mine had died down as quickly as it had come. The day meandered on as another dry, hot, calm one.

This was my first brush with what could have been my demise. My innocence, my ignorance of the events occurring around me, and my love of the wind had protected me. There was no panic or adverse emotion. I was simply detached from what was going on. It was just another great adventure.

While my Moslem friends thanked their God for my safe arrival, I had no time for religious dogma. However, I knew that something was protecting me; it always had. I was yet to learn to what that was, for the concept of the God of religion I had long dismissed as outrageous.

I came into the world born on a 21-mile square rock in the middle of the Atlantic Ocean knowing that there was more to life than what I could see, touch, and feel. From an early age, I knew much about the world of the unobvious. I remembered as a child that I came from elsewhere and that ultimately I wanted to go back there. I remembered past lifetimes and I did not understand why I could not return to them. I could vividly remember other places that I had no other way of knowing existed. I believed that my parents were not my parents and that my real parents would come back for me.

I was accused as a child of being "a know it all who always has the answers for things she should not know." I was born into a family who had low tolerance for "mouthy" children, and an education system that tolerated them even less. The criminal offence of physical abuse of a child was an unknown entity back then. I was subjected to beatings at home and at school for rambling on about whatever subject entered my mind.

I had a tumultuous childhood. My family and neighbours lived for the day, from pay cheque to pay cheque. They partied on Saturdays and some went to church on Sundays, although mine was not a particularly religious family. The children were sent to Sunday school a lot, but this was mainly so that the adults would have a Sunday break from us for none of them went to church except for weddings, funerals and perhaps Easter and Christmas.

There were the fun times of basking in the sun and swimming in the ocean from sun up to sun down, of raiding the gardens of our farmer neighbours and having "cook outs" in the trees with watermelons for desert. These summer days I wanted to last forever. We played games in the sea, swung from branch to branch in the trees like "Tarzan", and sent telepathic messages to each other. I had a large contingent of family and neighbours to run and play with. There was never a dull moment when we were exploring the hills, and jumping off the cliffs into the ocean below. I have the many bodily scars from being a child among children warriors to prove it. I had my head split open with a bottle, my chin busted open with a stone, and was thrown from a cliff. The other child warriors and I survived it all; none of us died, but there were some close calls from dog attacks, and near drowning.

I was considered a bright child who skipped class and succeeded in entering one of the best high schools on the Island. When asked by the teacher in religion study class (who happened to be the headmaster) whether I believe in God, I promptly announced that I did not. The God of the Bible was a punishing vindictive God who would allow people to burn in hell. I thought that was wicked and evil and I did not want to follow that God, and I never did.

My mother adored me. She was proud of the fact that I was cute, bright and "light skinned." Being a bi-racial child in a country founded on colonialism, racism and segregation meant that I would have a better chance to succeed than my "dark skinned" cousins. I was made to feel that I was special, could do anything, and should not marry anyone "darker then me." I rejected the marrying bit very early and chose never to marry at all, like my mother and some of her siblings had done. Children were sired without due regard for the institution of marriage. I grew to learn that being born within or outside of wedlock made no difference whatsoever as to how we functioned or did not function as an adult. It was a moot point in my family.

I grew up with three sisters and thirty-six first cousins. We were relatively poor, working class, and a force to be reckoned with. We were always getting into trouble in school. If there were neighbours of our school who had windows broken, gardens crushed or anything else that naughty children got up to, the headmistress would march us to the front of the assembly hall to confess our crime. I don't remember that we ever did.

Throughout my life, I had a deep and profound love for women (love, as I understood it to be). I was raised in a house of females with their children. Mine was a strong matriarchal family. Women were in control of everything and were clearly the dominant sex during my childhood. They were also more numerous than the men who they seemed to rule and dominate, although they suffered physical and verbal abuse from them. My mother, aunts and grandmother were all bossy. They displayed overbearing characteristics which I would later understand to be a form of protection. It was difficult to define their place. They all worked and in some cases were the only breadwinner for their children.

My grandmother, who left her 10 children, some of whom were quite young, to go and live with her lover, was feared. I remember her as beautiful and kind although aggressive sometimes. It was with her that I spent my first night away from home at age twelve. I was so traumatized at being away from my mother, sisters and cousins I could not sleep. At first sign of light, I was off running to find them. The thrill of adventure and change had not yet taken root.

I was not reared around male strength or kindness. The men in my life I saw were abusers of women, drunkards, and fathers who abandoned their children. I had one uncle who regularly sexually abused the girls in my family, another who slept with his wife's thirteen-year-old daughter and another who raped my eleven-year-old cousin. None were ever punished or ostracized for what they had done. The women stayed with their men while the child victims were sent to live with other relatives or had to stay in their abusive environment.

Unfortunately, the incest and abuse that occurred when I was a child was passed on to my generation. I have a first cousin who sexually abused boys, another who sexually abused younger female cousins and another who was having sex regularly with his thirteen-year-old daughter. The first and the latter cousin were sent to prison for their crimes unlike the abusers of my mother's generation. While I was not sexually abused, knowing what was happening to my cousins hurt and affected me deeply.

My father did not love me, and although I never knew him to drink alcohol, or sexually abuse children, he had abandoned most of us. He was certainly an abuser of women; I had seen that first hand with my mother. He did not play a significant role in my life. He did not know me aside from my very public life later on. He had eight children from three different women and did not interact with most of us. I did not know much about him until I was a grown woman. There were no phone calls on birthdays (I doubt if he knew the date), or spending time together.

My great-grandfather had left Italy at sixteen by boat, eventually landing in Bermuda and marrying my great-grandmother at age nineteen. She was on a boat that was shipwrecked there when she was eight. My mother's ancestry was a combination of Indian and Caribbean. My ancestors from both my parents were seafaring people who had left their homeland seeking a new life. Adventure, seeking the unknown, and something different, is in my DNA.

The men in my life when I was growing up seemed to bring about so much pain. It was a major shock to me when my father hit me with a broom at age seven for "dancing to Christian music." It was another shock when my 5th grade male teacher strapped me with his belt for "talking so much." I withdrew emotionally that year and went from being near the top of my class to 3rd to last place in a class with thirty children. I knew hate for the first time in my life for I despised that teacher.

In my adult life, my childhood influenced me in my natural love and preference for the company of women. However, I also grew to be an abuser, both verbally and physically. Genetic propensity and the social environment in my upbringing had its natural outcome. I was also very much into control, a do as I say kind of person, who was not happy if I did not get my way. My way or the highway was how I related in intimate relationships. I did not know how to communicate feelings, nor did I desire to. I was happy with superficial interaction - nothing too profound unless it was philosophical. I did not know who the real me was, and whoever that me was my sensitivity, insecurity and pain would not allow me to find out.

In spite of my childhood which was very often lonely and sad, I lived a great life. I grew to love adventure, and was motivated to get away from home to find out who and what I really am. I studied abroad and travelled all over the world. I attended university in Canada, the United States and France. I lived in Europe and spent time in the Middle East and many other places. I am a born adventurer who was ultimately searching for me. Even in all of my "fun" times, I was always aware that something was profoundly missing.

I grew to love different cultures, and the diversity of people around the world. I spent time in Egypt, India, the Far East, Australia, Central America, the Caribbean, the United Kingdom, Ireland, Israel, Palestine, Jordan, Saudi Arabia, and countries in Europe too numerous to mention. My travelling was a journey, a calling to find myself. I did not understand why or what, but I knew something or someone was beckoning me.

My twenties were filled with adventure and discovery. I partied a lot, and was sexually promiscuous. It seemed like the natural thing to do. I rationalized that unless I participated I was not qualified to talk about or to judge whatever the world was doing. It was the 1980's in Paris. Everything was so new, and exciting. I learned to speak my first foreign language, and had friends from around the world.

It was the time of all night disco dancing, drugs floating around and lots of drama and adventure. I was all about being in control of myself yet being wild with the exhilaration of the moment. I had difficulty committing to a relationship although I had quite a few over the years; relationships always seemed to get in the way of my "pick up and go" attitude towards life. I did not want to be tied down under any circumstance. Freedom was my mantra - freedom to be wild and undisciplined.

My love for knowledge was the only thing that kept me grounded. I loved studying, and learning new things. I would learn through experiencing places and cultures and through knowledge found in books. I learned about every major religion, travelling to many of the holy sites of the Jewish, Christian, Moslem, Hindu, and Buddhist religions. These observations, and experiencing the practice of religious dogma firsthand, only confirmed why I was never tied to any religion. I knew instinctively that there was more to life than what they had to offer. Therefore, while my three sisters, with whom I was raised, were all into different sects of Christianity I had absolutely no interest. My mother was like me while my father followed a Christian sect. The fact that my mother was not religious, and I was not raised as such, boded well as my future unfolded, for I did not suffer the profound guilt of many of my friends for what they perceived as "wrong."

Through my love of learning, I acquired degrees of high learning up to an honorary Ph.D in Humanities for my life work. I worked in various places, including Paris where I lived for almost nine years. I eventually came back to my country of birth to contribute in the field of business and politics. I believed that the political field was a way to help to evolve my country forward. I was elected in 1993 and served three terms in office during which I rose to be a Minister of Government. There were some great moments, but for the most part the political arena was a very frustrating time for me. I was always thinking and speaking "outside of the box" in my political career. Therefore, I was often undermined, ostracized and politically assassinated for it. However, that did not stop HRH Queen Elizabeth II from awarding me the lifetime title of "Honourable" before my name.

Politics, like religion, I soon discovered would not give me the impetus I needed to find me. Both are about controlling the masses, keeping them believing that all would fall apart without politicians or religious leaders to "guide" the way. Neither is about taking personal responsibility for all of the choices we make in our life. The inequality of the sexes, how women were treated by both was evident. Both the male dominated press and the political system treated women differently. There is an unspoken delineation of standards and expectations with respect to women politicians and leaders.

I had a very public resignation from the Cabinet when the Premier chastised me for defending a pregnant female member of the Cabinet. When I approached him to discuss his treatment of women members, including myself, he berated me with "you cannot get over me or under me young lady, I am the man!" I resigned on the spot; I was and am the woman! I resented him initially, but this incident actually brought me closer to my destiny that was calling.

Inequality towards women practiced by all religions was also disturbing to me as all relegate women to a lower class. Women are not allowed to be priests and can be excommunicated from the Catholic Church, the mother of all churches, for seeking to be one. There are no women Imams in the Moslem religion, and no possibility of a woman Dalai Lama. Who and what is the god of this creation, of inequality, and "tradition?" I often pondered. Once again, as I had done at twelve years old, I rejected that God.

Many memorable events took place on my journeys to foreign places in search for truth and knowledge. I mention a few which inspired my trek and hunger to know life. The fact that I created chaos and a near death experience in a sand storm propelled me forward. I simply went to where I was being led, always with a sense of adventure.

I have been to Egypt many times, during which I visited and studied the pyramids at Abu Simbel, Luxor, Aswan, and in Upper and Lower Egypt. I examined their interior but to this day not the three famous ones at Giza, although I went there a few times. What is the mystery of the foreboding feeling that I get whenever I go near these three grand pyramids? I pondered whether this was a rendering from an experience of another life. I do not know the answer but fate has kept me out of them despite three attempts to enter.

On my first visit to Egypt, my Saudi friend and I decided to horseback ride as far as the eyes could see into the desert while keeping the three huge triad structures of Giza in view. We raced the horses at full speed over the sand dunes, only to return to find the pyramids were closed. A strange gas was emanating from inside the structures so they would not be opened to the public.

On my second visit years later, I arrived for a visit to tour the three magnificent edifices. I stood in line to purchase my ticket, only to be told once I reached the counter that they had just sold the last ticket to the person in front of me. They had reached their quota for the day, and no one else would be entering. I felt indifferent and climbed them instead, peeped into the entrance, and walked away to climb and discover the Sphinx.

On my most recent visit, I was travelling with my ten-year-old daughter, and some friends. We had planned to visit the pyramids at Giza and take in the sights there. We drove to Alexandria, to go to the beach, to visit the great library and other cultural sites. On the day we were to set out for the pyramids we were delayed for some reason. We arrived in the early evening; the structures were closed so we settled for the magnificent light show on the outside of those three marvels.

I have visited many beautiful pyramids on my many visits to Egypt, including the beauteous ones in the Valley of the Kings and Queens. I have also visited many other wondrous structures, temples, ruins, and the like. The Avenue of the Rams with its numerous ram- headed sphinxes with the body of a lion leading to the temple of Karnak fascinated me. My tour guide, who was a renowned Egyptologist, could not answer my query as to for who or what reason the rams were there; they felt so familiar to me. The answers of why they were there, like why I had not entered the pyramids at Giza, remained a mystery. I had a mixed feeling of "déjà vu" and foreboding.

There were some other "too close for comfort calls" in life that were cause for pause. The Air India flight that was blown up by terrorists a day or so before mine; the flight that crashed in South America and never connected to mine. Taking one of the last flights out of NYC on September 10th., the day before the World Trade disaster, because "I just don't want to be here tomorrow." I often was near danger, but not near enough to be affected by it. However, an incident in Israel in 2004 was too upfront and personal.

Our arrival at the Allenby Bridge and the crossing over from Jordan into Israel was smooth enough. We were a party of seven, three men and four women with various nationalities. There was an Egyptian, an American, a French woman and me. I was travelling on my British passport. There were two Palestinian men, who also held American passports, and a Tanzanian. We were visiting Israel and Palestine for a few days. We knew that it could be risky as suicide bombings and shootings were common.

It was with eager anticipation that I crossed the threshold onto Israeli soil. This trip had been decided the night before as we dined with a good friend who is a special advisor to King Abdullah of Jordan. "Renee," he called out from across the table, "would you like to go to Israel and Palestine in the morning?" "The last time I checked the Pope was still Catholic," I retorted.

An early morning departure had been set up for the next day. Abe said that there was one problem: my Egyptian friend, who was travelling with me, would not be able to go since it was difficult for Arab Moslems to get visas for entry into Israel. I would not accept this fate for her, insisting that she be included and travel with us. It was eleven at night; we were to leave at 9 a.m. the next day. Miraculously, (or should I say it is who you know) the visa entry was arranged and off we went that morning. The Palestinian-Americans, along with the others, had their visas arranged previously. Khadija and I were to get our visas at the Allenby Bridge entry point which divides Israel and Jordan. We would be travelling with the others who were on a business visit to Israel and Palestine.

We checked into the Olive Tree hotel in Jerusalem and headed directly for Old Jerusalem. Jerusalem is a beautiful city, with friendly people from all over the world. While the others went on their business appointments, Khadija and I spent the day visiting some of the holy sites many of which you can see from each other. The Dome of the Rock, The Wailing Wall, and the Church of the Holy Scepter are some of the most holy sites of the Muslim, Jewish, and Christian faiths. Our trip that day included a visit to Bethlehem to see what is purported to be the birthplace of Jesus. We also visited the baptism site on the river Jordan and the crucifixion site which we had seen on the Jordanian side. We participated in whatever ritual was going on although neither of us is religious. We maintained respect at all times, although the Rabbi was not happy when he pointed out to me that I was taking a picture of Khadija who was sitting on Jesus' grave!

We were then headed for Palestine which we entered by a route over hills and dales. The two Palestinians with us wanted to avoid the border crossing from Israel. They feared confrontation with the Israeli border control officials who they viewed as dangerous and erratic. It was great to see the countryside and life as it exists there. We were on our way to the capital city of Ramallah.

I was amazed at the stark difference between Israel and Palestine. Israel projected wealth and hope, while Palestine emanated poverty and despair. There were fences separating them not just physically, but mentally as well. The city of Jerusalem was pristine, with European-style buildings, sidewalk cafes and a great nightlife. Now before us was Ramallah with worn out buildings, most of which are covered with bullet holes. We spent the evening in Palestine at the house of a Government official. We listened to stories of the tragedy of people who had been killed in the name of religion, and their fight for sovereignty. Fahad lived on the same street as Arafat's (head of the Palestinian Liberation Organization, "PLO") compound. We had a great evening of delicious food and wine with him and his family. We heard about the tribulations between the two countries.

As it was getting late, it was decided that Khadija and I would be driven back to Palestine getting dropped off by our Palestinian driver at the border, and picked up by our Israeli one on the other side. The others travelling with us were to spend the night in Palestine.

We approached the border into Israel walking between the concrete walls leading up to the checkpoint desk. Suddenly, we were hollered at and told to halt in Hebrew and Arabic as eight or so Israeli border police approached us with machine guns. Sirens were sounding all around us and we could hear people in the distance behind us running. There was immediate chaos. Time stood still, and so did we. Khadija, who was used to hearing and seeing such confrontations on the television, went into a complete panic. I calmly looked at her and said, "Nothing will happen to us. It is not my reality to die on the Israeli Palestinian border. This is not my fight and I will not die here this night."

In the meantime, I focused on the woman with the machine gun pointing at me. I was relieved to see that it was a woman holding the gun for in my mind there was no way a woman would kill me. I began to ramble on, making fun and light of the situation. I often do that in uncomfortable situations. The hot dry night with dusty streets, barking dogs and screaming voices eventually subsided and we were allowed to pass. The chaos turned out to be a drill - I had no way of knowing until it was over!

In 1988, while travelling through NYC on my way to or from somewhere, I met up with a friend who had introduced me to the teachings of her Indian guru. The last time I had seen her two years earlier, she had talked incessantly about this female guru. On this trip however, she spoke incessantly about her new teacher, "the Ram." He did this, or he said that. I was intrigued, particularly when she talked about him being channeled through the body of a woman. There was something very familiar about this. To this day, I can vividly remember hearing the name "Ramtha" for the first time in Brenda's car on a street in New York City.

She gave me the white book, *Ramtha,* which I immediately read. I loved it and I felt like I was reading my own story. I could not put the book down: its contents, like so many unexplained occurrences in my life, were familiar to me. I read it line by line, repeatedly, before moving forward, highlighting and making notes of the salient points that resonated with me the most. I knew this story and knew that I was a part of it. From that day, Ramtha The Enlightened One became a part of my life. I have read this book on his life many times over the years.

There was an event in NYC soon after that on November 12, 1988. When I flew there to attend it at the Marriott Hotel at Kennedy Airport, it had been cancelled. I began ordering books and videos from then up until 1993. I talked to Ramtha over the years and knew he was listening, even challenging him to appear to me.

I was elected to Parliament in 1993 and my daughter was born in 1994. My life took a new turn, and I became very busy. I continued to seek knowledge, and talked to the Ram but I did not try to attend another event. It did not seem to matter. I went to Seattle a few times on business over the years and would always lament, "The Ramtha School is near here somewhere," but never attempted to visit.

When I resigned from the Cabinet in 2004, I invited my travelling buddy to go on an adventure trip with me to Pyrenees Mountains in France. We stayed in a spa and did adventure activities by day. We climbed mountains, and rode bikes down them. We went whitewater rafting, and I parachuted from a mountaintop. During my parachute jump (with a trainer), I was acutely aware of how small we all are. Life itself appeared to be very small as the parachute circled drifting in the wind. I landed, folded up my parachute, and said aloud, "Now it is time for me to go to the Ramtha School." I did not know where the thought came from, but the plans were now in motion once it came.

Whether being in the co-pilot seat over the Sinai desert, whitewater rafting in India or watching the sunrise over the Himalayan Mountains there, meditating on Table Top Mountain in South Africa, flying around the world in private jets; meeting with Condoleezza Rice, Hilary Clinton, Jimmy Carter, Ted Kennedy, Tony Blair, Queen Elizabeth II, Queen Rania, and other leaders from around the world; or fighting for human rights or other causes, my life has been full of discovery. My cultural, religious, social, and political exposure has brought me to where I am today. I have lived a life of which most people can only dream, a life that has brought me to the realization that there is much more to it than what we live every day.

While on the election campaign trail in 2003, I was canvassing in one of the neighbourhoods that I represented in Parliament. I decided to stop by my brother-in-law's house. I could hear loud music coming from inside and began banging on the window where it was coming from. He finally came to the door drenched in sweat. "I was doing one of my disciplines," he exclaimed, "I go to a school in Washington State." "You go to Ramtha's School?" I interrupted him in shock. I knew John to be a staunchly religious elder in the First Church of God. I was enthralled with his stories of the orbs, the entities from the unseen that manifest, as he spoke about what had happened to him at his events. He, on the other hand, was taken aback by my knowledge of the Ram.

In August 2005, I attended my Beginner's Event in Italy, and then other events while still serving in Parliament until December, 2007. My adventure in the Ramtha School of Enlightenment, a grand school of ancient wisdom, has been a great one. I have loved every moment.

I have learnt much in this lifetime about the external of myself, but my conscious awareness is now pointed inward. The awakening of me who has been a sleeping god has begun. My search for knowledge and happiness has brought me back to myself, and back to my master teacher, Ramtha, whose teachings are a marvel. I now have a true understanding of the meaning of life, why I am here, and what I must do to find the god that lives within me. I am committed to learning about me, peeling away the onionskin of my past. It is an arduous journey giving up the known and going inward to the unknown. It is a constant journey of self-discovery and reflection. I am learning who I am and to love me.

Ramtha has spoken directly to me at events and in a question and answer session. The first time that he spoke to me he said " I want you to know that I have been with you in every lifetime." I was very startled and did not know what he meant by this. However, my acquired knowledge in the school has brought to the realization that Ramtha has been teaching me in every lifetime. I am determined to learn and live his consistent message of truth in this lifetime. The message is now clear, my god is inside of me, allign myself with it, change and become it for I am god. I finally get it!

Ramtha is the first man in this lifetime that I have truly loved. It is ironic that he channels through the body of a woman. He is the father that I never had. He is a friend, and a remarkable teacher. He is the one who has shown me the path to me, and the god that I am. He has taught and given me the desire to know and to love myself. Not the love defined by my past, but one that lives in the moment and always is. I now understand what Yeshua Bin Joseph (Jesus), who I once rejected, meant when he said, "The kingdom of god is within," and "in my father's house there are many mansions." There are many mansions of potentials in my mind. I can build, create and manifest them not by being in control, but by letting go and letting god. I am giving up my past and the emptiness I feel inside and filling that void with the love of myself. Yes, it is a long journey back home. My master teacher is giving me the tools to get on the trail and to go there. I now know what Yeshua meant when he said, "Be silent and know that ye are gods." My god dwells in the silence within me, and yet is everywhere around me.

The lanterns of the future now are burning for me. My master teacher awaits my return. My God awaits my return. I am humbled to be taught by such a loving being who just is. I am humbled to be sitting at the feet of greatness, learning such profound knowledge, and hearing such resounding wisdom. I am humbled by the love I am experiencing.

I know the long journey home is but a breath away. If I listen quietly, I can hear it in the wind.

I thank you Ramtha for being in my life, for your love of truth and me. I thank you JZ for the sacrifice you make to let Ramtha happen. You are both greatly loved. So be it!

MITJA KADOW
Germany

PILGRIMAGE TO MY MASTER TEACHER: MISSION OF MY LIFE

My name is Mitja Kadow. I was born in Hamburg, Germany. I grew up in a beautiful suburb by the river "Elbe," surrounded by parks and nature, in a very loving family with a big circle of friends.

I was engaged in many different sports and reached high levels of accomplishments in several of them. I was not the best student at school until the tenth and eleventh grade when we were able to choose specific courses and go deeper into the subject matter that we were interested in. My parents sent me to the most sophisticated school in town and after three years, I failed the tests, flunked the class and changed schools. My interests were sports and social events and I don't remember spending much time doing my homework.

I eventually got the point and started to apply myself better at school, became a pretty good student and succeeded greatly in the final graduation. My mother always made sure I learned how to play instruments so I started with the flute and after about six years moved to the clarinet for several years and then learned to play the saxophone. I took occasional piano lessons as well. For two years, I went to Bible class, as I was supposedly religious and had grown up in a Lutheran church, though we attended only three or four Sundays per year, including Christmas and Easter.

During that class, my bad study habits resurfaced again, as I don't remember much at all. I remember that I was taught that there is a God and that God was in me as well but I never personalized that message. The only time I communicated to that god was when I needed help.

I had a strong urge to learn more about Jesus and felt very drawn to him but never thought of it as anything special, since everyone seemed to love Jesus. I thought of him a lot at night when I was going to sleep because the only prayer my mother ever taught me and that I repeated before slumber was: my heart is clean, my heart is pure and you, Jesus, live there with me. I loved who the being Jesus was, what he did and what his message was to us. We had a weekly study of religion in school as well and we learned much about other big religions like Buddhism and Hinduism.

I was given a video tape with an esoteric speaker who truly impressed me because she put life and all religions into perspective. I was about 18 when I got really into learning about non-classical sciences such as quantum physics and natural healing, and I dove deep into that world.

I traveled much with my family throughout Europe and as a teenager by myself or with friends. I took a job as a leader for younger kids on bus tours to summer holidays and ski/snowboard trips which is where I found a passion to take leadership.

Over the last few years in school, I had developed hay fever and asthma which were hard for me being an athlete. I never thought that regular medicine was the right approach and I always felt that there must be a cure, not just a temporary relief with a pill. I had learned from my esoteric studies so far that all disease is a manifestation of our thoughts so I started to search for natural remedies. Being the son of a dentist father and a physical therapist mother, I was prone to learn much about health, though classical medicine was not what I was looking for.

My parents separated when I was about ten, which is when I had my first emotional hardship. They never learned to become friends again. It was very difficult for me because I was trying to build a bridge for communication between them but neither wanted to hear from me what the other had to say. I realized I could not fix the problem and was very sad about how they looked upon each other. It was a great learning in the long run about how a perfect world can change quickly and that we all see the world through our own eyes; that it is up to us to create what we want to see and never be dependent on somebody else. That emotional experience was the trigger for the hay fever and the inability to breathe freely without guilt - asthma.

I studied biology at school as one of my majors and knew that our bodies were created to be working perfectly and I wanted to find a way to help my body be in perfect health as it was designed to be. I found a naturopathic doctor that helped me to get much better but my asthma and hay fever never fully went away. This naturopath (Petra Ramon, and note the last name!!! RAMON) also gave me books to read to learn more about how we create disease in the body and certain philosophies about life. I got so excited about what I was learning that I decided to study naturopathic medicine and become a doctor.

It is mandatory in Germany for all males to serve in the military for one year which was quite an experience on its own. I felt like I was going to prison but I must say that I did learn much about survival, camaraderie and how to handle weapons.

During that time, Petra Ramon continued to give me books to read and eventually gave me a white book. It was called "an introduction." It was my first introduction to Ramtha and I remember crying while reading the first few pages. While marching for hours in the military I contemplated what I had read and started to say mantras like "consciousness and energy creates the nature of reality" for hours and hours. I could not stop thinking about the Ram and talked to him often as he said that he was the wind.

I got an urgent feeling inside and wanted to meet my chosen teacher. I remember listening to an introduction tape that was sent out at the time to people who requested information. I listened to it over and over, and over and I just wanted to pack my bag and go. The next Beginner's Retreat was coming up in May '96 and I knew that I had to be there. My duties with the army were done by the end of May and I was supposed to start my naturopathic education at a very expensive school in the middle of the month. I worked out my left over vacation time in the army and did many nightshifts to gain extra days so I could take of the whole month of May. I told the naturopathic school that I would be coming two weeks after classes began. I worked part-time evenings and weekends in telemarketing to make the money to buy my ticket and pay for my beginning retreat at Ramtha's School of Enlightenment. I believe that was the only beginning retreat of that year and it was a twelve-day trip with traveling time.

The closer the event got, the more impatient I became. When it finally arrived, I was more than ready to give up anything and go on to find my master teacher. I actually went with my girlfriend at the time, Joanna Ramon, who was the daughter of Petra who had initially introduced me to Ramtha. I have known Joanna since Kindergarten, and we kept coming into each other's lives and now we went on a pilgrimage together.

When we arrived for the first time in the United States of America in Seattle, a student of the Ram was there to pick us up. We also met a couple of other people on the plane on their journey to the great school. A gentle man named Paul from New Zealand picked us up and took us to 'the masters' center,' the local bed and breakfast for traveling students. We slept on the floor of an old church with many other pilgrims from many different countries. We made great friends and long lasting relationships during that time.

The day of the event arrived and I was humbled to be walking onto the holy ground of the school. I had a seat close to the door three, which is the door through which Ramtha enters the hall to come and teach.

At that time, Ramtha was teaching the entire retreat himself. When he entered the hall for the first time, I cried deeply as if I had found my long lost parent again. I later found out that that was actually true when Ramtha told me that I was one of the children that he took on as a parent in his life and my name was Basila. He gave our group a name: Elohim Ka Men Ra.

I knew that this was my home and that I belonged here. It was hard for me to leave after this event and go back to my new career as a naturopathic doctor when I had just learned the power of Blue Body® healing from Ramtha and that "consciousness and energy create reality" and that I am God. I had experienced that in fieldwork I understood the attitude behind my asthma and let go of that, which healed my asthma and I never had it again. I also released the hay fever. It only has come back a few times when I slipped back into that old attitude.

Ramtha came to me in several sessions during the disciplines and touched me or said things to me. At that time, I barely spoke any English and some things he said, I did not understand. These personal interactions almost made me faint and I had never felt honored like that ever in my life. I was committed to come to my Follow-Up and the big Assays and Boktau, the long event.

I made it to my follow-up, where Ram invited me to the house to participate in a special ceremony with a few selected students. That was it for me. Ramtha made me a red guard in one of the early events and I could now be at every event to study under him. Soon after that, I was invited to be one of his comrades in special group and eventually became a teacher which is still being a student just from a different perspective. I had found my master teacher, my true father and most respected leader and have been with him ever since.

My gratitude and humble thanks to JZ Knight for giving her life to the great work, and channeling Ramtha. I am most grateful and honored to be a part of this marching army of the mind into the future.

CHERYL NICHOLS
Washington, USA

FELLOWSHIP DES VOLS

The first time I heard about JZ Knight's ranch was at an elevation of 500 feet, flying low in a Cessna airplane, looking down. It was days after New Year's Eve, 1991, and we had special flying clearance to fly low over the entire Puget Sound region as a part of the Department of Wildlife's diving duck survey and census. I had been a volunteer for three days, waking up at 4:00 a.m. and arriving at Shelton's airport by six.

Every year in January, biologists count the diving ducks, and the Puget Sound region is especially rich in duck habitat. It was an honor to be chosen to help out, though I was only a freshman in college. We had flown for three days already, counting the diving ducks on lakes, ponds, fields and salt water.

The flights had been a little more daredevil than I had expected. Flying low over tree-tops was enough of a thrill for my first time in a four-seater. By day three, I almost wet my pants in Tacoma when we actually flew UNDER the Narrows Bridge power lines, banked a 90-degree right turn at the last minute, flew alongside the bridge, and ducked back under the power lines on the other side. The duck count was probably a little less accurate for this part of the Puget Sound; I don't think the biologists in back were breathing either.

In the plane, the biologists sat in the back seats, foreheads touching the window. They spoke non-stop into their tape recorders as they counted and named the ducks below. I was in charge of the transect map, following the coastline carefully and announcing when the plane had passed into another quadrant. The biologists could keep track of the data this way, and correlate it with the duck surveys that were happening simultaneously on the ground. The plane had to fly low enough for the two wildlife biologists to identify and count every duck that we flew over. The sound from the back of the plane was a constant drone that sounded something like "Transect 115, five brant geese, three mergansers, eight camelbacks…transect 116, two camelbacks, four buffleheads…"

On the day I flew over the Ranch, I didn't have to hold the map and read out transect quadrant we were flying over. I had been invited back, not as a volunteer, but as a tourist. We were scheduled to fly over the San Juan Islands, a place I had only been a few times in my life. A friend of mine had lent me his camera to take pictures of the Islands. I was excited to join the search for the wood duck that sometimes inhabits the island coves. Little did I know when I woke up that fourth morning at 4:00 that the wind decided to change our plans. I arrived at the airport to hear that an amazing wind had come up the night before, blowing all the fog off the fields in the Yelm area. The biologist was excited. Usually the fields in Thurston County were shrouded in fog during the census window. This chance was too good to pass up, so off we flew to the Yelm to count the ducks.

We headed south from Shelton's airport, the pink sunrise painting the sky. Soon Mt. Rainier, in her January blanket of snow, reflected some of this color back to our eyes. I probably took twenty pictures, as each time the plane turned, the mountain shone with greater intensity of pink and of shadow. I didn't know it at the time, but I was flying over my future land. I was looking down on the fields and rooftops of my future neighbors and friends.

When we flew over the Ranch, I remember seeing the horse shed just a few feet below me. When we flew over the annex and arena, I was intrigued. When we flew over JZ's house, I had to exclaim in awe. "What IS this place?" Her home looked like a beautiful castle to my small town eyes. It had spires and turrets that took me into the fairytale like magical feeling of Cinderella and Sleeping Beauty. "That is JZ Knight's Messiah ranch," the biologist answered. I hung there in the sky in that moment. The plane seemed to disappear. I logged that vision into the special place in my heart. I didn't know it, but I had a future to come there that would be wonderful and filled with love. I recognized it in my soul and remembered the future to come.

I had always been a deep thinking child. I didn't easily fit in with the crowds of kids, preferring one or two close friends. I loved playing for hours on my Commodore 64 computer, playing outside, and watching TV. *Mork and Mindy* was my favorite TV show when I was about eight years old. I liked how Robin Williams was unique, and that he was allowed to be different and not understand the social cues around him. There was a truth to his take on the absurdity of the silliness that are societal norms. I, too, thought some of the expectations of me and my life were absurd.

In the most poignant episode for me, there was a man who wore an A-board sign with the question "If Jesus came back today would you recognize him?" written on it. This whirled me into deep contemplation. I remember clearly grappling with the question of recognition. Just how would I recognize an enlightened man? I was very concerned that I would pass the moment by, pass him by. I concluded that someone would be different from humanity if he was detached from human emotions and loving beyond measure. I made a pact with myself to absolutely know greatness when I saw it.

Well, my worry was for nothing. Or maybe one could say that my concern for recognizing truth created the path for me to find it. Ramtha was written into my life's book before I was even a child. I had no need to worry if I would recognize him. The door to the RSE school found me when I was ready.

It was the summer before my sophomore and junior year of college. I was teaching nature workshops for the Whale Museum's summer program in the San Juan Islands when I became ready to find RSE. Since I was enjoying myself so immensely in Friday Harbor, my beautiful mother coerced her co-worker to fly up and get me. Having no excuses left to stay, I reluctantly agreed to be flown back home. She was right, the freedom of life on the islands was encapsulating! Camping at the wildlife rehabilitation center, biking into town to teach children, and spending the rest of the day taking care of baby seal pups could have easily kept me from returning to my college junior year! I didn't want to come home, but part of me was sending me closer to meeting my destiny in Yelm.

When I arrived home from the San Juan Islands, my friend was there with a Ramtha tape in her hand. A new co-worker who had come into the office had handed her the introductory tape and now it was being handed to me.

My first reaction was that the school sounded cool, but I was a poor college student, and figured that there would not be a way for me to come up with the money to go. My friend was all fired up because she was going to her Beginner's Retreat in September. I stayed aloof from the idea. If the money mysteriously came to me I would go, but I wasn't holding my breath about it. Of course, I went to the library and checked out the books I could find on the topics, JZ's *My Story* and Ramtha's *Voyage to the New World.* The co-worker also threw out a few kernels of intrigue about a breathing technique, so I tried my own version of breathing and manifesting my beginner's retreat into my reality. I laugh at the sweet clean desire in my initial intent. Not knowing anything, I really tried to come up with something close to what I had heard about.

A month later, just days prior to leaving for Western Washington University, I was at a house picking blackberries, and was stung by a wasp on the crown of my head.

Students from RSE were there picking blackberries with me and one student named Bodananda came to me and said that he could help me heal my throbbing headache and wound. He sat me down on the floor in front of the couch.

I followed his instructions…closing my eyes, I imagined that my brain had no borders. I heard a powerful breath and heat rained down on my head from his hot hands.

I became borderless. I just easily went to the edges of my brain and kept my awareness going. I found myself swimming fast towards a sunrise in black waters like an ocean without boundaries. Swimming faster and faster, I was pure joy. Abruptly I heard a "So Be It" and I fell backwards and snapped back into my body awareness.

Now this was an experience like no other that I had ever had. This vision was incredible. I could feel the rush of the water over my frontal lobe as I swam fast towards the sunset. It was an all-encompassing vision. I didn't remember who I was, there was no sense of self…I just was. But this was nothing compared to what I was experiencing now that I was back in front of the couch in my body that had previously been stung by a bee. I felt like I was being crushed into the ground by the gravitational field I was now feeling. Gravity was now pushing me literally down into my head and straight into the carpet floor. I didn't want to be back but I was also amused at this new phenomenon. I was aware of gravity for the first time ever, and I had absolutely no pain left into my head. Stunned at the experience that I had just had, I swore to myself that I wanted to learn from Bodananda's teacher. Even though I was a poor college student with no money, I was going to manifest a beginner's event at Ramtha's School of Enlightenment.

After exclaiming to Bodananda that I was feeling gravity as if it was the first time ever, he laughed and said that I was going to go far in the school. I was just beside myself with this awe of new awareness. What did I not know? There was so much that I wasn't aware of. I just must taste more of this unknown! I must come to this RSE school!

A few days later, I went to college at Western Washington University. My mother took me, and we went to the local supermarket to get some food for my fridge. There was someone in the checkout line with an "Infinite Voyager" shirt on and I could not help but introduce myself. I don't know who this guy was, but he obviously was not ready for my recognition of him and shirked away from my flamboyant "hello, I want to also be a student in the Ramtha school, do you go down to events often, can you ever give me a ride?" introduction!

In Bellingham, I set up an envelope that would hold the money for my future event.

Whenever I had change or extra money from my work check, I would put it in the envelope. I recognized that I had no extra money but that I would use my money wisely and dedicate any extra to going to my event. When it was full I would go to the event, but I didn't count it until I knew I was close to having enough. I took a Saturday morning job as a dishwasher on the other side of campus and would often find money laying on the ground as I walked to work. How did that money get dropped on the ground? I'd imagine kids pulling out gloves, late Friday night, not aware that their bills came out of their pockets. The mysteries are as varied as all of our journeys were to get to RSE. I know now that I couldn't have missed my doors to Ramtha and his school. It was my destiny to know about it and to make my own journey there.

INEKE BUSKENS
Netherlands

MY JOURNEY TO MY MASTER TEACHER IS NOT REALLY A JOURNEY...

My journey to Ramtha, my Master Teacher is not really a journey. Yet it is a long, long story that I really want to tell in the shortest possible way.

Beyond time and space and beyond hope and desperation, I always knew that life was meant to be beautiful and glorious, that real love exists, that I did not have to die. And that one day, I would experience that, on this planet, in this lifetime. There was this longing to be all that I could be, although I did not even know what that meant exactly. So I searched and found many teachers. And I left them.

"God is not a man."
I heard myself saying this at seventeen, when I explained to the choirmaster of my church why I could not sing anymore. I could not get another "he," "him" or "his" out of my throat. I remember that I was just as shocked as he was.

Yet when I fell in love, thirteen years later, I was married in a church by two men. Not allowed to visit Mary, mother to young brides, I lost something I could not name. We went to throw our bridal bouquet in the North Sea, hoping that the Raina do Mar would reach across the oceans from Brazil to Holland.

I got sterilized in India when I was 26. I wanted it. I wanted to give birth to myself, I was afraid that I would become like my mother, I was afraid that men would only love me for the babies I could give.

Yet when I fell in love, five years later, I had a repair operation two months before the wedding. I cried when I saw my belly cut open from one side to the other. And I accepted the patronizing, patriarchal attitude of doctors and nurses as righteous punishment for what I had dared to do with my body.

I have forgiven my father for leaving us when we were small, for the fact that I did not bleed, nor cry for seven years. I have forgiven my mother for not being the loving, allowing, respecting mother we wanted to have.

Yet I am still in the process of forgiving myself. Forgiving myself for having been hard on myself, for judging myself for all the things I did, which were really just experiences I needed to have, wanted to have, experiences which mature into wisdom when they are loved.

When I found an ashram in India where I could, at times, touch the God in me, I agreed to project my divinity on to the guru, wearing his photo around my neck. I gave up everything I had in my life up to that point: a promising academic career, family, friends, and lover.

Yet when the Ram came to South Africa in 1999, I had almost given up on my quest. So many roads I had traveled that were leading nowhere.

I nearly did not go. A friend, many years in school, convinced me to go and loaned me the money for the Beginners' Event.

And at that blessed event, somebody put my cushion in front.

At the feet of the chair where the Ram was going to sit.

We had a glorious event. I loved the disciplines, I loved the school's teachers, I loved the lectures, I loved the other students, the conversations we had. I wept when I was alone, when I purged myself of my self-acquired Catholic dirt: "I am worthy, I am worthy, I am worthy," I remember shouting under the shower one morning.

The moment came; the Ram was arriving. Everybody got up and started dancing and singing.

I looked in amazement and some derision: "They are all mad and what am I doing here?" Then the Ram caught my eyes; electricity jolted through my body. "Hah," he said, he had scored. I was on full alert: Never had I experienced power like this.

When he came closer, he looked at me and said: "Lady, move your body. Your God loves you." I could only look at him.

He started teaching. The words to ask a question were not even formed in my mind and he had already turned to face me. I realized that whilst he could see me, I could not see him. Yet I felt completely safe, challenged yes, but loved and safe.

At the end of our second evening with the Ram, he invited us to come and participate in the last great Boktau retreat, at the Great School in Yelm. Thirty-six days in Yelm would mean six weeks without income, at a time that the exchange rate between the US dollar and the South African Rand was 1 to 12.[1] I looked at him and he looked back, smiled and said: "Lady, you can do anything." Then he went on to say that he would make it possible for those of us who were sincere about our spiritual journey. He said he would send us a "runner" in two weeks time. I did not know what he meant by a "runner" but I accepted his offer: "So Be It!"

I wanted to go.

Yet I was afraid of losing my husband. I knew I would change. I would change away from him. My husband was the mother I never had, the father who left too soon. Even though we were lovers no more, he was my best friend. He was the sun to my moon. Life without him was unimaginable.

---

[1] It is about 7 Rand to the US dollar at this time.

When I got home, normal life enveloped me, as if I had never been away. As if the Ram's world was a different world, as if there were no place for a path with the Ram in my life.

Yet, then came this Sunday morning two weeks after the event. I got out of bed into our garden. It was misty, beautiful and mysterious, an exquisite autumn morning in the mountains of the Western Cape. I saw a strange white light close to my roses. Trying to figure out whether the light was something other than the mist, I heard a voice in my head: "Lady, go and stand in the white light." I replied: "Why would I do that?" I got back: "Just do it," and I did.

I did not feel anything; at least I cannot remember feeling anything.
But I went straight to my office and wrote a letter to my bank manager, telling her what money I needed, what I needed it for, why I needed it and what I would do to pay it back.

And after sending the fax, I got back in bed with my husband who was still sleeping. The next morning at 9:15, I got a call from my bank manager: she was going to give me the money!!!

When I entered the Great Hall in Yelm, Washington three weeks later, I saw written on one of its walls: "Just do it." I knew I had come home. And I also knew whose words these were. And I knew that these words are divine: they urge us on beyond thinking and doubting into the unknown of all that we can be.

There has never been a question in my mind that Ramtha is exactly what he says he is: An ascended God, a Hierophant, a 35,000 year old warrior channeling through a woman's body.
Even though I did not understand what that meant in the beginning.
And even though I still cannot comprehend the full picture of what he is.
I know that I want to be like he is, but then me.
I know that I want to love like he does. I have never seen anything like it.
I know that under his schooling I am learning to love myself.
I know that when I "just do it" I am becoming the woman I always knew I could be.

I know that I do not have to die. I bi-located, I experienced defeating space and time.

I know that I can be healthy, wealthy, happy and wise. I am becoming more so every day.

I know that I can do miracles. I have done them and will do more.

I know that I can be woman and divine: God-Woman Realised.

I know that I am my God-Self.

April, 2008, it will be nine years that I am in Ram's school.

Yet it seems there has never been a time that I was not in school.

When the student is ready the Master appears.

My journey to my Master teacher is not really a journey.

It is an unfolding into my Self.

Beyond time and space, beyond hope and desperation.

PS:

Yes, I left my husband.

Yes, that hurt initially and I got over that pain into more power, more joy and more love.

Yes, I paid my friend back and yes, I have gotten to a level of wealth where I can secure my own future.

And yes, I have accomplished all this by "just doing it." Just as the Ram said.

JENNY GIFFORD
South Africa

the lotus grows in the mud

A bunch of kids
who a moment ago
were happily walking down the street
are suddenly
in front of my 10 year old eyes
being stuffed
carelessly
into the back of a van
and driven away at breakneck speed.
they are flung hard to the back of the van
crying and shouting.
raucous brutal laughter blisters the air
and
absolute confusion reigns in me.
oh no, i think
what can be happening.
and every fibre in my body
spiraled into a tight frightened powerless moment

i cannot bear to think of it

a triangle of the most delicious looking chocolate cake
you could ever imagine
filled with large dollops of creamy white icing
and big chunks of chocolate on top.
a gift to my teacher.
sat on the desk
right under my 5 year old nose
for
what seemed to me to be the longest hour.
unable to concentrate
and tormented by my taste buds
into my tiny suitcase it went.

home seemed to me to be the perfect place to experience such deliciousness
and at least i wasn't being
taunted by a piece of chocolate cake any longer!

they found it

in my little suitcase

and i was severely punished
by a big committee of big people.
the headmaster
the teacher
and both my parents.

do school mistresses usually
have to check that
your panties match your school uniform.

that line
every monday morning
filled me with a creepy dread

the girl students walked in circles
bikini clad.
and the boy students drunkenly and gleefully
looked on.
in a disassociated haze cloud
i gathered
that
the boys were choosing
the beauties.
i can't remember what i scored out of 10!

the birth of jealousy and rage maybe?

i became the under 16 year old rhodesian breast stroke swimming champion
practicing long hours

unable to participate in the olympics
because i was a white racist pig.

i was able to win over the admiration of my dad though

by 18
i was dignosed by top opthamologists
with impending blindness.
100% blind in my right eye already
i started to practise braille.
a visit to london was planned by my parents.
appointments made with the top harley street physicians.

they apparently knew it all.
the best they could do
was suggest that I join a group
of other bloated, sick, sad, cortisone drenched, anti organ rejectory drug filled people.
they could give no cause

on the way home to our hotel
i threw my pills out of the window of the double-decker bus
never to be had again
and never again to see the doctor or the group.

as a special london treat
we sat in the front row
of a play called
let my people come.
i found myself staring at large penises
haircurlers in fannies
large bunches of bananas
and gang bangs

THIS PLACE WAS A STRANGE SCARY MYSTERY TO ME

WHY ON EARTH WAS I HERE

WHAT WAS I DOING HERE

what was i meant to be doing here
what is sinning
why was i feeling so bad about myself
where was the joy
how could i ever fulfill the ten commandments
why did i feel so helpless

where was my power
how could i help myself
and be of use in the world

diets made it worse
sant mat
bhuddism
kryon
fortune tellers
clairvoyants
religion
tantra
power of positive thinking-norman vincent peale
elizabeth clare prophet
melchizedek
denise linn
sai baba

my studio
was piled high with every conceivable book
and workshop pamphlet
that might offer a lead
i scoured pages night after night
trying to make some sense of this barrage of madness
and voices in my head that made no sense at all
except at best in small pieces

everywhere did i hunt
driven
and tireless
i had to find some meaning to it all
in february 1999

RAMTHA
came to south africa
and
these words i will never forget

THAT WE HAVE NEVER SINNED

THAT WE HAVE ALWAYS BEEN LOVED BY GOD

THAT WE ARE GOD
BECAUSE EVERYTHING IS GOD

i was drinking the longest coolest most nourishing pristine glacial water i could ever
have imagined

and
that contained within us all,
are all the god genes we need
to be anything we choose.
to be immortal
to be unlimited
wild
kind
compassionate.
to be free
heal ourselves and others.
bi locate
levitate
become invisible.
to be a totally present and loving presence.
he taught us about the grid that i had seen in a lot of stephen hawkings drawings.
the void

universes of existence
all time being simultaneous
inspiration and
mystery.
he instills passion in my heart, veins and mind.
about awesome storytelling
grand parties.
he loves me
even when i don't love myself!
showers me with the power of presence.
shows me what hope for the world means
he has taught me
about the
joy of rain, rainbows, snow.
being wet
the night sky
and camping under the moon
the joy of a veggie garden
my potential
that i have a neuronet for yellow.
about ground hog day
to own my past.
for a glorious new life
about personal power
and
personal truth.
i want to be with THE RAM and his fairy friend
EVERY BLISSFUL MOMENT.
that lightning looks the same as the brain having a thought .
to share without resentment
and what a beautiful community of like minded beings is
10,000 years into the future.

to remember
all that i am.
to take responsibility for the reality i have created.
that we are fundamentally creators.
to create our day every day as the gods that we are.
and that words matter.
how to see the future of a deck of playing cards.

this magnificent loving hierophant wizard
ascended
my beloved master teacher

THE FUTURE
is golden
and i am hooked on it

JENIFER PRESTON
Ohio, USA

THE ROAD LESS TRAVELED

For years, I have always been on a spiritual quest to find the true meaning/purpose of life. I finally got into transcendental meditation - participating in a small focus group in Columbus, Ohio. It was led by Dr. Hari Sharma who is now a fairly well known author covering Ayurvedic medicine and its applications to life. He has written books on averting cancer before the disease ever hits. He is a pathologist at the Ohio State University but was a devout student of Maharishi.

In the early 90's, I had a very successful, large allopathic veterinary practice in central Ohio. One day I had a client walk into my office; she and her husband were in the process of adopting children from Guatemala. I decided at that moment that this could be an opportunity to help innocent third world children. I contacted their attorney and began the adoption process on my first son. This attorney, by the way, is a special representative for Haiti at the United Nations - a very compassionate fellow.

My first adopted child, Andy, arrived in March, 1984. My life, of course, changed greatly from that moment on. I was thrust into motherhood with an infant son, trying to save the world in any way I could. After this, I decided I could help the world even more by adopting more third world children!

All of my children, except one, were adopted from underdeveloped countries where parents never know where their next meal will come from, let alone food for their growing, hungry children. I would contact an adoption attorney or an orphanage and apply for a child. I always told them that I would take a child that no one else would want. These would usually be children who were handicapped either physically, or as I later found out, emotionally. I truly wanted to give the "unwanted" a loving home, proper medical care, a healthy environment, and a chance to be educated—all things that were not possible wherever they came from. Most of these kids were not really 'orphans.' Their parents had a lot of kids but not a lot of groceries. They would literally take their kids to an orphanage or contact an attorney who would "compensate" these people for bringing their children in for adoption - specifically foreign adoption.

Pregnant mothers would actually contact attorneys to let them know their newborn would be up for adoption as soon as the birth occurred. The attorney would compensate them, help them with nutrition, and arrange for an actual hospital birth to guarantee a live delivery. Most of the time, hospitals were well beyond the means of these mothers. Good nutrition was beyond their grasp too. This was a great arrangement for the mothers, who had no form of birth control, and knew that ultimately the child might die due to malnutrition, massive parasites or community/family violence. They truly cared for their unborn children and wanted beautiful lives for them that were never possible for themselves.

It was also a great arrangement for the adoption attorney, who usually had a list of adoptable families in America. The real fly in the ointment would come if the child was disabled in any way. Who would adopt such a child?? You can understand their excitement when I volunteered.

Total Adoptions:
Four from Guatemala - three of these from one family. All of these children were given up for adoption because the parent/parents had no means to support or FEED the children after they were born. The older siblings had actually died from parasites.

Three from Chile - two with epilepsy and special needs. The third was a girl that a Catholic orphanage gladly sent to me. Little did I know she had been sexually abused since she was an infant - even while living at the orphanage. This does not create a mentally stable teenager.

Two older children from India. One daughter with polio; she came along with her anti-quated braces and crutches. One son - an amputee and young beggar from Calcutta. He had been pushed off a moving train and lost his leg in the incident. He also had a strange and painful prosthesis.

One older boy from Colombia. He was a severe burn victim unable to get proper medi-cal care. When I went to Bogotá to pick up my new son, I saw the cardboard hovels - whole neighborhoods of cardboard dwellings. This is where the boy had been raised. It was common for the mothers to go off to work, being maids in the well-to-do homes in Bogotá. Their children would be left alone in the 'hovels.' It was also common to cook with gasoline - the only fuel available to these needy parents.

The stoves would often explode; hence, my son's severe burns. 'Marcos' was taken to a local hospital for treatment. The single parent, having no means to compensate for the treatment, never returned for her son. The hospital had done all that it could with its meager supplies and expertise. An American hospital would be greatly needed for full recovery. NO ONE asks to adopt these children. Those were the ones I sought -I knew there had to be many in such circumstances. The orphanages were equally GLAD to find me.

One boy was actually from Ohio. The local juvenile judge asked me to consider him as an addition to my family. Born of drug addicts, he lived his first few months in a car until authorities took over. He had eventually been adopted but disrupted; no one wanted him - he was nine years old and not much to look forward to. Of course, I said okay.

My last three adoptions were from the neediest country of all - Haiti. I adopted one physically normal baby, one three-year-old girl unable to walk, and one tiny baby with spina bifida that was absolutely UNADOPTABLE. The orphanages in Haiti are over-crowded with very few medical supplies. They customarily do not accept handicapped babies or children into their facilities because they get NO requests for such adoptees. The typical white, affluent families that apply to adopt are not ready to take on the additional burden of disabilities. Adopting from third world countries is enough of a challenge for many.

One day in early fall of '88, I stopped into my office on my day off just for a very few moments when my private line rang. I answered it and an orphanage in Haiti that I had contacted was anxiously speaking on the other end. A mother had just come into their facility with a very handicapped daughter, hoping desperately to find help for the tiny child.

The child was paralyzed from the waist down and desperately unhealthy overall. The mother could barely feed herself, let alone nourish this needy one. Medical attention or care was not even an option. Would the orphanage be able to help the distraught wom-an? The spokeswoman for the orphanage explained that they did not usually accept handicapped children because there were never any requests for them from potential adopting families. They only accepted 'place-able' children, for there was only so much room and limited rations. She knew the mother's only chance lay in my acceptance, for she knew I had different expectations.

I asked her what would happen to the baby if I did not say 'yes' right then and now. The woman explained that they would tell the mother to keep going; they flatly could not ac-cept the child. The grim part of this story was that it was almost Halloween. During this holiday, it is a voodoo practice to 'sacrifice' handicapped children. After these events, there are no disabled children left in the poverty-stricken neighborhoods. That tiny girl's destiny was in my hands at that very moment. I only had to consider the options for a single minute. Of course, I agreed and committed to the adoption.

When 'Marty' arrived, she had fairly severe spina bifida with an untreated hydrocepha-lus. She was suffering from hepatitis and severe kidney infection. She had little moments without severe discomfort. Her status slowly changed under proper medical care and guidance. Today she is a sophomore at Evergreen State College in Washington State. She has also been a student of Ramtha's School of Enlightenment since she was nine.

All of these adoptions (except one) had to go through rigorous immigration documentation and tremendous personal expense - both of which would have been incredible obstacles to many potential families. I enjoyed the challenge - even the one-on-one interviews with the immigration officials who couldn't believe my motive!! Why would any single woman want to help so many unfortunate homeless children???? Also not all orphanages are willing to work with single parents.

I lived on a large, beautiful farm outside Johnstown, Ohio - a suburb of Columbus. I employed another family to look after my children while I worked - many hours. Unfortunately, this was a fundamentalist Christian family that had more religious influence on the children than I realized. It wasn't easy finding someone to watch fourteen children.

Even though I was busy with a huge veterinary practice and the logistics of nurturing a large family with their many diverse medical, physical and mental needs, I still had an underlying NAGGING spiritual quest. I had helped many individuals in the world, but I was not satisfied personally. Even with all my children, I still had a drive within myself to do something more with my life.

I investigated and pursued meditation with the small group but this did not fill me spiritually. I was an avid reader—mostly new age, "spiritual" books. I devoured Jess Stearns' works, Edgar Cayce biographicals, volumes of past life readings, and UFO encounters. In high school, I had somehow obtained an actual recording of Bridey Murphy's hypnotized recall of past lives. I was mesmerized!! This was all the proof I needed of reincarnation; it blew Christianity out of the water for me.

I even read a book that purported to be a directory of channeled beings. I remember reading one chapter on an entity in Yelm, Washington. The author described how the channeler charged huge sums to attend her sessions, drove around the tiny rural town in a luxurious car, and lived in the berg's only mansion. I passed that chapter by completely, thinking that a truly spiritual entity would not act that way.

One weekend, I even drove my whole family to Washington DC to have a session with one of the well-known authors / therapists of past life regressions. Thinking this might possibly be an answer to my quest, I drove 700 miles, with family in tow, for my one-hour 'session.' Much to my disappointment, the therapist could NOT hypnotize me. NADA. What a wasted trip.

One day in 1992, I had a rare thirty-minute break between patients at my office. This was indeed an infrequent occurrence. I was really looking for another 'spiritual' book to read. I hastily drove to a tiny new-age bookstore not far from my office. I had about five minutes to browse the tiny 'channeled' section. The ONLY book that caught my attention was *Voyage to the New World: An Adventure into Unlimitedness* by Douglas Mahr. The bookseller highly recommended it; I purchased it and raced back to my office.

My life and my destiny changed *that* day. With this book, I had a proper introduction to Ramtha, a truly channeled being. I immediately ordered every tape I could get my hands on. Andy and I listened to these tapes over and over - amazed at the knowledge within.

In 1993, my nine-year-old son Andy and I flew to a Beginner's Event, telling our Christian family that we were going to a veterinary convention. We spent much of that exciting flight to Seatac discussing possible questions that we would pose to Ramtha when the opportunity arose. Most of the tapes we listened to over, and over were dialogues. We had no idea that most of our time would be spent 'blowing' or trekking through sleet, cold, cold rain and deep mud in a vinyl-fenced field.

To my dismay, at our Beginner's, we had a FIVE-hour session of disciplines - which my body/personality thought were exhausting. This was almost the end of me. I did survive, with a lot of credit to my young son Andy who never lost sight of the whole goal.

We are still here fifteen years later. I have more passion for this school and my teacher now than I ever had before.

After our Beginner's Event, Andy and I flew to more and more 'veterinary classes' in Washington State. One of the most beautiful retreats we attended was a 'dimensional mind.' Then Ramtha announced plans for the first month-long Boktau (a Boktau is a very intensive, 30-day retreat. This is quite the event to hone your mind). With this lengthy retreat in mind, I decided right then to sell my practice. I made a focus card and within weeks, found a large corporation to purchase my entire business.

In 1997, my son Andy and daughter Joy and I moved to Tenino, Washington. Daughters Marty and Heidi joined us several months later. All joined the RSE school with my son and me. The rest of the family stayed in Ohio, convinced that we had gone to join the 'Antichrist' or 'devil' that resided in Yelm. Rumor at my office was that I had gone to live underground with a cult out West. No one really communicated with us to find out why we had really moved out to mountain country. To this day, no one inquires as to our true reason for uprooting and moving to Tenino.

I now have a holistic veterinary practice - a 180-degree shift from regular medicine that I practiced for so many years in Ohio. Holistic medicine, whether for animal or human, is more aligned with restoring the body to its own specific frequency. Instead of padding the wallet of drug companies, I strive to recreate the normal, healthy body. In this way, I am utilizing what I have learned in my school to help alleviate disease and pain in the animal world. I am giving back to nature.

I am still head on with my spiritual journey. Thanks to Ramtha, I finally have the right direction. Instead of meditating for hours on 'nothing,' I am focused on my future destiny. I love my school more than anything. I have changed my destiny and the destiny of my children. Four have been students of the Ram; two are still current. We owe our lives, our future, and our wonderful destinies to our school and our teacher. We love Ram greatly with all our heart and all our being. We are truly students of the great work; we are going home.

CATHERINE MAGNIN-MOURIER
France

THE WINDS ALONG MY PATH

I t's August of 2005. I'm breastfeeding my six-month old daughter in the gym of the athletic centre of Sportilia, Italy, where 700 people impatiently await the arrival of RAMTHA. The atmosphere is electric with anticipation and curiosity. A happening is about to occur and I have no idea of its significance. This is our first retreat and our first encounter with Ramtha.

How have Laurent and I come to this retreat? What has led us here? We have each decided to set forth the experiences which brought us to this great day in August, 2005.

My first memory of a "spiritual experience" goes back to when, at the age of fourteen, I made my first communion in the Catholic religion and participated in a three day "retreat" during which I recall being smitten for the first time with a great impetus of passion and love, discovering a thirst for knowledge and a yearning to go beyond my limits. It was during those moments of introspection that I deeply felt a faith in the future and in who I was. It was a magical moment, full of joy, exaltation and of love for the whole world.

But unfortunately, this spiritual uplifting didn't last very long. My school life regained the upper hand with all its habits, and I rapidly became mired again in the daily trudge of life. It seemed as if my parents, teachers and friends dragged me into a daily routine full of sadness and sameness. They constantly fed me back a world without surprises, where nothing would ever change.

At seventeen, I discovered writings such as those of the Prophet Khalil Gibran, and I decided to get an education. I felt like living life to its fullest, travelling, discovering other worlds, and I made all sorts of plans. But, I became pregnant, and a wedding was hastily arranged. I soon found myself married and the mother of a little boy at the age of eighteen! Suddenly, my life had taken on a completely different direction. But very quickly, motherhood became quite satisfying and I decided to breastfeed, much to the consternation of my friends and family. I had always wanted a natural and healthy existence. My own mother did not breastfeed us, but I considered it absurd not to.

I also made up my mind to follow correspondence courses, even though I found myself surrounded with little encouragement. They did not understand my choices. Why slave away to "learn" when one is "married with children?" I was never able to find a single person to encourage me in my choices!

At this stage in my life, my father suddenly became confined to a wheelchair as the result of a surgical error. Therefore, I needed to attend to my parents' news shop/bookstore. I no longer had time to study, nor to send back my homework, and so I quit just a few weeks before the baccalaureate exams.

I focused fully on my family. As I was convinced that I didn't want to raise an "only" child, my second son was born some twenty-four months later and the third, three years afterward. At twenty-three, I was the mother of three boys.

In the meantime, my husband, a pastry cook, and I bought a pastry shop in the village of Jura. Little do we know that we had signed on for years of hard labour! We were treated as foreigners and moreover our competition was well established and respected. The residents patronized him naturally. We had become the victims of the fear of change, as people are little inclined to take on new habits! I was twenty and I didn't understand such attitudes. My obstinacy was compounded by the years of personal difficulties and the lack of funds. I threw all my energy into attracting clients. I no longer read; even though at times I had occasional philosophical thoughts, I was up to my neck in survival. I had no one with whom I could communicate. My personal goals were repressed to the lowest nadir of my being. Nothing at this stage of my life helped me escape. I had too much to do. I would wait till business got better and the boys grew a little before starting any new plans.

It's as if during all those years, I hadn't seen the light of day! Finally, I was able to poke my nose out of the mud! As I suffered from having quit my schooling, I now searched for ways to improve my lot. A psychology magazine article caught my attention and I made plans to learn about Neuro-Linguistic Programming (N.L.P.), for which I needed to go to Paris, where I met new people, made new friends and more importantly, talked about something other than the weather!

I finally was able to begin to learn who I was, to learn about human nature, and how to interact with others. A new world opened up. More than a breath of fresh air, I felt alive and rediscovered my youth's exuberance. Life took on a new tack!

I was thirty and, armed with my hard-won experience of managing a business, I started to offer training courses for pastry shop personnel throughout all of France. These training courses on the sales, presentation, and communication would permit me to finance my own continuing educational training courses that I took on NLP, as well as the purchase of many books!

And so, little by little, I begin to develop self-awareness, despite the hostile environment, my background, and my own fears. But the true spiritual path hadn't yet opened up! For the time being, I lived mostly in the acquisition of new knowledge, of understanding the real meaning of our communication, even though I was not yet engaging in self-analysis. During these years, I was simply learning, acquiring and piling up knowledge. I discovered new models and learned different ideas. Fairly quickly, the training I conducted was more focused on pure communication. It became instinctive. I felt the need to communicate all my newly acquired concepts to those who shared my trade and who encountered the same problems.

By the same token, I also felt the need to change, to begin anew. I was more and more intolerant of passivity around me. I expected others to change. I also delved into the study of kinaesthesia, which opened up a new horizon: everyone could free themselves by sheer mental willpower! Human beings were more than just what their personality expressed.

Following a three day seminar by Anthony Robbins and his famous "walk of fire," I concluded: it was time to change my life.

A ditch had opened between my husband and me. We no longer lived at the same rhythm. Even though he would be hard-pressed to admit it, my filing for divorce relieved him. I left the business and established myself as an independent trainer. I launched myself into a new professional and passionate life.

My teenage boys stayed with their father. A new era of difficulties began: we had no money, and I missed the boys terribly. I felt lost, although I desperately held onto all that I had learned during the last few years. Although I lived some twenty miles away from my sons in order to be able to see them as often as possible, it didn't happen as I would have liked; their father's bitterness provoked lots of problems in our relationship.

I immersed myself in my work, working night and day to develop new courses. I was driven to impart my discoveries, to help my student/trainees, most of whom were heads of their own businesses, to see the world from a different point of view, to give them my know-how. Thus they were happy to have access to other ways and to possibly improve relations with their employees as well as their clients.

At that time I was able to read a lot on the subject of human relations, personal conflicts and communication in general. I continued to take a few seminars in the general area of NLP. I built up my know-how and thought about putting it into action, but in fact, it stayed on the surface and I was not able to integrate it into my daily life as easily as I would have liked. I realized, it's not enough to have the knowledge and to teach it, but it is absolutely necessary to really live it (walk the walk). In such moments, I discovered many new ideas and I believed my life would change, but it was only an illusion! My inhibitions and fears of not being recognized were still there. Yes, I had come a long way, but there was still a long path to travel, to truly find myself!

I had swum in the waters of knowledge but I hadn't always drunk at the source nor internalised it. While my thirst for knowledge, my frenetic need to prove that I would succeed and that I was different, served as the driving force, my ever expanding ego prevented me from making a stand and taking the path of real spirituality, the path towards Truth through an approach of humility and the joyful recognition of who I was. In conclusion, there were still many bridges to cross although, without a doubt, I could allow myself to be led to the Source if I were to let go a little…but I wasn't sure.

I would need to endure many more disappointments in order to discover that I was still perhaps on the wrong path, that I had nothing to prove. I was still not fully able to differentiate between my head and my heart, between knowledge and experience, between what I saw and what I felt.

My love life had been full of ups and downs; I searched to live through others, to be recognized as a woman, while up until then I had lived the roles of mother, business manager and trainer.

I still didn't know myself very well, and I still suffered without realizing it. I gave the impression of being independent and sure of myself but in fact I was deeply into CONTROL.

I moved to the department of the Drôme at the end of 2000, where I bought a house. How I was able to obtain a mortgage was a minor miracle. A quieter period began. I found time to contemplate my behaviour, which seemed motivated largely by fears and defensiveness, that which I wanted and that which I didn't want. Books such as *Conversations with God* and *Life and Teachings of the Masters of the Far East* were helpful. I wanted to leave my companion but it was difficult as I was into the chemistry of the emotions.

Learning that I had seriously overpaid my taxes, I decided to use the money to take a trip to India organized by a Belgian painter who had lived in India for thirty years, read Sanskrit and was regarded by the locals as a "sage." During a trip he made throughout France during which he conducted painting courses, he talked about a trip devoted to holy shrines and a week to be spent painting in an ashram. I was taken by his erudition, his knowledge of India and his program. There were nine of us who would join him in Bangalore in December of 2001 and I looked forward to spending three weeks relaxing in self-contemplation. I met Laurent on the trip and our love was born in a timeless space, in a cocoon of our own making.

As soon as we returned, we decided to live together and Laurent moved from over 500 kms away to join me. My life took on yet another turn! I had finally met someone who could listen without judging and who stood up for me. Our long conversations helped to break down existing barriers of fear and incomprehension. I learned to let go little by little, to accept and to grow. We shared the same ideals, the same interests; I like to say that we have fostered a beautiful communion of souls!

Very quickly, Laurent introduced me to his friends, among who was Vincent, whom he has known for fifteen years and who had just recently met Valerie. We would become very close friends during the following years even though we were not immediate neighbours. In September of 2002, Laurent would be best man at Vincent and Valerie's wedding and six months later, Vincent would return the favour at our wedding.

Valerie had been reading the teachings of Ramtha for several years as well as the *White Book.* They attended their first retreat in 2004 and talked to us about their experience. The concept that we each create our own reality awoke in me a vital need to become more independent, to rely on nothing and no one. At that moment, my ego was still trying to assert itself.

We decided at the last moment to attend the Beginner's Retreat in Italy in 2005. Our daughter was a beautiful baby of six months old and we hesitated to engage ourselves for nine days. I certainly didn't want to separate myself from her. We called the French coordinator to sign up; then later we called back to cancel. We had a hard time deciding. But I will always remember the emptiness, the feeling of loss and of everything crumbling when we called Norma to cancel! It was horrible to realize that we would not go. However, the message from our inner powers became clear and we soon called back to reinstate ourselves. Of course, all the bunks were then taken but we were nonetheless allocated a whole room for ourselves in the centre's infirmary!

I believe I can affirm that, without being particularly conscious of it, my whole life has been spent searching for myself. It has been a long progression to dare to fix a rendezvous with the divine incarnate being that I am. To discover the self is to discover my wisdom, my humility and my humanity. It is a life long trip to the essential, towards the heart of the matter and to be able to savour each step of the way. It was the right time for our first meeting with Ramtha. As they say, it had to happen! I was finally ready to go beyond and to let go of the superfluous.

At the moment I write these lines, we are preparing to leave France to live in Yelm, Washington! We will be there this summer, three years after our first seminar in 2005 which was such a new and grand adventure for both of us, but that is another story!

BABU JOHN SAMUEL
India

HOW I MET MY MASTER TEACHER *AGAIN*!

I say 'I met my Master Teacher *again*,' because like a lot of my fellow associates, I believe the Master Teacher and I really met prior to my being born here…this plane called Earth filled with experiences and adventures that offers stunning beauty and pathetic lethargy and cruelty… that perhaps few places of existence offer. The people I have met and the subsequent interactions experienced along with the magnificent nature scenes I have witnessed make coming here a worthy choice indeed. And the adventure continues…

In my visualization into the past, I see the Master Teacher conversing with me over my future Earth lifetime. Of course, at the end of it all, I made the dubious action of exclaiming, "You are my Master Teacher!" I can see Ramtha smile for it gave him the right to 'use any means to achieve the end' through all sorts of experiences. Indeed, on this plane I have been a reluctant warrior-adventurer…entering the web of a large family system when I really enjoy my own privacy, with fields of study that I did not particularly enjoy like engineering when I wanted to be a pilot instead …seeing my first love of flying disappear as a career in the Indian Air Force due to a knee injury…facing the challenges of western habits for an eastern youth…entering a marriage that I did not particularly want…having kids when I thought offspring were for the 'others,' and entering corporate life where I spend many boring hours, trying hard not to fall asleep.

Well, at this time, looking back, I do enjoy my privacy now, but I have also enjoyed the company of dozens of my family members, uncles and aunts, cousins and in-laws, who turned out to be delightful entities. Although in a conservative family, I was able to take off on a motorcycle alone at the young age of twenty-two, completing 7,500 miles of mostly two-lane roads throughout India and escaping death through potential accidents almost a dozen times. On weekends, I experience my first love, flying ... as a private pilot and accumulating 550 hours with my instrument and multi-engine ratings. I'm now able to understand the laws of the universe better, thanks to my engineering background and I met a charming woman whom I initially ignored but eventually married. I keep telling her that she is the only one who could tolerate my unconventional ways... and we have had two offspring who have proven to be absolute delights, offering their own experience opportunities to enable their 'dad' to reach higher levels of tolerance. To top it all I am an independent Business Consultant requiring all the skill and knowledge I possess to make people change and turn their companies around to profitability . . . or face a hasty departure into the street . . .

Well done, my Master Teacher!
Splendid performance and experience-situations and I thank you!

Prior to realizing I am a God and could manifest my own destiny, I used to visit psychics. In one chilling session, I was told I have a Teacher who had been with me a long time. He had a name beginning with R and I would be given great knowledge by a woman. Hmmm . . .

While a rebel most of my life in a silent and unobtrusive way, I gave up religion long ago. I felt that the Jehovah described in the Old Testament could not be any God I want to worship and conducted my own research into the 'Truth.' I was introduced to classical spirituality by a friend who had experienced her share of gurus, masters and sacred places. She showered me with books and tapes, particularly by the Masters Abraham and Mafu. Finally, she said 'you are ready for the *White Book*.' I liked this publication, which is the first book that Ramtha authored and which has been distributed worldwide. I thought Ramtha was 'indeed interesting' and added it to my library, smug with further increasing my string of knowledge.

I lived with my realization, secure that I was indeed a *'great guy'* with all this accumulated wisdom and thinking. I really did not need any help, particularly from so-called Masters or Gurus.

While I did get the brochures from the Ramtha's School of Enlightenment, I felt the time was not just right. Convinced that I was born in this place to 'do some good,' I proceeded in my persistent efforts to accumulate wealth. I felt there were some future projects that represented my true destiny. Initial efforts turned out to be somewhat frustrating. Having accumulated great assets in real estate along with subsequent liabilities, I then saw the 'whole house of cards' collapse in front of me. The joy of being pursued by creditors including the IRS turned out to be an endearing experience indeed!

In the meantime, I joined the cadre of Business Consultants, and then interacted with 720 businesses over fifteen years, helping some 30,000 people including dependents to lead calmer, more organized and hopefully more fruitful lives.

So, while consulting in the faraway land of Florida, I finally scheduled to attend RSE's weekend-introduction starting on a Friday, 3,000 miles away in Santa Barbara in California. Before I left for the airport, the client had incessant questions and between missed flights and the rental car drive to Santa Barbara, I arrived at the late hour of 10:00 p.m.

I discovered that Ramtha had indeed been there, given a rousing teaching to the shocked participants and had just left! I went on to continue the weekend session with the remnants of the RSE staff including Father Miceal and Dr. Joe Dispenza, both experienced teachers of the School. The information given was indeed intriguing. To top it all, one of the exercises was to draw your dream symbolically on a card, place it on the wall of the room and then be blindfolded. At this point, I was turned around by the teachers and told to focus on the card. Without stumbling too much into the furniture strewn around the room, and with a couple of false starts, I found myself in front of my card. I was so startled that I took out my pen and drew two lines next to the symbol to match the color of the ink. Yes! It was my card! Excited cheers from the staff were followed with long congratulatory hugs. Life was looking up again!

The second session was in Yelm. This time, I again planned to leave my consulting project on the east coast and arrive in time on the opening day. However, by the time I collected my luggage in Seattle and drove to RSE it was late at 9:30 pm. I was just in time to see Ramtha exit the stage! I had missed him again!

The next session was back at RSE months later. This time I knew what to expect and I was fully prepared. Ramtha arrived and in the midst of the cheering and clapping, it was satisfying to finally hear him for the entire session, but not without controversy.

In the session as he walked around the arena, he pointed to this older, disabled woman sitting in her wheelchair and told her to leave the comfort of the wheelchair and get up and walk! The woman stared him in silence but did nothing. I was in a state of shock. Having been taught to help the elderly and speak politely to the disabled, I stared at Ramtha. *'How could you possibly talk like that?'* No one else in the audience seemed unduly perturbed.

During the first few years of coming to RSE, I was still intrigued but not convinced about Ramtha and his wisdom. Master Teachers seemed far away and somewhat interesting. After all, I had done twenty years of research on UFOs, life in general and spirituality! Ramtha appeared knowledgeable and he was certainly entertaining.

During one session, suddenly the cry went out, "Ramtha is here!" I remember thinking, "Darn! He's here just when I was looking for a restful break! I bet he's here for another long eight hour-session. " In retrospect, I was in that state of mind which did not fully recognize or appreciate Ramtha. I was mentally agreeing with some of his statements and in my apparent great wisdom, disagreeing with others. I settled down at the end of the Hall and I noticed Ramtha staring at me. I looked back at him with some trepidation to realize that he was not looking away... *'Darn! Looks like he's figured out my attitude...or lack of it...no fooling this entity!'*

It's strange to look back now when I join the rest of the students in rejoicing at Ramtha's coming and realizing the depth of his great experience and knowledge. Every moment with this entity is a joy!

I realized that in six months of his teachings I had accumulated more knowledge than in the twenty years of lop-sided and intermittent research on my own. I know more about the meaning of life... where I came from and where I am going, and about manifestation, and about disciplines practiced by great yogi entities from my own country, about extra-terrestrials, UFOs, Jehovah, Id and Yahweh. I also saw JZ Knight, who channels Ramtha, blossom separately as a Teacher. I've had a lot of fun learning and experiencing in the five years that I've been in school, seen miracles happen and met some fascinating people from all over the planet!

And having had this great opportunity to meet my Master Teacher, what do I do for the rest of the fellow inhabitants of this Planet? At every chance, I tell people about Ramtha and the school, particularly the people I like, because if they ever came to the RSE sessions, they will manifest their dreams. Since I am in the School, I have written three books, two of them novels about world situations. The theme always manages to include mysterious subjects like the God within, manifesting your dreams, UFOs, underground tunnels in the Earth and life after death....any means to convey information to a sleeping human civilization...the forgotten Gods!

In fact, when I visit my family in India, I tell friends and acquaintances about the School. They are generally shocked and tongue-tied. They don't know whether to be rude and challenge me or ask for more details... while my family appear to be in mental anguish to be involved in the conversation. In fact, this became so frequent that I am finally prohibited from talking about Ramtha to visitors to my home and to my wife's family. "For God's sake, don't talk to them about a 35,000 year-old entity...talk to your family.

They already think you're nuts!"

So when visitors ask "…and Babu, what are you doing in the US when your family is here in India?" I say, "Well that's because I go to School there." After a couple of glances at my silvery hair, inevitably, someone will ask, "School! What School is that?" Then I grin and tell them all about Ramtha and RSE… *'I just can't be rude and ignore them, can I!'*

Yes! Meeting my Master Teacher has been an unusual experience. I am amazed that he takes time out to spend with us. I guess he really loves us…and believes in us!

I have manifested most of my dreams and there are more coming. I do my disciplines, some days more regularly than others. Times are exciting and ever-changing! I spend time between India and the Pacific Northwest having moved to Onalaska, in the Yelm area and life is magnificent.

More intriguing, in my limited interactions with Ramtha… there is something else he knows about…regarding my own destiny…why I am here. There has been just a drop of a hint here…a gesture there. It is intriguing and exciting…something is brewing for me… but for the present, the future is *now!*

BETTYE JOHNSON
Texas, USA

Awakening: A Memoir

I t would be fun to begin this by writing, "It was a dark and stormy night," but this was not the case. I was born on a hot summer night in Dallas, Texas—July 28, 1929. My parents had no money for a hospital; therefore, a doctor came to the house to deliver me. Apparently, my parents wanted a boy because I did not have a name until I was three days old. My paternal grandmother called on the third day and asked, "How is Bettye Ann?" My mother gave me the spelling of Bettye and I bless her for this.

Not too long after my birth, I developed colic and cried incessantly. I was unable to take my mother's milk and was given goat milk. At age one year, I became ill with scarlet fever, which is a rash from a strep infection. When I became an adult, I learned that the basis of all illnesses come from emotions. I realize now that I came into this existence as an angry being and it did not get better.

My sister was five years older than me and I remember hearing my mother tell people that when she went to the bathroom or outside to hang up clothes that she had to take either me or my sister with her, because she was afraid that my sister would kill me.

At age four, I developed pneumonia and remained at home under a homemade oxygen tent. I almost died. Then when I was five, I had my tonsils removed and almost hemorrhaged to death. There was something within me that wanted to die, but I did not die. Now I realize I had a destiny, or I should say a date with Ramtha.

My father was a bombastic bigot and although he rarely spanked us, he lashed my sister, my young brother and me severely with his tongue. Some label it psychological or verbal abuse. I could never do anything right and was told repeatedly that I was dumb and stupid. My mother was too afraid to say anything because she was psychologically abused too. I remember her walking around with a frown on her face and her shoulders slightly bent. We were all in fear of my father and tiptoed when he was around. I thought of her as old even though she had been a vibrant beautiful young woman when she married my father at age nineteen.

The Great Depression is said to have begun with a major crash of the stock market in October of 1929. I did not realize how poor we were until I grew up. My father's older sister and my mother's family subsidized us. Mother made my clothes and my sister received hand-me-downs from cousins on my mother's side. On my father's side, my sister, brother and I were the only children.

My father's family lived in Dallas and one of my aunts taught elocution, also known as expression. Mother enrolled me in her class where I learned public speaking by reciting poems and acting them out. I was also in small musical programs although my family told me that I could not carry a tune.

When I was six, my father found work 200 miles west of Dallas in a small town named Winters. It was there that I earned my spending money by picking cotton in summers. As a family, we began attending the Methodist Church. There were no Negroes in the small town and I was not really aware of segregation. I have no idea where the belief came from, but I became afraid of God. I thought that if I thought about God that He would strike me dead. Therefore, I tuned out much of what I heard in church and this was a blessing in disguise.

We had lived in Winters for three years when we moved to a larger town fifty-four miles away named San Angelo. I later learned that we moved because my father was fired from his job and was in trouble with the law for stealing from his employer. My mother lied and gave him an alibi, so his case was dropped.

During this time in Winters, I triggered a genetic gene and began gaining weight. I was teased and ridiculed. I retreated inwardly and developed a passion for movies. I remember searching the alleys in San Angelo looking for pop bottles, which I turned in for money. I would take a bus and go downtown by myself to the movie matinee. I also dreamed of traveling all over the world and pored over travel brochures that I sent off for.

I never had a sense of 'fitting in' with children of my age and often felt like I was on the outside looking in while others appeared to be having fun. In the fourth grade, I cultivated a love for reading and in the summer, I would take the bus downtown to the library with my brother accompanying me. My mother was instrumental in creating my love for opera. When there was a performance at our civic auditorium of various artists of the musical and dance world, she took my brother and me whenever she had the money for tickets. I was exposed to great violinists, pianists, ballet and opera singers as well as plays and other forms of entertainment.

The surprise bombing of Pearl Harbor by the Japanese began the involvement of the U.S. in WWII. I remember I was playing outside in our front yard when someone came from the house and told me. This was a change for our family. We experienced gas rationing and ration cards for items such as shoes, sugar, coffee, butter, flour and other items. My mother went to work as a bookkeeper for a wool warehouse where my father was working. Our finances improved and by the time I graduated from high school in 1946, I was able to attend the Texas State College for Women—now Texas Women's University located in Denton, Texas.

I was not a brilliant student and lost interest in my studies when my father would not allow me to change my major. The world turned upside down for our family when my father left my mother to marry a well-to-do woman. Divorce was an unheard of thing on both sides of the family and it was traumatic for my mother, which spilled over to the rest of us. I left college and went home to hell. My father and his new wife lived within six blocks of us and my father had custody of my brother. He threatened suicide if my mother did not give in and she capitulated. In retrospect, I can see that all these adversities moved me into another phase of my life.

After leaving college, I found a job as an office clerk and met a man who I began dating. He was Greek and frankly, the first man who was attracted to me. We married and I escaped from one hell into another. I loved the Greek people and we had a small community in San Angelo. I soon learned I had married an emotional, unbalanced man and after eighteen months, I divorced him and moved to Houston, Texas. Fortunately, there were no children.

For the first six months in Houston, I lived with my sister and her husband. By this time, my sister and I had become friends and observing my ballooning weight, she placed me on a diet and managed to get diet pills. I soon found a job and from May to September of 1950, I lost fifty pounds and I often said, "Life began at fifty - 150 lbs, that is." Later I will write about another aspect of that statement.

I began dating and life was interesting and enjoyable. By this time, I worked in the U.S. Civil Service for the Navy Department in downtown Houston. One morning while on my coffee break, I read a small item in a Houston newspaper. The item said that there were recruiters in town from the State Department seeking overseas office workers. I mentioned this to a co-worker and she urged me to apply. On my lunch hour, I went to the hotel where interviews were conducted, and filled out an application. After taking an aptitude test, I was sent to the nearby FBI office, where I was fingerprinted. This was in April of 1952.

I had almost forgotten about the interview and the application, when in July I received a telegram offering me a job as a code clerk. I had no idea what a code clerk job entailed. I accepted the job and in mid-August, I found myself on a train for Washington D.C. Little did I realize I was moving into a new neural network in my brain.

I moved from a world of segregation, bigotry, prejudices and low self-esteem to a new world. Once I was sworn in, eight other young women and I found rooms in the same boarding house near DuPont Circle. My real education began. I learned to encode and decode secret messages. I learned that not all black people were segregated or ignorant and many worked for the government.

My uncommon education became full swing when I was assigned to the code room in the embassy in Paris. Without intending to, I discarded most of my Texas accent, racial prejudice and bigotry. In retrospect, I understand why I easily lost most of my Texas accent, because I had no one to mirror back to me the sound of it. I had shifted my neuronet.

Paris, and a new mindset. In the communications center, we worked shifts. The day shift was followed by the evening shift and then the midnight to 8:00 a.m. shift. The embassy received wire traffic from all over the world and was the largest U.S. communications center outside of Washington D.C. The French were fighting in Indochina—now named Vietnam. The U.S. was fighting in Korea, the French were also dealing with unrest in Algeria and Senator Joe McCarthy was conducting witch-hunts in the U.S. for communists and homosexuals. Adding to this was the U.S. relationship with Russia—it was the time of the 'cold war,' and Europe was still recovering from WW II.

There were days when I worked double due to heavy code traffic, and this meant sixteen-hour shifts. In the midst of this, I took advantage of experiencing all I could of Paris. I became sophisticated, or so I thought. I primarily dated American Marines at the embassy, because they also worked shifts. Those of us in the communications center did not really attempt to develop relationships with the French because of the sensitive nature of our work. Therefore, I saw a part of Paris that many Americans did not see, bar hopping from Place Pigalle to the Left Bank, and learning the art of social drinking, but never having sex with the men I dated. We were out to have fun and yes, there were male-co-workers and Marines who had French mistresses and no one condemned them.

In addition to my social life, I spent hours in the Louvre and other museums and art galleries, perusing the shops and attending the opera, Folies Bergere and visiting the various cathedrals. I was not a religious person and had no real affinity with God. I visited these cathedrals because of the architecture and curiosity. I enjoyed the trips made to England, Germany, Switzerland, Belgium, Holland and Italy as well as other places in France. I was educating myself and I thrived.

During my last year in Paris, my bubble burst. A man who was dating one of my co-workers came to my apartment and I let him in because I knew him. I wondered why he had come to see me and I soon found out. He raped me. I was ashamed because it had been impressed into my belief system that it was always the woman's fault for being raped. In one sense, this is true and for me it was because I allowed him in. When I found out I was pregnant, I was devastated. Abortion was an unknown to me and I thought that if I told my family that they would disown me.

With the McCarthy witch-hunt in full swing, I knew if it became known that I had been raped and was now pregnant that I would be fired and sent back to the U.S. in disgrace. Finally, I told one of my supervisors because he and his wife had become my friends. They were my only support during these dark days. I wore clothes to work that did not reveal my swelling stomach and Brad placed me on the midnight to eight shifts. He also found a doctor for me and after he examined me, the doctor told me I would have to have a caesarian operation. Brad helped even more by placing me on vacation with the story that I had gone to Italy.

The baby was delivered in a Catholic hospital and the nun who attended me after surgery would not tell me if the baby was alive or dead because I had signed my rights away. Brad had helped me find a foundling home for the baby before I delivered. I remember her malevolent glare. No one would tell me if it was male or female. I went back to my apartment and cursed God—thinking God had deserted me and I was a sinner.

Soon after I recovered, an opportunity came for me to move into an apartment with a co-worker. I accepted, and thus began another phase of my life. I was not so lighthearted. Our apartment was within the building of the widow of the famous singer Chaliapin. My life began anew as I placed the event behind me and moved forward. It was easy not to dwell on the experience, because I had never seen the baby or even known if it was alive or dead or its sex. Therefore, there was no attachment. Except for my supervisor and his wife, I held my secret for the following twenty-five years.

When my tour in Paris was completed, I transferred to the embassy in Tokyo. This was a new experience and the communications center staff was small. It also became party time after work and there were no shifts—only staggered hours. I lived in an apartment complex owned by the U.S. government.

I enjoyed the difference of Tokyo and Japan. It was a new adventure. I purchased an American auto and had it shipped to Japan. I learned to drive on the opposite side of the road and to maneuver my way through the narrow streets, honking my horn just like the Japanese. I refused to ride on their commuter trains because it was like packing sardines in a can.

I dated a Marine guard and we developed a friendship that was not love. It is interesting the choices one makes. I carried the guilt that I was a 'bad' woman, and when the opportunity came to have sex—we did. Bombshell! I learned I was pregnant. I was horrified and told him. I sunk into a deep abyss of despair. The long and short of it is that we married and returned to the States. I silently made a vow to myself that I would be a good mother and wife, and I was. All of this was a blessing in disguise.

This man, a career Marine was away two-thirds of the twenty-three year marriage and this was a blessing, because we now had three sons. I developed self-reliability skills and I was able to bring my sons up my way. I learned how wonderful male children could be. I learned to be self-sufficient and take care of the moves from base to base, paying bills and enjoying my time alone after my sons went to bed at night. Occasionally I took my sons to church. I still had no relationship with God and one could say I had a neutral attitude, but felt a duty to expose my sons to religion.

After the death of my mother in 1976, I contemplated her life, and I knew I wanted more than what I had observed of her life. When I was forty, a thought flitted through my mind, "By the time you are fifty, your life will be different." This thought came to me off and on over the next ten years.

On my fiftieth birthday, I held my 'coming out' party celebrating my divorce and my fiftieth year. The statement I had uttered in previous years came to pass: "Life began at 50…" My sons were out of high school and I was working again for the government. Freedom! Before my divorce, I had gone to Overeaters Anonymous where I learned the 12-step program. I was beginning to connect with the spiritual aspect of myself. I also knew this was not the stopping point in my new life.

My sponsor introduced me to metaphysics and Religious Science. I felt like I was learning a new language. She gave me a book by Ruth Montgomery, *The World Before,* and everything in the book resonated with me. I had an image of everyone being created at the same moment as points of light with each of us connected with a thread. I now know that I was beginning to see a web, or a grid. I began to learn about the power of the mind, meditation, holistic health and psychic abilities. I began having a relationship with the God within me. I remember reading a small book that said, "God is within everyone" and I accepted this statement as being so.

I recall a very meaningful moment. I was now divorced and alone in my condominium one evening. I do not remember what I was contemplating, but energy came through the top of my head and it grounded me to the couch. I was unable to move and it felt like I was held in a vise with no pain - only a powerful energy.

Mantras began coming into my thoughts and I would silently repeat them over and over until a new one replaced the previous one. Two in particular that I remember are, "I know I know, I know that I know," and "I am that I am."

I attended a government-sponsored workshop in Los Angeles about self-esteem, it was based on the book *I'm OK, You're OK.* When I left the event, I was flying high and had my first experience of a glimpse into another reality. I was driving in the middle lane on the freeway to my home in Orange County when I glanced over to the fast lane on my left. I saw an old truck with a large carousel on the back and it was going round and round. I looked back to my lane and when I again glanced to the left, there was no truck. It had disappeared - poof! We were not near an off-ramp and the truck was not ahead of me or behind me in either of the lanes. It was something to contemplate and I know now that I tapped into a parallel timeline.

I became a sponge, soaking up new knowledge and yet I knew that what I was learning was not the final step. Religious Science, Unity and Divine Science taught me the power of the mind or positive thinking. I explored many modalities of thought and a new concept of God began forming within me as I gradually threw out all of the old programming I had received.

In the spring of 1980, I enrolled in a class to learn about using psychic abilities. We had exercises of psychometry, remote viewing and sending and receiving. In the sending and receiving exercise, we chose a partner. One week, partner A sent an image to partner B and the second week we reversed. I was partner A and when it came for me to receive what my partner was sending, I began seeing an image of a little girl in a pink dress; I had a most unusual week. Everywhere I went, I heard the French language. There were also articles in newspapers and magazines about France. When we came to class, my partner told me that she had no choice but to send me what she did and did not understand why.

I knew immediately why and that it was connected to the birth of a child in Paris over twenty-five years previously. I began to cry. I pondered the meaning and went to see one of the teachers of the class. He was psychic and closed his eyes. I sat quietly and when he opened his eyes, he told me I was forgiven and to move on with my life. I accepted what he told me and did as he said - I moved on in my growth. I also knew that my God had not deserted me, but carried me through all the adversities.

Soon after this class, I was invited to attend a class of a Divine Science ministerial school in Arcadia, California to see if I liked the philosophy. I attended and it resonated within me. I decided that I wanted to be a minister and enrolled for the fall class. This led me into a new adventure of becoming a minister and a program director for a holistic health center.

The class was held two nights a week and began in September. Little did I know what was in store for me. Within me, I had a deep desire for intimacy in a relationship. Although I met and dated men, none turned me on until I sat next to a man in this Divine Science class. We were married in December and I call him my Mr. Magic because he gave the experience of what I had been wanting. We were able to talk about everything. I felt like I was an open bottle pouring forth all that had been suppressed. He also gave me the intimacy I wanted. He is now deceased, and although our twenty-year marriage was not all a bed of roses, he gave me a beautiful experience. This is how I remember him - Mr. Magic. I have outlived my three husbands and I have no regrets.

Adversity is interesting in many ways. I grew up fearing my father and I had a sense that something had happened when I was around three years of age. After I married my late husband, we attended a workshop and were asked to draw pictures of our fathers. I was shocked at the anger coming from me. I took my crayons and drew red and black scribbles. I then began a search to find some avenue to reveal what unfinished business I had with my father who had passed in 1967. Not too long after this workshop, I was gifted with another workshop and I did not want to attend but my husband encouraged me and I went.

On the last day of the workshop, we went into a process where we stood up and as questions were asked regarding attitudes of our parents, we were to take the body position as to what we thought their attitude was. The questions were simple, such as what was your mother or father's attitude towards money. When the time came for questions regarding attitudes of my father, I did well until I was asked the question, what was your father's attitude towards sex?

I came unglued and screamed, "You raped me!" I began crying and became hysterical.

Fortunately, I received loving support from the workshop leaders and those attending. They were loving, but not interfering. When my tears subsided, I went home and my body was wracked with the energy of volatile anger for three days. On the third day, I told myself that this was enough and I gave the anger up. I had held this anger inside of my body - my cells - for fifty-two years. The revelation and the release were necessary for me to find my way to my Master Teacher.

For our second anniversary, we chose to attend a spiritual weeklong workshop given by Dr. Brugh Joy and David Spangler. This occurred the last week in December, 1982. The evening of December 30, we were told that there would be three people channeling their entities who would speak on peace.

I was not at all into channels or mediums. I lay back on the floor and ho-hummed when the first and second mediums supposedly channeled their entities. The third person was a pretty blond named JZ Burnett from Tacoma, Washington. I did not realize that at the time that she actually left her body in front of us. When her entity took over her body and said, "Indeed," I sat up as if a string had pulled me. I was mesmerized, because I knew I knew Him. I did not know from where, but I knew he was a Master Teacher, and that I had heard him before. His name was Ramtha.

After the conference, I lost touch with JZ Burnett, now JZ Knight, until the summer of 1985 when I viewed the Hawaii Ramtha video. I recognized my teacher, and I knew I could only learn from him. In 1986, I knew I was through with my ministerial career and retired from the ministry, which had many adversities and learning lessons. My husband was retired by now and we were drawn to Washington State, because we had friends living here. In October, 1986 we moved to Washington. The rest is wonderful history with its ups and downs.

It is a challenge to write what I have learned. I became a dedicated student. I know that from adversity comes a jewel. We only have to look for it. It is a grand journey.

I am most appreciative to JZ Knight for channeling Ramtha and giving us students the opportunity to learn from this Master Teacher. I have written more about my journey into awakening and this book, titled *Awakening the Genie Within,* will be published soon in 2008.

JACQUI DAVIS
Guyana

THE RISING PHOENIX

I was born in a beautiful country located on the northeastern coast of South America bordering Venezuela and Brazil. The weather is sunny all year round with monsoon seasons.

My father could see into the unseen realm and told my siblings and me lots of tales. So I grew up with a knowing that there was more than my eyes could see. My father's job took him away from home often. My mother decided when I was about five years old that she would live in London, England so she left my father and my siblings and me were raised by my grandmother, my mother's mother.

My grandmother was into the church. So every Sunday I had to attend morning church and afternoon Sunday school. This I did not like because to me Sunday was another sunny day that I should be outside playing and climbing trees for fruit. I noticed early in my church life that the congregation, including the minister, had a hard time living up to what he preached from the Bible. I questioned God early in my life and did not like HIM much since he was the reason I could not play on Sundays.

I did, however, believe in the aspect that "ask and ye shall receive," and when I was nine years old I wanted to attend a music festival at school. All the children at school wore the same uniform and white yachting shoes were a part of that uniform. My white shoes needed to be replaced for this festival. My father was away at the time and he was the one I needed to pay for the new shoes. I went into the toilet, closed the door, got down on my knees, and started to pray to God to send my father home so he could buy me these shoes. As I was praying, my aunt, my mother's sister opened the door and saw me praying, and proceeded to say quite loudly, "look at this sinner praying." That remark brought forth shame.

I was what they called an unruly child. I questioned the grown-ups about things like where the trees, moon, stars and sky come from. I questioned where babies came from and they always told me children are seen and not heard. I came out of the toilet feeling this shame, but I also knew that there was a place inside myself where grown-ups and their opinions could not touch me. My father showed up and bought me my shoes, and I attended the festival and my school won for the best singing. That experience was a pivotal juncture in my upbringing.

My sisters and I always walked to school and we always took a short cut through someone's property. On this property, there was a great house and this particular day we wanted some money. As we passed by the house, this beautiful woman with long silver grey hair stopped us and spoke to us and gave each of us a very shiny shilling and we were happy. Later on we found out there was no such woman that lived in this house. Another memory that was pivotal.

I finished high school and told my parents that I wanted to go to college in the United States. My mother felt I should study in London but I insisted on going to the United States. Destiny was calling.

I moved to the United States and graduated from Secretarial College, and went on to study Political Science at Queens College in New York. This field of study my mother approved wholeheartedly. However, after three years of college I got bored and became a stewardess. My life as a stewardess was the beginning of my awakening. I saw, experienced and learned greatly because, since I was visiting places where I had no past and no one knew me, I let loose. I partied and burned my candle at both ends in Europe and in New York.

I now know that everything I created was preparing me for the great work. Without these experiences, there is no way I could have lived in Yelm. I drew from the wisdom gained from my past. My roommate in New York was also a stewardess and she gave me a book to read, *A World Beyond* by Ruth Montgomery. When I finished reading this book, I felt apprehension; like I had forgotten something very important. It was my wakeup call. That day I promised myself that I would plant my feet firmly on the earth and I started my inner journey. I engaged in a therapy called Primal Scream. When I came out of my first week of this experience, my boyfriend said, "I don't know what you are doing but keep doing it." I looked years younger because during that week there was no television, partying or seeing any of my friends. I only saw my therapist and went back to my hotel room. This therapy regressed me back to memories where my energy was stuck. My deepest regression was to the void. I reclaimed a lot of my power. When I was done with this part of the journey, I quit the airlines.

I lived in New York City and owned a popular and fashionable yoga studio off of Fifth Avenue. Many of my students were into gurus and would do their best to convince me to attach myself to one of their gurus and I would often say to them "I am only interested in teaching postures, for GOD is in those legs and thighs that you want to tone." One day my assistant came with a VHS tape and told me I MUST watch this one because it was different and I would LOVE it. She stated that it was a spiritual teacher being channeled through a woman and I told her I did not believe in channeling. She, over a period of days, persevered and I chose to watch this tape.

I saw a beautiful young woman dressed in white sitting on a chair and after a few moments, it seemed like she had collapsed. Then the body started moving one leg wide to the side and then the other leg wide to the other side and with hands on knees, it started the deepest breathing I had ever heard. This being started talking and caught my attention until he was done and long after I turned that television set off I sat staring into space knowing that something just happened to me.

There was a movement around my heart area and later I was told it was my soul re-membering. I shared this tape with three other beings; all came to RSE, two are still current and the other passed on, bless his soul.

I said to my friends, "I am going to see this Ramtha and I will lock eyes with him and I WILL KNOW if he is a SCAM. So we registered for the last Question and Answer dialogue in Seattle and attended the workshop.

We stayed in the same hotel where the workshop was being held and arrived early the following morning so we could get good seats. As soon as the doors opened I dashed into the room and became "Goldilocks." The first seat was too something, the second seat was too something and the third seat was just right, which was a seat in the front row center of the stage. I then started to check the room out and as I turned my head, sitting on the stage was the Ram and he and I locked eyes. For me, time stood still and I became very quiet in my being.

He, the Ram, gave one of his finest teachings, that I AM GOD and again I was so fo-cused on what he was saying that it surprised me. When he opened up the audience to questions, I was the fifth one he chose. I told him I was interested in ascension and asked him how to do it. He answered, "why do you want to ascend" and I said because it is the ultimate and he said, "the ultimate, little entity, is A LIFE WELL LIVED" and in that moment I knew I was in the presence of the GRANDEST teacher on the planet and to this day, the RAM has been the greatest gift I have chosen for myself in this life time as he continues through his LOVE and WISDOM to show me that I AM DIVINE.

PETRA RAMON
Germany

MY CALLING TO RSE

December, 1993: Hamburg , Germany.

I t was a good day - working with my patients, taking our dogs for a walk. The evening was quiet, my three children were busy with their friends and I had just sat down to relax. There was something oddly different in the way I felt this evening though - some sort of ... quiet anticipation? Suddenly - unaccountably - a question popped into my mind: if someone would come now and tell me that I had a free choice to travel wherever I desired, where would I want to go? I had no idea. I just felt empty, or maybe bored - certainly not inspired to go anywhere. This was very unusual for me because I loved traveling.

That night I woke up from a deep sleep, hearing bells ringing. All kinds of thoughts went through my mind - what could this possibly mean (maybe the Third World War had broken out and people were gathering in the church, and I had missed it all!)? I got up and went outside to find out from where the sound was coming, but it had stopped. I went back to sleep and the same thing happened again. This time I was outside like a rocket, but again, no bell ringing to be heard.

Back in bed, I made a plan that if this happened again, I would turn my head onto my right side; because I can't hear with my left ear, any sounds I then became aware of would be sure to be coming from inside of me. That is exactly what happened; I heard the bells ringing clearly again even though my right ear was covered!

For some reason, I felt quite excited about this experience. It didn't scare me at all. The sound of the bells was pleasant, and in fact, for the next few months I looked forward to it when going to bed. After a while, the sound was also with me when I was working with patients - not always though.

In March of '94 I participated in a weekend seminar in southern Germany. It was all about diagnosing and balancing the energy flow in the meridians. The seminar building was in a country setting next to a church.

I heard the bells again, and I was sure that everyone else in the room could, too. I turned to my neighbour and remarked, "Hey, do you think they want us all to join the mass? They are ringing those church bells forever." He turned to me, saying "What bells?"

Back home in Hamburg I was invited to another event. A friend of mine had a book-selling booth there and I helped her afterwards to pack up. She picked up one book and said: "You should read this." I kindly refused: "No thank you, I have a bedside table piled with books I want to read." She insisted: I would be very interested; it was about channeling, etc. . . . I refused again, telling her that I had just read Jane Roberts' Seth books. My friend still insisted, giving me the book anyway - I could read it at my leisure.

It was the German translation of *Ramtha: An Introduction.*

Because I don't like having things around that don't belong to me, I began to read it immediately so as to return it a.s.a.p. Well, I did read it very quickly, not because I wanted to return it, but only because I was captured by the message of the book. I ordered all the Ramtha books that had been translated into German at the time. In reading them, I was absolutely fascinated and wanted more. So I requested informational material from RSE.

How excited I was when I finally received it and could actually listen to the included audio tape of one of Ramtha's teachings. I listened to it at least three times a day.

The next logical step (for me) was to register for a Beginning Event in October ' 94 (embarrassing to say that I didn't even know about the State of Washington and that Seattle would be my flight destination. Thank God I found out just in time - otherwise I would have landed in Washington D.C!).

Arrangements for a B&B for my first RSE event had been made in advance for me by a local business; I was to stay in a private home on the second floor. The whole night long before the event, I was entertained by a multitude of "wind-chimes," with which I had been unfamiliar in Germany. Their sound was just like the sound of my "bells!" Later I learned how Ramtha experienced becoming the wind and that he calls himself the Lord of the Wind. Some students told me how they playfully call wind-chimes "Ramtha detectors."

From that moment on I never heard the bells again.

My Beginning Event was magical. At one point I flew back and forth between Hamburg and Seattle at least four times a year to attend events at RSE.

Exactly five years later, in October '99, I moved to Yelm.

MONA SAUBIDET
France

PATH TO THE UNKNOWN

I was invited to dinner. The door opened..."Hello Shit-Face," said my Dad. "You're full of shit" was another thing he liked to say to me.

How I reacted and chose to feel brought out all the insecurity and unworthiness I had to own. "Ok, I am a piece of shit! So I guess I'm fucked up!" was my thought. I realize how I soaked up and took on all my father's hate and anger personally.

My mother never corrected him, nor took my side. It was in her education not to contradict him. I was not allowed to express my anger; or if I did, she'd say, "You should be ashamed of yourself."

My father was, in my view, the supreme authority. I used to fear his moods and whims. He could sulk for days in his whiskey, casting a dark cloud all around him. I knew that we just had to wait until the sun came out again. However, in the beginning, Dad wasn't like that. I had a very happy and wonderful childhood.

I was born in 1959, the year the TV series *The Twilight Zone* started. I was the first girl to come into the family of a young couple who had emigrated from Argentina to the United States of America. My mother, with my three elder brothers, was getting ready to move again to join my father working in France. We were on a march. This was just the beginning of a life of moves. We weren't going to settle more than two years in the same place or house.

In France my younger sister was born. Then a year and a half later, we moved to England. My first memories go back to a beautiful old English cottage in the countryside. We had a big garden and I'd spend hours looking into the throat of flowers, watching the bees, catching spiders, climbing trees… all the things a child can do in a beautiful garden. Nature was my friend and I was conscious everything was alive and aware. I remember telling off one of my brothers when he tried to destroy an ants' nest. I said to him that he too, at one point had been an ant, and therefore he should not destroy their nest.

I loved all the girls' toys but loved the boys' games too. I played with my brothers' war games with guns; we were "special commandos," shooting and playing dead.

One day a boy at school chased me to kiss me. I ran so far and when I reached the end of the field, I stopped and turned around and I said to him, "You know, I always wanted to be a boy!" He forgot the kiss and ran back as fast as he had come!

I had a Catholic upbringing and went to a Catholic school in the beginning. All the teachers were nuns except the music teacher. I went to Church on Sundays with my parents. The mess . . . I mean the Mass in Latin was endless. You had to kneel, stand up, sit down, sing, and stand up again… I never understood all the rituals. But I believed in God somewhere, somehow.

At home, I was allowed to watch all these science fiction and futuristic TV series (*Dr. Who, Thunderbird, The Twilight Zone, The Invaders,* etc). For me it was clear that extraterrestrial life existed. Furthermore, one night while climbing the steep stairs to go to my bedroom I looked out the window and saw …What! A flying saucer! What excitement! I came tumbling down the stairs saying: "Mummy! Mummy! I saw a flying saucer!" My mother gave me an explanation: it was a toy factory next door trying out their new toys. "Oh there's a toy factory? Yeah? In the middle of the night?" I thought to myself. But I believed her and forgot the whole thing until it popped up back into my memory about ten years ago. I even went as far as to ask her if we had ever lived next to a toy factory. She replied in the negative.

Furthermore, my brother José had a telescope and a book with pictures of the planets and the stars. He had bought a "Ticket to the Moon" in a machine in a station in London and he would brag: "I'm going to the moon, not you!!" The idea that there was life out there in space seemed a natural thing to us children.

There was a lot of music in the house: on weekends, my father listened to Brazilian jazz music like Jobim and all the great Jazz classics like Armstrong and Ella Fiztgerald.

My eldest brother Daniel was entering adolescence and he'd listen full blast to all the pop and rock on the pirate radios. We were in the middle of "The Swinging Sixties" in England. I watched all the music programs like *Go Steady Go and Top of The Pops.* I remember the first worldwide TV broadcast with the Beatles singing "All you Need Is Love"! John Lennon was living next door to a friend and one day all of the kids went together with his son Julian to the cinema to see *Yellow Submarine.*

By now, we had moved houses and changed schools for the third time in six years and were living closer to "Swinging London." It was the days of the Hippie movement and "Flower Power." I remember going by car past houses and buildings that must have been squats because big bright colorful flowers were painted on the walls and longhaired people wearing long Indian style shirts were hanging out on the sidewalks, smoking.

My brother Diego too started growing his hair and inviting friends over to party when my parents were out. The next morning we found a mess of empty glasses and bottles and cigarette studs. Wow! Was he in trouble?

Now, my father decided to leave his job and he got hired by an Australian company to work in France once again. We arrived a couple of months after "May 68"- the great students' and workers' movement in France - and moved to a place near the border of

Switzerland in a little village called Ferny-Voltaire named after the famous philosopher and writer who used to hide out there when he needed to escape King Louis XIV.

La France! It was a bit of a culture shock for me after the modern sixties of Great Britain. I was plunged into the language, this new culture, which had different codes, traditions and mentality (Just to give you an example: in England, it is polite to eat with your hands UNDER the table while in France it is polite to eat with your hands ON the table. One day I was invited to a girlfriend's house. They were six girls and the last child was a boy. There I sat, with the father to my right at the end of the table, and his son in front of me. The father would hit his son on the head every time he forgot to put his hands on the table. I'd pretend to wipe my mouth, grabbing the napkin all the time because I had forgotten to keep my hands on the table!).

I went to the little village's school. The teacher would punish and hit some of the pupils with his ruler or grab them by the ear. One day I had taken a ring of silver with turquoises that belonged to my mother and I wore it to school. The teacher came up to me and said, "What is this?" I answered back in perfect French: "It's the ring of my ancestors the Incas." My God knows why I said that because after that he never bothered me again.

We had a vegetable garden and for the first time I tasted the delicious homegrown tomatoes, strings beans and strawberries…

We lived in a chalet, a wooden house surrounded by mountains. I had a view from my room of Mont Blanc. I fell in love with the sunsets that turned the distant snowy high tops into different shades of purple, orange, pink or carmine. I'd paint them every evening. I had bought fluorescent colors to be able to portray the beautiful powerful colors I saw.

In addition, of course I learned to ski. With the school, every Thursday all winter we would go, be it blizzard or shine. In the summer, I would run and play hide & seek in the cornfields with siblings and friends or jump up for a ride on the farmer's tractor. On the holidays, we'd go to the Olympic swimming pool. There I learned to conquer my fear of diving from heights. We would also train ourselves to hold our breath as we swam under water from side to side: 25 meters.

Armstrong had stepped on the moon and I watched him on TV, but I was upset to see that they did not encounter any other life forms. "How come?" I thought to myself.

Waterloo: that is where Napoleon's last battle took place and that is where we lived in Belgium. I loved it! It was wonderful! We were right next to a big forest and we could go for long rides on bicycle with all the kids. Just in my neighborhood there were several American families and there was Danny Ascona…. I was in love with him! He had the darkest, most mysterious eyes you'd ever seen and the blackest wild hair. This wasn't my first kiss but…when he wanted to go further and I just wasn't ready…. and he wanted to stick his finger up my …I didn't even know I had a vagina! And well, that was the end of that. He never talked to me again or came round to see me. Needless to say I chose to feel rejected, of course.

I started shoplifting. We would go with the kids of the neighborhood and I would steal Barbie Dolls and all the toys I wanted plus sweets and other things to eat. I would make myself invisible; unnoticeable … I never got caught but my sister did. Boy.

I loved my school: there were Canadians, Swedes, Dutch, and French and Americans. I had two great girl friends with whom the sole idea was have fun. We would invent many games and disguises just to have our dose of laughter and every moment was lived with rare intensity and appreciation of our time together.

My schizophrenic aunt came from Argentina, to live with us for a year. She was a great artist and painter but her sickness plunged her into a day dreaming, into some sort of forgetfulness; she was absent, caught in her thoughts. One day I saw her walking in the street with her stocking hanging. She was superstitious and would buy all these lucky charms. She must have expected some magic to happen and maybe save her, I thought.

It was summer and as I was settling into my new room with my sister and I had this thought. What is death? I wanted to know what death was like. So as I lay in bed, I started contemplating what it would be like if I were dead. What would it be like… It was neither depression nor a morbid motivation, it was the desire to know what lay beyond this life. So that night, I focused on a spot on the ceiling thinking, concentrating on what it could be like to be dead. Soon it all went blurred and I felt like I was lifting up. I saw this whirling tunnel of light and started gravitating through it. I had the sensation of being aspirated, sucked up and out of my body. I got scared and I fell back down into my body. This was a taste of something "elsewhere"!

I was in my early teens, and I was concerned about nature and pollution. I was aware that the future was about living in harmony with nature so, with one of my girl friends, we imagined the ideal community that we'd like to live in; we would make our own pottery, grow our food, bake our own bread, in short; be self sufficient. I didn't want to be a consumer. I bought secondhand clothes at the flea market; I'd make skirts out of old pairs of pants, I'd wear my shoes till they fell to pieces, I'd do patchwork. My big brother bought me a book for my birthday on environmentalism. It had practical and technical instructions as how to adapt and survive in nature.

One of my other brothers was now in a band and I sang the backing vocals and started playing guitar, learning songs. We did a couple of gigs for his school and a contest.

I was living in the provincial birthland of Joan of Arc and of the Art Nouveau.
I didn't have many friends in school so I hung out with my big brother.
He was now at the art school "Beaux Arts" and we would paint, draw and sketch together with his friends. I spent a lot of time at my little desk in silence with my creations. One day I felt a hand on my shoulder. I turned around. There was no one. I imagined it that it was my long gone deceased grandfather, a painter, who paid me a visit. But maybe it was my own observer.

During a period at night, I would go down to the living room when all was quiet and I would lie down and stare at a spot on the ceiling without making a single movement.

"Just focus on the spot! Be the spot." I felt as if I went right into it, into that black spot and came back down.

We were all now, adolescents and on the weekends, my mother always accepted friends for dinner. It was a noisy and joyful table.

My first boy friend was a gypsy-like young man with beautiful light green eyes. He sold jewelry in the markets. He gave me my first guitar and my first acid. I saw and walked through gardens filled with roses everywhere while strumming my guitar, which sounded like crystal water! One day he told me he was leaving for India. He never came back. I saw him many years later; he had taken one acid hit too many and never came down.

I started writing my own songs in French and later did my first concert at a film festival in a northern town where the old steel factories were. I started performing also with a professional theater troupe and we won a prize. One day after school I hitchhiked to Paris with my guitar and a friend. I was walking in the streets of Paris fantasizing about being an actress when to my surprise, this director came up and offered me a part in a film with a famous actress. That was an instant manifestation!

I met another boy who wanted to go around the world on boat. I told him I wanted to sing, so I said we'd only have a short "journey" together. I didn't know how to express my feelings and was afraid to speak up when I wanted to break up with him. After the confrontation and his vivid refusal, I ate all these pills and found myself in the hospital. However, that summer we traveled together by auto stop to the south of France, to St Tropez, and to the "Cote d'Azur" where I went busking with my guitar in front of the cafés, singing my own songs and others'. When we came back, I was pregnant and he took me to the hospital to abort the baby. I had just turned 17. Again I wanted to break up. I came to tell him but he got mad again and sequestered me for a whole evening. When he finally let me go, he told me he would kill me if I didn't come back the next day. I went home that night, terrified. My parents saw straight away something was wrong. When they asked me what it was, I burst out into tears. They nearly laughed but reassured that I was out of danger. I guess I concluded it was dangerous to tell the truth sometimes.

My father was working now, in the North of France in a town called Lille. He came home on weekends. Again, he was gloomy and his moods would frighten me. Sometimes I thought he hated me. One day I came down the stairs. I had put on some eyelash and some lipstick. "You look like a whore like that," he said in an angry voice. Now why would I believe him?

I started smoking, hanging out in bars, dropping out of school, drinking too much, acting . . . like a whore. One evening, a guy I sort of knew invited me to his place and offered me a tea. I woke up the next morning in his bed not knowing what had happened. I understood later that he had drugged me. I had no memory of what had happened. It was frightful and I felt shame, dear mother!

I got hired as a singer in a small Jazz band with my brother on the double bass. We played in little festivals, in cocktail lounges or restaurants. Then I started singing with an orchestra band on weekends. We would go to these little lost villages in the countryside to do what the French call "Le Bal Populaire" (Local Dances). The repertoire ranged from disco to rock to disco to waltzes and "musette" (French traditional music). Sometimes the Maier welcomed us and we'd be served rich meats, cheeses, and wines of the area. We would perform till two or three in the morning. There would be fights sometimes and the boss of the band would get drunk and one of the musicians would take over the driving in order to get us all home safely… sometimes in the winter snow.

My parents were getting ready to leave and go back to Paris as Dad was out of work again. I had left school when I met Ziggy. He had shoulder length dyed black hair, plucked eyebrows over big blue painted eyes, and was dressed all in black leather. He looked androgynous. We started dating. He had a little house of his own and threw parties. He was working in a psychiatric hospital and he would sneak out pills and experiment with them with others.

After I moved in with him, I still managed to get my end of school diploma. In his cellar, he had synthesizers and we'd jam with others, until one day we decided to do a band. We wanted the music to be different and we auto-produced our first vinyl record on a big tape machine. We conceived the cover and sold it through a record shop's label. We also produced our first concerts. We played behind a big plastic sheet that I'd paint and cut while singing or doing all these weird sound and light effects. Our second record got more response and press, so we went to Paris to sell our first album. I was sure I'd get the record released no matter what. We were a "post new wave" duet with synthesizers, guitar and rhythm machines. We finally signed with a major company.

I remember that one night I was hanging outside of a concert hall jumping up and down on a small wall getting into some sort of trance and conceiving in my mind an abstract concept of what I wanted to experience. Indeed the free radios were bursting out in Paris in the 80's and they were all playing our tunes. Later when we actually went to England to perform, I entered the hotel room and turned on the radio ...our song was playing.

One day I was invited to a well-known English artist's house to dine. He threw a dart right into the bull's eye on his first shot. He bounced around, shouting, "I'm the King. I'm the King." He turned to me and, handing me a dart, he said: "Here, my dear, your turn." I remember thinking something like, "Well, I am not afraid of being ridiculous and really, I've got nothing to lose." Then my mind went blank, I must have gone analogical: the dart was in the bull's eye, right next to his!

We toured in several countries in Europe: Denmark, Holland, Switzerland, and Italy... and even played and recorded in New York. I had shaved part of my hair off, and I was smoking a lot of hashish and drinking. I was living in a suitcase, not seeing much daylight and I still didn't have a home of my own. We weren't earning enough to rent a place and furthermore all the money went into new equipment. It was such a life of contrasts: you'd be driven in luxurious cars and taxis, you'd dine in fine restaurants, all expenses paid, you'd be on TV and yet you'd go home at night to sleep on a mat at a friend's house. That's the way I had created it! I loved it for a time.

Then people, friends, starting looking up to us, to our image and I was getting restless inside. I was feeling caught up in my own creation. I could sing and bring out wild energy to a big wild crowd but I was still so insecure and filled with a feeling of unworthiness. Whatever I did was never good enough for me to accept myself. As a result of that, I refused big contracts. I started hating and blaming myself, my boy friend. I didn't want to admit I wanted to stop and get off this "merry go round"! I seemed to put myself down all the time; I was depressed, paranoid and thinking of death. I thought I might end up like my aunt; my head was full of... Shit! As my dad said! I was fulfilling his prophecy!

Furthermore, I had read George Orwell and I thought the end of the world would happen in 1984, so nothing was worthwhile. I was one of the living dead: "No future," said the Punks; so shouted the voices in my head!

Then a friend in the business lent us a house in the middle of the woods in the south. I started watching myself, looking at my movements, watching nature, feeling the heat of the sun on my skin, and observing the shades it made. There was a bird that came every day and sang a beautiful song on the same tree. I'd meet with it every day that I could. Slowly I started changing. I wanted to change. Then a publisher told us we could share an old water mill outside of Paris with another artist who seldom came. It was in a valley at a dead end road where no one ventured. I continued to witness my train of thoughts. I would oscillate from hate to adulation, from ups to down and I battled with myself. Little by little, I won. I started changing my thinking patterns.

Little by little, I began loving myself, at first through an imaginary love. What would it be like to be loved, to feel love, to have the sensation of a fulfilling and loving relationship? I imagined somebody sitting next to me as I drove the car alone. I imagined and figured out what I would feel inside, right down into my cells. There wasn't a face or a body. I created an imaginary ideal and abstract presence by my side.

That summer at the mill, an old friend of ours came to visit us with his friend Ulli. They were both living in Berlin and they had driven all the way. When the day came for them to leave, I decided to go to with them to visit Berlin, leaving behind my boyfriend and all.

Berlin was such a wild city in the 80's. It was an island in the middle of communist East Germany, surrounded by a wall. Here and there were buildings, mansions, houses abandoned since the last war and lots of squats with marginal people and artists. The day and the nightlife were intense to compensate for lack of liberties on the other side of the wall. In some parts of the city, the sidewalks or the tram railways were covered with grass. I loved it; to be in a city where nature was slowly taking over. In certain places of the city, you could sense the past still alive and tangible; the morphogenic field was holding the memories of the past. Not all of them felt pleasant! I found the German culture and its Gothic writing, its great philosophers and composers so fascinating. Berlin had once been the center of Europe.

How did it happen? Well, I stayed with Ulli and… all that I know is that I never saw his body and that when we made love, he never ejaculated. We were eye to eye and present with each other, with each breath, each movement. We made love for hours, for days, for weeks . . . the energy would go up so high! Kundalini rising? Heat and sweat. He would go so far and then stop and we'd start again. He was full of respect and attentive to me and just a touch of his hand gave me a thrill. We were like two virgins experiencing this cosmic adventure. It was new. We were surprised by each other and ourselves, shinning and vibrating like electrons in rotation.

Every time my ex-boyfriend called I was deeply affected and felt empathy, but I could not go back to him.

Then came a moment where I decided I had to leave Berlin and Ulli. "There must be something more than this!" I must have thought. I went to a friend's house in Manchester, England and cried for days. I cried all I could. What was I doing? Who was I? Where was I going? Whom had I harmed? What was important? Different questions were bubbling in my head.

I could not go back to Berlin, so I went to stay in Brixton, the Jamaican quarter in London. I loved it there. It was beautiful to see and meet the children, the generations of the mixture of English and Jamaican blood: light brown skins with blond frizzy hair and green eyes! Their parents had had to confront all the prejudice against color and race that is still going on.

It was a joyful community but had also the reputation for mugging and dealing drugs. I was visiting a girlfriend, looking out the window onto a garden and dreaming of having my own apartment and little garden…I must have gone analogical 'cause very soon my friend told me she knew of a place where I could stay and she had the key to it!

So there I manifested this apartment for free in London. It was in a big old house. I was on the ground floor. I had a bathroom and a big room with a kitchen and a mezzanine. I was the only one in the building to have a decent bathroom (yes, it was a sophisticated squat!) so the neighbors would come and take a bath from time to time.

I had view of a lovely park that was in front of the house. There was this tree that I loved 'cause it was all twisted, and its branches went in all directions, a bit like how I felt myself to be! I talked to it each time I walked by. There were Japanese cherry trees on each side of the street and now it was spring and they were all in blossom. I watched the wind blow all the petals, creating a pink snowfall whirling. It was the first time I had a place of my own and it felt so good. I could do what I wanted, when I wanted, and I allowed myself total freedom.

I started fantasizing about what it would be like to live without a past. Since the past had made me suffer, I decided to let go of it and my identity. Every day as I woke up I thought and said: peace, love, joy, abundance, health…Then I'd ask myself the question: "What would you really like to do right now? What would really make you happy?" I didn't know. I had to find out who and what I wanted! "Who am I? What am I?" I questioned myself and little by little, I turned to God in me and started talking. I started sensing the presence of something in me that was sparkling, fresh, pure, and light. I'd sit for long hours, maybe all day, just gazing out through my eyes watching, observing… my thoughts or non-thoughts. I started conceiving ideals of who I could be, seeing myself through the eyes of a loving parent, talking to myself as a loving parent would talk to their beloved child. I was bringing myself up, raising myself.

It was all just so simple: a walk to the market would become a source of joy and adventure, a moment to express deep appreciation. In the queue at the post office, I would find delight in waiting, living the moment in patience and gratitude. I could walk at night through the park in pitch dark and say to myself, "You'll be fine. Have no fear. No matter what, you are protected in all situations." Sometimes I felt a tingling in my third eye, my frontal lobe and I loved to feel that tingling as I was focused on the present.

I was always in search of that sweet connection to God in me. I was so immersed in my own self-discovery that even reading a book, watching TV or listening to music appeared totally absurd and incomprehensible because it would only take me away from the presence observing and loving me and that I also was (however, it is funny: the only book I bought at that time was a book of quotes, and there amongst others' words, were my Master Teacher Ramtha's words!).

I had contacted a deep state of bliss never experienced before and it was not triggered by anything or anyone; it came from within. I had a sacred relation with my God. I would question, I would pause: "What would God have me say, do?" I would look at people in the street and say to myself: "They are God. Look! See!"

There was to be a series of events that threw me off; I hadn't yet understood or mastered my emotional addictions as our Master Teacher teaches us, and I fell right back into a pattern of guilt, self-blame and auto-punishment and denial. I had another abortion but this time I chose to feel, to live it as an abortion of my own self torn out of the belly of my own God.

After that, I didn't go back to Brixton; I couldn't face it anymore. I came back to the past, to Paris and its noisy streets.

I accepted an invitation to work in Florence, Italy for a year but the beauty of the city didn't help my state of mind. I was being my worst enemy, tortured by my mind, dwelling in unworthiness. I had lost my way again.

I had had an abortion but the ex-girlfriend of my Italian boyfriend was pregnant and was having the child. He asked me to leave; he was the father and was going to live with the mother. What irony!

I was angry with God and was blaming it for my downfall from grace. I was hard on myself and so life gave me more of the same. I was near "Place Blanche" and "Pigalle," the area of the music scenes and shops and prostitutes of Paris. I experienced life in the messy Parisian squats. My mind was also messy and squatted.

The war in Iraq broke out and it was like the war in my head. I felt the dread.
Had I forgotten all the wonders I had lived and discovered?

The desire to have a child had started to grow in me. I met the man who was perfect for me. I knew his limits, 'cause I sensed an underlying anger in him, but I thought we'd make a good team together and give each other affection, since he presented himself as the victim of his two former wives. I thought I might bring him some sort of relief, I might save him and in exchange he'd offer me the security I needed and all would be fine. But of course my soul couldn't settle for that.

One month before I delivered my son, my husband won the custody of his younger daughter, whose mother was a heroin addict and didn't present herself in court. When he asked me, I answered, "Yes, I'll take care of her."

I gave birth to my beautiful boy by cesarean. It was the first time I heard my doctor laugh. He was telling a joke to the midwife while he was sewing me up at the same time. I loved my baby with all my heart and was so happy to have given him birth but I had the baby blues. I felt I had ruined the delivery because of the caesarian. I had not stood up for a delivery in a clinic of my choice, with the possibility of delivering in water. Instead, I had accepted my husband's family doctor whom on top of everything else, I did not like.

But my son's birth woke me up. I thought, "What in the world have I been doing with my life?"

I was now with a little girl who just turned four and my baby son. I had never had anything to do with kids before, and this little girl was afraid of abandonment and would panic if she lost sight of me. She needed a mom and reassurance and caring just like my little baby son...just like me! So there I was for the first time; two kids in one go. I did the best I could and I took it all on with pleasure and joy. I discovered maternal love and I loved them both deeply. I received so much in return.

I became a vegetarian. I was dogmatic and tyrannical and at the same time I would play the victim. I was searching outside of myself for God but at the same time didn't really seem to want to find it. I started going to conferences, to seminars on all different topics. I did Rebirthing and met Babji devotees, (- not Sai Baba-) who explained that you create your own reality. I met the inspiring Jasmuheen The Breatharian who's a living proof that you don't need to eat in order to live. I listened to a Deepak Chopra lecture at "la Sorbonne" university heard him talk about immortality.

There was an evening with a video presentation in Paris of Ramtha and JZ Knight. I didn't understand that there was a school. I must have zapped it out of my head, believing I couldn't go. I don't know if I understood much, but I remember being mesmerized by Ramtha and JZ's flamboyant appearances.

One day an acquaintance talked to me about *The White Book* with great passion and I bought it straight away. I read it and read it and underlined it and underlined it...this book is the book I have read over the most. I hid it under the sheets in the cupboard. I was playing the good housewife and thought it was too controversial for my husband to see. Furthermore, I feared his judgment and disapproval, just like I feared my father's. I wanted to separate. My husband didn't want another marital failure and threatened to take my son away. "I'll prove you're mad and you'll end up in the gutter all alone!" he threatened. I was afraid. Every day there was an event that stimulated the terror in me until I heard him call the bank and tell them, "Deny all access to my wife. She is in a cult, she is sick."

I felt like a gazelle that had to run for her life 'cause the lion was after her! I went with the children to my parents. No one wanted to go back home. Sophia's Grandmother came to fetch her. I had no legal right to be with her. She was now only eight years old. I stayed with my son. The divorce was on. It would be pronounced after four years.

I had what I thought to be hemorrhoids. I was often bleeding. I went to visit a doctor who told me I had cancer, a tumor in the anus. I believed him. I knew it had to do with my thoughts and my attitude. I wanted to heal myself by alternative ways but nothing would work 'cause it was all about attitude, and furthermore I was too casual about it. Three years went by until the tumor broke out to reach the size of a fist. I was in pain all the time, bleeding, losing blood; I couldn't even take care of my son anymore. I was a like a monster of selfishness in my desire to be a victim, to be right. I had nearly reached a point of no return when my sister called and said that a psychic had told her that if I didn't do anything now, I would die. It hit me; I could really die! No! No! I woke up!

I realized it was I. I was responsible for all this. I started crying, calling all my ex's and my ex-husband asking for forgiveness. It was dramatic.

I decided to go to the hospital. I chose a doctor who said he could heal me. After fifteen days, a round of chemotherapy and two blood transfusions, the tumor had disappeared. The doctor didn't want me to get too excited but he told me that I was a special case. He had never seen someone heal so quick and had showed pictures of the progress in the tumor's regression to his colleagues. The treatment was scheduled for six months. But here I was; back to life.

My neighbor and best friend Christine, who was the mother of one of my son's girl-friends, had studied with Dr. Gerard Athias and Dr. Sabbah, who held the same line of thinking as Dr Hammer; they were all decoding the emotional origin of sicknesses.

Christine and I would spend time together exchanging books and knowledge while sharing delicious meals, drinking wine or having tea. One day I was ready to share the most precious read: *The White Book* by Ramtha. She loved it so much that we started reading excerpts to each other. She bought several copies to offer to friends and family. We were now both passionate.

I remembered a woman I knew who had gone to the school and I called her up. She lent us some videos. We watched them during a weekend; studying, taking notes, we were totally excited by what we were learning. Then I checked on the internet for the school's site and discovered there was an event scheduled in Europe, in Belgium.

"Let's go." I said. So we registered, feeling the joy bubbling up of making known the unknown. My friend later admitted she was afraid to go, afraid of being caught up in a cult. But two months later, in January 2005 we were at our first retreat.

When I came out of that retreat after blowing, doing C&E and with all the knowledge I had gained, I felt like I was floating and that my feet were not touching the ground. I had my head in the sky! My consciousness was expanded! So many revelations, so many questions answered as to the mystery of our origins to history of our neurons. Whoosh! We came back to our homes filled with joy, with active frontal lobes and the burning desire to share this with our children.

That summer we went all together by car to Italy. The children and even Christine's mother came along too. Ramtha and JZ Knight were to be there! It was the first time I was going to see Ramtha for real. I was so excited I was dancing with joy and shouting, shaking my personality around, but when Ramtha came through the door and into the room, I went blank. I was flabbergasted, stunned. I couldn't utter a word or move. I stopped. Heat rushed to my cheeks, sweat was pearling. Something in me knew this entity. It was like my whole body was remembering... thirty five thousand years ago. "You made it! You kept your promise! You came back!"

I have blessed myself in this life; I am grateful I made it all the way to my Master Teacher Ramtha! He has given me answers, opened up my mind so much and has pushed me beyond my own wildest dreams, to live a fantastic future now, beyond all the world's changes, to continue the unending adventure of eternal life, to the 23rd universe and beyond and to realize Christ immortal in this incarnation and many more wonderful adventures yet to be conceived and experienced. But most of all he has given me the tools and the knowledge that allow me to know and understand myself more and more and to redefine, sculpt and acknowledge my Divine Self. I understand I am all that he is, that I am God, that we are all that he is. We are all Gods and although I know this I have yet to *know* it!

HANS-JACOB MOLLAND
Norway

THE JOURNEY TO FIND MY MASTER TEACHER

I was born into my genetic line on the fine morning of August 21st, 1973 in Oslo, Norway. I didn't know it at the time of my birth, but 1973 was a chaotic year on the entire planet due to the conflicts in the Middle East. There was a worldwide oil crisis and when it was time for my baptism, my parents told me they needed a special permit from the government to drive the car to church because of fuel shortages. What a great time to arrive on planet earth. ☺ Norway was a beautiful country to grow up in and the economy was booming because of the newly started oil production in the North Sea. There were only four million of us in a country rich on fish and oil. So I was raised in a safe and secure environment with a prosperous future for the country as such.

Although I was baptized and grew up in what would be considered a Christian (Lutheran/protestant) country I would not consider my parents to be religious in any way. Sure, we went to church on Christmas Eve and for funerals and weddings, but that was it. The very same year I was born my father started up a German company in Norway. He soon became very successful and so my parents decided out of tax reasons that my mother should stay home with my two sisters and me whereas my father would take care of finances. After that, my father spent a lot of time traveling and working. That was challenging for me because I always sought his recognition and approval. The lack of that laid the foundation for some of my challenges in life as well as "the way out."

Because of my father's job, however, we traveled a lot so I was fortunate to see the world at a young age. Looking back, I can see how much perspective it gave me to get to know different cultures and mentalities before I was molded and shaped into the mass consciousness of Norwegians.

Before I was two years old, we moved to a very nice neighborhood on the west side of Oslo and that's where I spent most of my life. I grew up in an inspiring environment. My friends all came from the upper middle class and wanted to do something with their lives. They wanted an education, to travel the world and live life fully. So did I.

I went to nice public schools, had some great teachers and some not so great ones. I did pretty well in school and because I did a lot of sports, I always had a lot of friends. We would meet up after school and play soccer every day. I think I came home with bruises on my body just about every other day. My mother got used to it after a while, though.

I remember I was very interested in science and the universe at a very young age. The first book I ever read (that I can remember) was a thin red book about the solar system. I knew everything about the planets (according to the acquired knowledge back then), how far they were away from earth, the circumference of the planets and their nature. In elementary school, I started subscribing to a magazine called "Illustrated Science." It came out monthly and it was like having a birthday every month when it arrived in the mailbox wrapped in plastic. The information was exciting and I was filled with a lot of facts that could be considered useless (like how many whales it takes to fill the Empire state building).

I don't really remember a lot from my childhood, but I remember that at the age of twelve I started pondering the meaning of life and wondered if this was all there was. Life seemed challenging and kind of meaningless already at that age. Anyways, life went on.

After I graduated, I moved to Germany to work for six months. I had the opportunity to work for a big German company through my father's contacts and I was very excited. I was eighteen years old and this was the first time I was away from home over a long period. I went through all the different departments to learn how a company works. It was fun. I was in another country, made new friends, learned another language and got to know a different culture. I felt free.

During this time I began reading a lot of philosophy. I read about Socrates, Plato, Aristotle and Diogenes. I loved Plato's allegory of the cave and what Diogenes told Alexander the Great when they met. When Alexander the Great asked Diogenes (who was a beggar) if there was anything he could do for him since he was so poor, Diogenes replied "Stand out of the sun." It made me laugh and fitted well with my dislike for authorities. It was fascinating and for the first time I was able to read through several chapters of a book before I became impatient. I became a seeker of truth and knowledge and so it began.

I moved back to Norway after six months, but I got the sweet taste of being far away from home and taking care of myself. I loved it and it seemed carefree at the moment. No one to tell me when laundry needed to be done, or bed sheets needed to be changed. I made my own rules. So I decided to study in Germany.

At the age of twenty-one, I moved to Saarbrücken, Germany to study economics. I chose Saarbrücken because there were hardly any Scandinavians there. I wanted to move to Germany to hang out with Germans and not Scandinavians. I was playing a lot of pool at the time and it was through this passion that I met my new friends. The first person I met was a very nice guy who was to become my very best friend. We met at a big pool hall down town and started shooting some pool. His name was Andreas and I have to be honest, he wasn't a very good pool player. He told me he played for a club and that they could use my talent. I joined the club and started playing league games. Andreas was an odd character. He told me he used to live on the streets and that he only had a few years to live because of heart problems. I didn't believe him. A few years later however, he died of a heart attack at the age of thirty-five.

One day while playing pool Andreas started asking me all kinds of questions about who was really running the world, who controlled the money and so forth. I really hadn't given it much thought at the time other than the fact that I had given up on politics and believing in authorities. I knew I didn't want to join the army simply because it didn't make sense to me. I always wondered why people wanted to be bullied around by authorities, but I hadn't thought about the fact that I was being bullied around by an invisible group of rulers called Illuminati, The Establishment or Secret Government if you like.

I was playing pool and didn't pay much attention to Andreas going on and on about his conspiracy theories, but when he finally took out a book called *Secret Societies and Their Power in the 20th Century.* I thought it looked interesting and brought it home to read. The book was so fascinating and definitely resonated with something within me. The author had extensive knowledge, lots of references and always repeated, "don't just take my word for it, go out and search the truth for yourself." The book was written by a young German who grew up in an occult society. After having read about the Illuminati, their story and the background behind wars and major happenings on the planet I couldn't help but feel watched by Big Brother himself. I became a little paranoid actually.

However, the author, who wrote under the pseudonym Jan Van Helsing, had a way out for those willing to change the way of the world. I have to mention that the author chose the pseudonym Van Helsing because Van Helsing in Bram Stoker's *Dracula* was the vampire slayer.

In the last chapters on how to get out of the bankers' grip, he suggested spiritual growth and awaking to the true self. He referred to several spiritual leaders, authors and teachers both alive and deceased. He referred to Baird Spalding, Madame Blavatsky, Drunvalo Melchizedek and many others. However, one sentence stood out when he referred to Ramtha. It said, "If you want to know God, go look in the mirror." On some level, it made a lot of sense to me, but I didn't truly understand and so I wanted to know more. This was back in 1996 and the only books I could find on the Ram in Germany were *UFOs and the Nature of Reality* which was my first book, followed by

Last Waltz of the Tyrants and then *Financial Freedom.*

Needless to say, the newfound information brought about a great change in my life. I eventually gave up on my studies because they didn't make sense to me anymore. After all, I had just read about how a small group of people controls the population on the planet through money, energy and education (amongst others). After having read about the history of money, I asked some of my fellow students if they really understood what money and interest rates were. I couldn't find anyone who could give me a good answer. Not even people working for banks could give me a good answer. I knew I was on the right track so I packed my bags and went backpacking for six months in the Far East. I read a vast amount of spiritual material on this trip and met the most exciting people I had ever encountered up until then. When I finally reached Bali, Indonesia, I participated in my first spiritual retreat ever. This was in August, 1997 and the workshop was called "The Flower of Life." It was about sacred geometry and the activation of the so called "Mer-ka-bah," the light body. I was blown away. It was forty-two hours of video teachings with some disciplines in between. I never knew math could be so much fun and that you could actually understand so much about consciousness and life through geometry.

I moved back to Norway after the six-month trip and did the same workshop again in Sweden a couple of months later. It didn't take long before I finally settled down in the "normal" world, studied Information Technology, started working, found a girlfriend and so forth. I never forgot what I had learned, but I "fell back into the old world" for a while. It didn't take long before I was bored with normal life, but it wasn't until a few years later that I picked up a cardboard box full of my "crazy" books on The Philadelphia Experiment, the history of money and the Ramtha books. I realized I had to go to the bookstore and get more "spiritual fuel."

My life wasn't very fulfilling and I had always been a big dreamer, knowing that there had to be more than the drama we play out here on planet earth. I picked up more Ramtha books and other stuff. Particularly Eckhart Tolle's *The Power of Now* put me back on track for good. I started going back to retreats and did a couple here and there, whenever I felt like it. I remember doing a retreat in Italy on co-dependency and understanding relationships. I have never seen so many people cry at one time, but felt a certain joy of seeing people release their suppressed emotions. Later I went to see a Zen master in Greece. He talked a lot about being present, the importance of balancing the left and right brain and had us working in the garden when we thought we were on a break. In his library, I found a book written by Dr. Joseph Murphy. It was called *The Power of the Subconscious Mind* and was about using affirmations to create reality. I loved it and soon upon my arrival in Oslo, I jumped straight into a Silva Mind course to learn more about the power of the mind. The Silva Mind course was interesting enough, but like every other discipline I had learned I never kept up with it for very long.

All of these events made me remember that special teacher I had read and listened to a few times - Ramtha. I remember a few years back when I was curious to see if there was a Ramtha website so I checked it out on the internet and found out there was a school that taught exactly what I wanted to learn – HOW TO CREATE MY OWN REALITY. I called the school and they sent me a cassette tape of a Ramtha teaching. I listened to it every night on my walkman (yeah it was in the late 90's and a cassette tape was what I got) before I fell asleep and was absolutely astonished by the teacher and his words. I was totally fascinated by the prayer at the beginning of the teaching and I wrote it down so I could repeat it to myself every day.

It wasn't until summer 2006 I decided to go to Yelm for my Beginner's Retreat. I had absolutely no idea what to expect. I had found the Ram through a reference from another author. I didn't know anyone in school and at that point, I was not familiar with the movie *What the Bleep.*

I arrived at SeaTac with an open mind and a heart filled with hope. I have to admit I was a little nervous because I was moving into an unknown. However, I was excited as well. I didn't know it at the time, but this was the last eight-day beginner's and it literally changed my life forever.

I met some extraordinary people, made new friends, listened to fabulous teachers and learned great disciplines that I have kept up with rigorously till this day. I knew I had found something unique and special and there was no turning back now. I came back for another event one month later. Then I did a follow-up in Belgium in November where I actually met two fellow Norwegians . . . well, the teacher had everybody from each nation stand up and when Norway was called, I saw two other people stand up. One of them turned out to be from Costa Rica and the other turned out to be from Denmark. They just happened to live in Norway. Anyway, we became good friends and met up once, or twice a week to do disciplines, make food and share some oaky red wine. Finally, I knew some people in my own country to share stories, realizations and thoughts with. I kept coming back to Yelm for more retreats with only weeks, or a few months in between. I had clearly become an addict. As we speak, one and a half years after discovering the school and twelve years after having discovered Ramtha I have participated in more than twelve retreats, moved to Tenino, Washington and my life will never be the same again.

So Be It!

DEBBIE CHRISTIE (A.K.A. MASTER OF MUSIC)
Arkansas, USA

MY JOURNEY

At the time, my Mom and I were both seeing a local psychic. She called us one day to tell us that if we were interested, a friend of hers who had just returned from California had a video she was interested in sharing with others. The video was of a forty-year-old housewife from Tacoma, Washington channeling a 35,000-year-old warrior from Atlantis.

Mom and I went as we decided we didn't have anything better to do on a Sunday afternoon. It was shown at the Little Rock Public Library on February 17, 1985 which I later came to find out was also the anniversary of Ramtha appearing to JZ in 1977.

The moment I saw Ramtha, I kept trying to remember where I knew him from. He was very familiar to me and I thought maybe it was because he reminded me of E.T. I had seen the movie a year prior and walked out of the theater contemplating those magic words, "There has to be more to life than what I know."

I assumed that I would walk away and let what I saw pass from my mind. However, I couldn't stop thinking about it. There was this constant chatter going on in the back of my brain and I had to have more. So I ordered the set of videos – Hawaii Dialogue 1984.

They were $100 and I didn't have it, so I decided not to pay other bills and get the set of videos. When I balanced my checkbook, there was an extra $100 in my account.

The videos couldn't come fast enough and when I got them, I watched them every day and started ordering the specialty tape cassettes. I also started showing the videos to everyone I could get to watch them. In listening to some of the tapes, I found Ramtha to be a bit chauvinistic in calling men "masters" and women "ladies" and this pushed my buttons a bit. It definitely did not turn me off to the teachings, but I did wonder about that.

Mom and I looked at the schedule as to when we could attend a live event and found July 21-23, 1985 in Phoenix as one we could attend. For us, it couldn't come fast enough either. At the end of the event, we all received a pearl from Ramtha and when I was standing in front of him, he just stared at me with the grin. I turned to walk away and something told me to look back at him. When I did, I saw that he was leaning towards me. I looked at him and he called me, a woman, "Master."

I was working as a teacher and coach at Mt. St. Mary Academy in Little Rock during this time and finding out that it wasn't where I wanted to be. I put in my resignation at the end of the school year thinking it was time to find a university to get my doctorate.

At the Intensive retreat in July, both Mom and I knew we wanted more and having run out of money, I started delivering Domino's Pizza to make my way to the Estes Park, Colorado retreat in September. I made it to that retreat and I was assigned a room with a long time student who lived in Seattle. She invited me to stay with her to see if I wanted to move to the area and possibly get my doctorate in Washington. By the end of the retreat, all I knew was that I was moving to Seattle lock, stock and barrel and I was going back to Little Rock to wrap up my affairs there.

After returning and announcing my plans to my family who were not at all happy with my decision (but I have been blessed in this lifetime with an allowing family), I had to move; I was compelled to. I continued to deliver as many pizzas as possible to make enough for the move. And a week before Christmas I loaded all my belongings up in my car and took off across the country. I left at that time because I had a friend who needed a ride to LA and I needed the company. I was only twenty-four and had never driven that far away from home before. But, I had to do it.

Shortly after returning from Estes Park, I had a very lucid dream where I was at an event and sitting in the back of the room on a box. Ramtha had the audience turn and talk to their neighbor, which at that time he had not started doing with audiences. And in the dream he walked to the back of the room towards me while the people were talking. He came up to me, looked into my eyes, grabbed me and started dancing with me. To me this was another confirmation of my decision to move. Many years later, I found that I was sitting on a box in the back of the room (we call it the audio riser) while the audience was sharing with their partner. Ramtha walked back straight for me, looked me in the eyes, grabbed me and started dancing with me.

I arrived in Seattle on my newfound friend's doorstep on Christmas Eve. She put me up and a week later, I was sitting on her couch staring at the wall wondering what the hell I had done. But things started to work out and I found a Domino's to work for just down the street.

I applied for my teaching certificate and moved to Yelm the following fall after many runners and adventures, some of which were not fun. Homesickness had left me contemplating a move back to Little Rock where my first nephew had just been born. After a visit home, I decided to see what would work out for me in Yelm and hold off a little longer on moving back. I sort of bargained with God and said, "If this is where I am supposed to be, then something needs to happen that makes me want to be here more than I want to be home with my family or I am moving back."

I started coaching, and substitute teaching in the Yelm School district and not long after that I packed up my truck with camping gear and a Texaco Credit Card and headed off to Snow Mountain for a retreat even though I didn't have the money to actually attend. When I arrived, there were several of us who were there who didn't have money to attend, but Ramtha told the staff to give us all a duty and invite us to attend the retreat.

This was May 1988, the first retreat of RSE. I was assigned to watch the door next to the audio table. A couple of months later I was asked if I would like to do some work duplicating tapes for the audio department. Of course, yeah! A couple of months after that I was asked to play music for all of the C&E sessions at events. And the rest is history. Needless to say, I did not move back to Arkansas.

MARIA AUGUSTA INIGUEZ
Ecuador

HOW DID RAMTHA COME TO MY LIFE?

M y mother fell ill with chickenpox (varicela) when she was pregnant, and that affected my health. I was born with something called "capillary angioma." This can look like a burn or a purple spot on my right leg. By the age of six, I understood that this made me different because it was then that I experienced rejection. The first time my schoolmates saw me wearing shorts for gymnastics class, they got scared.

From this moment, my life took a very special course. I began to wonder why God did this to me, why I had something like that in my body and I let it affect me. Later, I experienced very serious diseases that involved my angioma, among them rheumatic fever and purple hemorrhage (I could die from bleeding caused by a simple prick). My kidneys were seriously in danger and the doctors gave me six months to live. My parents practically resigned many of their dreams to save my life. I was never afraid to die.

When this happened, I knew a woman named Susan who was a Jehovah's Witness. She looked very pretty and nice. She was beautiful and when I saw her for the first time I thought she was an angel that was bringing me God's answers to my worries, so I paid attention to her when she was speaking about "The Biblical Stories" and showing me drawings in the book that represented them. I used to dream of being God's angel!! I used to look all the time at the sky, thinking that I was flying towards God to meet him again when the Sun was setting.

I began from that day my search for God. The name didn't matter, only what he is. I thought he was invisible like the wind in my face, but equally powerful. I knew that he was listening to me all the time. I knew it.

Since I was eighteen years I had tried many religions, but none answered the most immediate questions that I had in my mind, such as: who are we? What is the reason for being alive? What does God expect from us? Why doesn't God show his face and speak to us directly? Why did he let Jesus die? Why do we sin? Why didn't he make us good? What did we have to do to become angels and return to the skies? I returned to the Jehovah's Witnesses because they answered most of these questions.

I got married while I was pregnant and this was an extremely serious act in my religion. Later, when I decided to get divorced from my husband because of his infidelity, the pain was so big that I lost the sense of life. Not even my daughter managed to fill this emptiness that this crushing experience left in my soul. Suddenly I began to feel hatred and desire for revenge. I turned into a mental murderer and then the guilt feeling came for not having been an intelligent enough woman to keep my husband by my side.

It was at this point when I decided to study the Bible with more intensity to find more answers and consolation. I involved my daughter in this because doing so assured me that she was going to be a good person and she would not do what I did.

Jehovah's Witnesses are a tremendously strong organization. Through the literature of the Watch Tower Society, they infuse what the Bible calls "pious dread." You must be afraid of Jehovah without doubting so He can recognize you as his serf.

Twelve years of inexplicable pain passed, raising the question: how long will I have to pay for my mistake? Then the weight of the loneliness came. I fell into an economic crisis. One day I asked one of the elders: if Jehovah is love, why does he allow me to suffer this much? The answer was as fragile as my love for Jehovah. I was so afraid of him until I got fed up with it and revealed myself. I recognized my need for answers that were not there.

To leave Jehovah and wholly revolt against him, I did exactly the opposite from what I had learned in his teachings. I wanted to hurt him because I wanted him to feel the pain and distress that existed in my soul until he understood how tired I was of praying to him with no answers. I wanted to be bad, very bad, to hurt God for not listening to my petitions of pardon and to let my tears be caused by something really serious, not by having loved the wrong man.

After six months of therapy with a yoga psychologist I was ready to return to life, releasing guilt for everything that I did wrong, but the fear of Jehovah was still in my mind; nevertheless I was in my fight to forget him forever.

One day (the most unexpected one) I went to the house of a friend of my best friend. I did it because she insisted that I go (instead of having the will to do something else). It was in this moment that Ramtha sweetly came to my life through love, since the owner of house was someone that I had known years before when he also was a Jehovah's Witness. I knew the daughter of this man and he had a picture of her in the living room. While I was looking at it, he came to me, asking why I was paying so much attention to the picture. I reminded him that we both had shared the same religion and we began a great conversation. When he knew that I stopped loving God due to my resentment with him, this man gave me the biggest adventure of my life up to today. He took a picture of me with his mobile phone and said to me: do you want to see God? Look … you are a God.

While we were talking, he showed me the book called *The Sublime Plane* and I noticed with amazement that I had always thought about the things the book was saying, but many people believed that I was mad. I wanted to know who the author of the book was. He was very cautious in saying that he would help me to find the answers I was seeking but I had to be patient.

Three days later, this man invited me to have lunch and then he took me to his place to show me a few cards he had drawn and found while he was blindfolded during a discipline at RSE. I was in one of them. The two of us were dreaming so much of a home of our own and he had found me. One week later he became my boyfriend and a month after that got engaged. The magic of unconditional love had come to my life as well as the accomplishment of my dreams.

My greatest joy came when I went to a weekend RSE workshop. I still had fear of Jehovah but, when I saw JZ Knight channeling Ramtha, her face was somehow familiar to me and his voice frightened me. The thing that disturbed me the most was that he was confirming that I was a God. In my still "low self-esteem reality" this possibility did not exist. I was so scared and simultaneously I knew that the man who loved me would not take me to anything bad. To see that he had totally left Jehovah helped me. Everything that Ramtha was saying touched me like a lash in my soul. I cried a lot the first day, and I didn't want to return to the workshop.

The following day, when we did a specific discipline I felt that my dead father took my hand and I began to enter the void. I felt my father took a burden away from me because I promised him something that was fulfilled some days after he passed away and I believed that he never saw it. When I felt my own energy in this practice, I cried so much because it was like discovering that I was alive, that there was power in me. I felt God's love for having created me.

While my relationship with my fiancée was continuing, things started to become sadly weak and all the time I was looking for more Ramtha. I wanted him to address my boyfriend's change of attitude, his manipulations and my suffering. He began to get bothered about my spiritual growth. He didn't appreciate my observations about what he was doing versus what I was learning. This way, I loved every teaching because they were my thoughts. Someone was finally speaking about what I believed and thought that life was supposed to be like.

The book *That Elixir Called Love* woke me up and accelerated the ending of my relationship, especially since I repeated for fifteen days a prayer mentioned in this book by Ramtha to liberate myself of the need for dependence on men and to be the owner of my own life. This ending caused me great pain because I felt in my soul that a line of time was remaining undone. Nevertheless, the mastery turned into my dream. I saw myself with Ramtha all the time talking to him like I could never do it with Jehovah, not even in my prayers. All the time I was shouting to my dear Teacher: " I love you baby. Do you know it?"

The magic came to my life as subtle as a soft wind. In my dreams, Ramtha has spoken to me and anticipated events that came to my life (such as my desire to go to the Follow-up workshop in Argentina). When I was there, everything was like this dream. When I came to this place, I knew that I had already been there and all I wanted to do was to intensely enjoy this gift from Ramtha, since in the dream we made a deal. I had to change my life and trust in myself to be able to achieve my mastery. Indeed, when I came back to Ecuador everything changed.

I hope that on a not very distant day I can share my mastery dream with the Ram. In my soul, I know that this is my bigger longing.

I am happy with my new life, with my God, with my mission and with the real love that came to me without my suspecting it. Fear has already turned into a memory of the past. It's not my way of life any more, and through mastery, I know that I can go back to God, and turn into this being of light that I already am. *Thanks, Ramtha for reminding me of who I am. I love you. Do you know it?*

HEIDI SMITH
California, USA

THE PERFECT STORM MEETS A MIGHTY WIND

The first time I met Ramtha face to face, I wanted to run away. Rumor had it he knew everything about us – every word, every thought, every feeling and action, including the ones I'd hoped were my little secret. Now as I stood in a line of other students on the last day of a retreat in Snow Mountain, Colorado, a line that was drawing inexorably closer to this master teacher, it was beginning to seriously feel like the Final Judgment. Although he'd repeatedly told us throughout the week how much he loved us, I had my doubts. I knew my private thoughts, not to mention words and actions, and "lovable" was not the first word they inspired. Maybe it was a trick, and when I got to the front of the line, I'd be struck by lightning.

Furthermore, as the line inched ever closer to him, my brain chose that exact moment to go haywire and was now sending me thoughts so vile that I couldn't have even made them up on a normal day. No, no, no. My one moment in front of an ascended being and this is what my brain comes up with? Could I get any less enlightened? Could it get any worse? It could, actually. Now he was looking at me, while my brain screamed odd obscenities and my body lost the ability to move.

Based on my reaction, you might think that I was an axe murderer or petty dictator of some sort by the time I came to Ramtha's school. In fact, I was a twenty-one-year-old girl fresh from my university. I'd finished college one week earlier and, loaded with champagne and some trepidation, headed from California to Colorado straight from my graduation party (fortunately, my mom was driving for the first six hours, or we'd never have made it). I'd turned twenty-two during the retreat. I'd also learned that my parents were separating. Altogether, it was an eventful week.

I was one of the youngest people there, and the other students tended to project their misguided assumptions about youth and innocence on to me ("you precious angel!"), little realizing that I was already a hardened reprobate. The week had served to confirm my suspicion that while other people's gods loved them unconditionally, mine didn't even like me very much. In the spiritual Olympics, I was a non-starter.

Given my attitude, you may wonder what I was doing there at all. I wasn't looking for a master teacher. I was violently anti-religion and had little interest in "God," based on the actions of his many followers. It wasn't any passionate desire for truth or knowledge that drew me. I was there for only one reason: to save my life.

It wasn't in danger from some mysterious outside force or a squad of hit men. The situation was quite simple. Ever heard that uplifting Nirvana song, "I Hate Myself and Want to Die"? I exaggerate, but only slightly.

To understand how things got so dire so quickly, it helps to know that for all intents and purposes, I was Catholic. My genetic line is one large collection of smart, talented, well-intentioned guilty people. My uncle was a priest and my dad, in a sincere attempt to understand the nature of God, joined a Jesuit seminary for nine years. The church rewarded his efforts with a chance to participate in weekly bouts of self-flagellation. Thursdays were official "mortification of the flesh" days, which also involved wearing chain metal bands around the thigh with the chains cut and the points facing inward. Nothing says divine love like deliberate self-torture. It's safe to say that my genetic code had a few kinks.

After he left the seminary, my dad joined the Catholic Alumni Club in San Francisco, which is where he met my mom, a (Catholic) teacher with a Masters' Degree from UC Berkeley who had lived in Europe and dreamed as a girl of being a park ranger. Both had skipped several grades; my dad went to the University of Chicago at age fifteen and graduated when he was eighteen. Both were older than the norm when they got married in 1963; he was thirty-five and she was twenty-eight. Perhaps most importantly, both had a wide variety of interests and talents and they successfully avoided repeated attempts from their peers to pin them down to just one.

After they'd been married for several years, they decided to leave the church, a decision resulting from my older brother's impending first communion. My dad considered his six-year-old son; he considered the church. Why would he ever allow his kids to be indoctrinated into an institution that he still had nightmares about? The decision didn't sit well with either side of the family, but it did free my parents to explore various aspects of the human potential movement that was sweeping America in the early 1970s.

Theoretically, my brother and I escaped Catholicism. After age four, I never set foot inside a church unless it was for a wedding, a funeral, or a visit to a European monument. But in fact, our genetics (which of course, we signed up for) were not going to let us get away that easily. Much later, we discussed some of the basic assumptions about life that we'd had even as children. Number one: You're wrong! When in doubt, it's your fault. Actually, whatever "it" is, it's always your fault (in fairness, this does provide a comforting degree of certainty: you never have to waste time searching for the culprit). A friend of mine recently told me a story from his childhood about dreaming that he'd committed a crime and had to turn himself in. He woke up, put on his clothes and rode his bike all the way to the police station, only to suddenly realize that he hadn't done anything wrong. That's kind of how it was with us.

If I thought about God at all, it was in terms of religion, for which I had neither time nor tolerance. The older I got and the more history I learned, the more inexplicable religion became. It seemed so obvious that all of the wars that had occurred and were occurring in the name of God had nothing to do with him/her/it. Then there were the Spanish

Inquisition, the back and forth bombings in Lebanon, and the Saudi Arabian princess getting publicly executed under Islamic law for the crime of disobeying her family's wishes. It all seemed like madness and hypocrisy, and still does.

On a personal level, I was never a fan of rules, and religion seemed to have an awful lot of them. It wasn't that I wanted to kill anyone or covet my neighbor's possessions; I just didn't want anyone to tell me that I couldn't. Legislated morality put my back up, and does to this day.

At the same time, I had a huge sense of fairness and justice, and would often get just as outraged over events that happened hundreds of years ago (i.e. slavery, the Salem Witch Trials and the Crusades) as if they'd happened yesterday afternoon. In fairness, I enjoyed getting outraged and self-righteousness remains part of my personal charm. Still, anything to do with human rights, freedom, and standing up for truth, regardless of the consequences, fascinated me.

In my early years, life was going along swimmingly until my parents made a shocking and fateful decision, one that would introduce my brother and me to horrors yet undreamt and eventually threaten our very existence: yes, they moved us to the suburbs.

Anyone who's seen a movie or television show set in the suburbs knows that life there is never as it seems. There's usually some serial killer lurking behind the smiling face of a soccer mom or a white slavery ring being run out of the scout leader's basement. The better things look, the more twisted they are, guaranteed. That was bad news for us, as we moved in to a two-story house with a white picket fence, a swimming pool and two palm trees in the backyard. Cue the theme from *Jaws*.

Los Altos, California sits in the heart of Silicon Valley, which in the late 70's and early 80's was just exploding into international prominence. The high school parking lot was dotted with Mercedes, Porsches and BMWs in addition to humbler vehicles. To all appearances, we were living the American dream. But as you might expect, there was a snake in the garden - in this case, a group of ten-year-old boys. Whereas the kids in our old, working-class neighborhood in Campbell had been a nice and fairly harmless bunch, the new crop of suburban kids in my brother's grade were more like a malignant growth. In fact, many of them have since died from unnatural causes or gone to prison and several were bona fide budding sociopaths. Welcome to the neighborhood! My brother fell in with that crowd and soon he was getting into trouble – at school, at home, and in the community.

I, meanwhile, was a very athletic nerd, obsessed with Greek mythology and interested in things like rocks and vocabulary when I wasn't racing up and down a soccer field. My teachers wanted to skip me ahead but my parents refused, based on their own childhood experiences. I was the defender of the meek and even beat up the school bully when he was hassling someone smaller. At age eleven, I was the master of my little universe.

But all was not right in our world. My brother was in trouble. His crowd was into drugs and petty crime and his once sunny disposition was turning dark as his view of the future dimmed. Somehow, he didn't seem to feel that he could escape the influence and pressure of his peers and change his circumstances. In truth, there were very few other kids to hang out with and it would have taken a huge act of will on his part to break with the ruling crowd, especially at age twelve. As it was, he became increasingly sullen, angry and withdrawn.

As he got older, his crowd moved on to harder drugs and more dangerous past times. For me, seeing first hand what was happening was just plain scary. Although I was still in elementary school, drugs suddenly seemed like an inevitable rite of passage – one that I desperately wanted to avoid. I loved my brother and was worried about him, but at the same time cared immensely about what he thought of me. At that time he was the most influential person in my life.

On his end, several things were happening simultaneously. In big brother fashion, he felt responsible to warn me about the dangers that lay ahead (which effectively scared the shit out of me), but at the same time found my naïve self-confidence beyond irritating, particularly when he wasn't feeling too hot about himself. As he later told me, "Something would rise up in me that just wanted to destroy you." Whether consciously or not, he set out to eradicate my self-confidence through relentless verbal assaults. Whatever I did, it wasn't good enough, and I began to seriously doubt my own worth.

Right around this time I was visited by the multiple plagues of braces, head-gear and acne (I'd like to speak to the inventor of head-gear on behalf of demoralized thirteen-year-olds worldwide). My prior confidence disintegrated into a morass of insecurity and I became chronically apologetic. I slunk through junior high school, praying not to attract too much notice and hoping to make it out without having to do any drugs.

But at fourteen, a small miracle happened: my braces were removed, the acne medication worked, and the head gear found its way to the trash. I was a new being, or at least I looked like one. And now I had a new problem. Arriving in high school, I began to attract immediate notice from males, some of them substantially older than I was. Perhaps inevitably, some of them were my brother's friends.

This is where things get a little warped. Although I was afraid of the effects of drugs, I wanted to be cool so I ignored their continual presence in our house. And, while I was too young and naïve to handle the attention that was coming my way, I was also full of hormones. Meanwhile, during the summer before I entered high school, I'd discovered alcohol, and while drugs were never my thing, booze seemed to have been invented just to ease my social path. Intellectually, I was undaunted. Put me in any academic setting and I was the opinionated loudmouth I remain today. Socially, however, my brother's comments had gotten under my skin. I felt inept and uncertain. Drinking seemed to be the only thing that gave me the courage to express myself in social situations, especially with guys. Lying in wait like a ticking bomb was some unfinished soul business related to being an unworthy female. Altogether, it was a perfect storm.

By the time I was a sophomore, our house had become a mecca for drugs and alcohol. Our parents both worked full time, leaving us ample opportunity to get into trouble. I became a habitual liar (although my mom assures me that I was never any good at it) and a thief, "borrowing" her possessions to such an extent that she put a lock on her bedroom door. Cocaine, acid, mushrooms and pot rotated through our house on a regular basis and it was common to come home during school lunch when I was fifteen and find a group of guys sitting around the kitchen table snorting lines. It was always rather surreal to return to social studies or P.E. after that. Still wanting to be cool, I never said a word and allowed my parents to carry on obliviously, despite the fact that our house was continually being disrespected (by me, among others – it was just a matter of degree).

Although I wasn't into drugs, my teenage years nevertheless became an exercise in self-destruction, including a close encounter with the F.B.I, high speed chases with cops, multiple near arrests, car crashes and an ongoing love/hate relationship with alcohol. In the midst of the chaos, an old soul program got activated that would have repercussions for years to come. For reasons of his own, my brother informed me that, "Everyone is having sex." The obvious implication was, everyone but me. As it turned out, that wasn't true but at the time, I believed him and in some twisted way, wanted to impress him. What better way than to lose this pesky virginity? So I did – with one of his friends. It probably goes without saying that this was not the kind of guy you wanted your sister hanging out with.

Before long I'd worked my way through several more of his friends, as well as a number of other guys (moderation has never been my strong suit). It was one of the worst things I could have done to him as a brother and a male, but it was also subconscious payback for messing with my head so badly. The sad part was there actually was some piece of me that was trying to say, "See? Your friends take me seriously. I must really be okay." Years later, my brother and I could only imagine that we'd made some bizarre agreement before we ever incarnated this time around to help each other overcome some very old and painful attitudes – by experiencing them and inflicting them on each other. It probably seemed like a good idea at the time.

Before long, my reputation preceded me. Far from seeing myself as smart, athletic, funny and worthwhile, by sixteen I believed that the only thing I had to offer was sex. It probably didn't help that I was reading brain-rotting romance novels at the time. Now there's an excellent blueprint for how to deal with men! The worse I felt about myself, the more important it was to be beautiful. In the grand tradition of so many California girls, I stopped eating.

That experiment wasn't destined to last. After a summer of pursuing the skinny, tanned look popularized by refugee populations in Africa, I returned to school in the fall and made a discovery: soccer and borderline anorexia are incompatible. Since soccer was one of the only things that was still working in my life and that gave me joy, something had to go. I started eating again and gave up my ambition to become the world's most beautiful sixteen-year-old (this was before the onset of chin hairs, but I guess that goes without saying).

The interesting thing is that it didn't matter so much what I did; it mattered what I thought about it. Many people have done drugs, had abundant sex, and have drunk themselves into oblivion without self-judgment. I doubt that Mick Jagger, for example, woke up during the height of the 60's after some drunken encounter with a groupie thinking, "I feel terrible about myself." But I was not Mick Jagger, and I did feel terrible about myself. Everything in my genetics and my basic view of life told me that I was being a very bad person. And being a teenager, I was naturally inclined to take the entire situation much more seriously than it deserved.

My parents were deeply confused and increasingly afraid. Where my brother's self-destruction was withdrawn and quiet, a white dwarf imploding in on itself, mine was more like a supernova – flamboyant and impossible to ignore. I became the front-runner for the position of Problem Child #1. Should they send me to an all girls' school? Lock me in my room until I turned twenty-five? They had no answers, and neither did I.

I was definitely no picnic to live with. Swinging wildly between rage and despair, accusations and apologies, I was the ultimate tragic drama queen and I was pissed – *at everything*. My mom, raised not to express her feelings, had no frame of reference for me, and since she wasn't constantly emoting like I was, I thought her cold. My dad was more inclined to be a disciplinarian, but they couldn't agree on what to enforce or how to enforce it.

It's easy to look back now, after almost twenty years of working with teenagers, and identify what was needed: purpose and a challenge, a good kick in the ass and the opportunity to do something demanding, preferably something that served other people or some greater idea. Also, it wouldn't have hurt to have locked my brother and me in a room for forty days until we'd either resolved our conflicts or given them up out of sheer exhaustion. But this was the suburbs, where the common goal was to give your kids everything. So instead, my parents sent me to college. Would the torture never cease?

Despite all the drama, my teenage years had many bright spots. When I played soccer, I could fly. I was strong, physically tough and fast, fast, fast. I still dream about it sometimes. Soccer also gave me my first taste of the power of focus. When I was a freshman, a senior boy from our school won the all-star player of the year award for the county. I decided then that I would own that award by the time I graduated. Sure enough, my senior year it was mine – a long-held thought realized. On the field, I was the captain – respected, admired, reliable. Off it, well.

Then there was writing. I discovered the school newspaper, and with it, an audience. The newspaper room was my favorite place in the entire school and I frequently cut other classes just to hang out there, which as the Opinions Editor I could sort of get away with. Computers were barely coming in to common use, and at that point we would painstakingly cut and paste our copy, using Exacto knives and glue. The day the newspaper came out was like Christmas and my birthday rolled into one. Even the faculty was reading my articles, and I could make them laugh.

My high school employed some of the best academic teachers I ever had. My humanities, history and English teachers taught me how to write and how to think, but above all they absolutely engaged me in what they taught. They were smart, passionate and funny and knew exactly how to deal with teenagers. When I became a teacher myself, their example was never far from my mind.

But at the time, there was some question about whether I would even graduate. By the time I was ready for college, I was only eligible for a few. My test scores were high but my grades reflected all of the chaos of my personal life plus my tendency to skip any class I didn't like ("Thirty-six absences in chemistry, Ms. Smith? That must have been some flu"). I never much cared about grades, which seemed to reflect effort more than anything else. Several university soccer coaches were sniffing around based on my athletic awards, including one from UC Berkeley, but I finally wound up at the California State University, Chico, a decent but not brilliant school.

The first year was a case study in getting what you resist. At last, I thought, a life away from drugs! Not that I had any plans towards clean living; I just wanted to be able to commit myself more fully to sneaking into bars and going to parties without the distractions that other controlled substances seem to bring. However, I soon discovered that my new roommates' favorite pastime was dropping acid and shoplifting (for what it's worth, they were both vegetarians – they didn't want to pollute their bodies). My freshman year I made the university soccer team, and occasionally, I'd come home from an intense practice to find the entire dorm room bathed in smoke, a gravity bong in the sink and my roommates chuckling over what sort of pizza to order. Déjà vu!

My own habits didn't change much, particularly when it came to liquor and men. Observing my lifestyle, my sophomore roommate, a prudish accounting student, solemnly informed me that I was going to die before I was twenty-five. Although living fast and dying young sounded romantic, I decided right then that I would live longer, just to piss her off. Meanwhile, my parents discovered Ramtha.

Since leaving the church they had explored numerous avenues, including *est*, which we did as a family, and Wingsong, a spiritual group based in Oakland. On breaks from college, I attended a few Wingsong meetings and listened to esoteric teachings. The concepts of channeled beings or other lifetimes made at least as much sense to me as religion, and *est* was always pushing the idea that we are responsible for everything in our lives, no matter how big or small. In a way, the stage was set for the Ram.

The first time I saw a Ramtha video, I was twenty. As I watched this odd but somehow familiar being jerkily making his way around the seminar room, temporarily occupying a petite blonde body but emanating an unmistakable otherworldliness, I recognized truth. I knew that I was seeing the real deal. It never occurred to me that he wasn't exactly who he said he was. Returning to school, I never mentioned a word to any of my friends, but he was there, in the back of my mind.

Meanwhile, graduation was approaching, and with it, a growing sense of doom. I didn't know what I wanted or where I was going. Although I'd settled down a bit and had held a steady boyfriend, like a steady job, for two years, I still felt deeply unworthy. The closer we got to graduation, the more nightmares I had about driving my car, completely out of control, and crashing into a wall. Something was telling me that if I didn't change, I was going to die – very soon.

In the midst of that, I received a phone call. My parents offered to send me to a nine-day Ramtha retreat in Colorado. It would mean leaving the very same day that I graduated from college. Did I want to do it?

There was never any real question. I didn't so much want to do it, I *had* to. I only learned later that my parents had to borrow the money to send me – and had already decided to separate. But mother's intuition told my mom that I was in trouble, and she was right.

The event was a revelation. We could have anything we wanted, I learned, if we just focused on it. God lived inside us. We had never done anything wrong and our God had never judged us. Fine, fine, great, but I judged me. When I tried to imagine what I wanted enough to focus on it, the only things I could come up with were completely based on my image. I was confronting my own self-loathing and need for recognition, which at times was almost comical. Whatever story Ramtha told about his lifetime, I immediately decided that I had been a key player. His mother? Me. His soul mate? Me again. His dog? Okay, I don't know if he had a dog, but if he had, it would have been me.

Now, on the last day of the event here I was, standing in front of my master teacher with all of my self-judgments, convinced that my past had rendered me beyond all hope and taking it all very, very seriously. Standing in front of him, I could barely think, and given the existing state of my thoughts, was afraid to try. Into my mind came the words, "Help me." He looked at me for a moment and said, "Think not of who you are today, but of who you can be." I shuffled off to contemplate the dismaying prospect of who I actually was rather than who I was pretending to be.

My life after coming to school was radically altered. I moved to Hawaii, worked with teenagers of all nationalities, ethnicities and income levels (including some who, unlike me, actually *had* killed people) and traveled the world. I led wilderness service trips with kids and eventually became a teacher. My parents both continued as Ramtha's students, and my brother came to school in 1992. He fell in love with nature, which is where he's spent most of his time ever since as one of the world's premier whitewater expedition leaders. With a lot of truth and effort on both sides, we forgave ourselves and each other, and Ramtha's teachings have provided a context for understanding what we did. It hasn't been all sunshine and roses, but we now can see our respective roles in co-creating that reality.

Throughout all of the self-destruction, I believe that there were three things that kept me alive. One, clearly, was an unconscious appointment with a different destiny, one that involved Ramtha. The other two came from my parents. Even though we didn't understand each other at all at the time, my mom and I did have a bond; when I was really in trouble, she instinctively knew it, and also knew the exact thing to help me out of it. Some of the most satisfying and rewarding experiences I had as a young person were through opportunities that she presented to me.

At the same time, my dad taught me about non-judgment. At the height of my wild behavior, when I was convinced I would be severely punished and was ready to resist to my last breath, he would sit me down and ask, "Are you okay?" It was so unexpected that it broke through all of my defenses and I would actually talk to him about what was going on in my life, the doubts and fears and confusion. It's a lesson I've used over and over in my own subsequent work with teenagers.

And then there's my teacher. I have never talked with him face to face since that moment twenty years ago, except in my dreams. Yet, somehow, I became the teacher of many of his children, teaching history and English for four years at the Children's School of Excellence, an institution created for the children of Ramtha school students. I choose to take that as a vote of confidence. Somehow, the wild child settled down (sort of) and became the teacher of others younger but wiser.

As for the Ram himself, he is the ultimate example of unconditional love, patience, power and clarity. From him I am learning what it truly means to be a God. Contrary to my medieval expectations, he laughs – often (of course, we give him plenty to laugh about). He also dances like he invented the art and has a greater appreciation of nature in all of its forms than anyone I've ever encountered, coupled with an ability to describe it that is beyond poetry. His point of view is endlessly refreshing, because it is unconfined by human considerations. In short, he manages to pull off something I never would have believed possible twenty years ago: he makes being God seem cool. No harps, no sitting around on clouds staring at eternity, but a continual, ever-changing journey into the unknown. I should also mention that in all this time, not once has he struck me with lightning.

I suspect that if I were to stand in front of him today, he would tell me the same thing he did then: Focus on who you can be. Because of my teacher, I continue to have a greatly expanded sense of who that person is.

JENNY BENNETT
Canada

EXPERIENCES OF A CHILD IN NORTHERN ALBERTA

Most of my childhood is a blur. I don't remember much of it and what I do remember was not the norm. Although I thought it was normal and I thought most people could see what I saw, it wasn't so.

One of the earliest experiences that I remember was when I was fairly young, five or six years old. My mother took me to the little white church that was one mile down the road, because two small children, a brother and a sister, were ice skating and had fallen through the ice and drowned. They were my age. There were two small white coffins at the front of this church and I couldn't understand why everyone was crying. The priest had this long white gown on and was preaching, but his words didn't make any sense to me because these two small children were playing tag with each other and running around the coffins. They would lift up the priest's skirt and dart under. They were laughing and giggling, and I wanted to play with them. I started giggling as I watched them, and I nudged my mother and asked if I could go play with them.

The lady in the pew ahead of us turned and glared. I got slapped by my mother, and I didn't understand. I saw them alive and real. I wasn't allowed to go to church after that.

I had many things like this happen to me over the years and they're the only things I clearly remember. I saw ghosts floating above the ground and going through buildings all around me outside. I asked about this but was never given answers. When I saw things most of the time, they were future things that would happen and it was like watching live TV. I saw the events take place in living color and action as if in a real movie.

One day my brother that was four years older than me was going to go flying his plane. I told him not to go that day, because he was going to crash. He told me I was stupid and went anyway. He had built this plane himself. It had a cockpit that you pulled over your head like a plastic bubble. The pilot sat in the front seat and directly behind, one passenger could ride. It was painted like clouds underneath the wings and was green and beige on the top wings that looked like the ground. He had to land it at ninety mph.

He went flying that day and it had rained, so the field was soft at the neighbors' where he started and landed it. On landing, the landing gear buckled and he crashed. The plane was totaled but he walked away unhurt. I was beaten with a broom by my mother and called a witch when she found out he had crashed.

Pictures would just flash in front of my eyes and I'd see things which would all come true. I saw my dad and mom come home with a large bull moose with huge horns on his head in the back of our '52 Chevy pick-up. I also saw them sitting up in a tree and my dad shooting his gun over my mother's back to shoot the moose. Her hearing was affected after that, which is probably why she yelled all the time. I saw it exactly as it happened.

When I was about twenty-two years old, my husband was driving a rubber-tired backhoe down a steep hill that crossed a river with a longer bridge on it. As he was coming down this steep hill, his brakes failed and he thought he was going to go into the Smokey River. At the same time, I was working in the Peace River Hospital in the lab, pouring Petri dishes for the bacteriology department. I went into a trance and saw him coming down the hill with no brakes, so I applied the brakes for him and saw him cross the river. Tony, a lab tech I was working with, asked me what happened. He saw me trance out, so I told him what I'd experienced.

I went home that night and never said anything to my husband. He came home from the bar and said he'd almost died that day because his brakes failed. I never told him what I saw or did. I was always beaten in the past, so I said not a word.

We never had power, a phone, TV or running water; we heated our home with wood and coal. For the first seventeen years of my life, we never had electricity.

I remember large eyes appearing over the dresser and the ceiling opening up, and being taken time and time again. There was a large circle behind our house where nothing grew. Our neighbor Rick commented on it, wondering why not nothing grew in the circle. I never said a word, although I saw them land there. They forced me to drink a bitter white liquid that looked like milk before they brought me back. I hate milk to this day.

They always came from the east and left to the west. The sky cracked like lightning, flashed, and played tunes, but it never rained. My sister admitted to seeing them, ran inside, and left me outside. I always searched every night under my bed and in my closet before going to bed looking for them. They showed me things I never quite understood but wanted to know, and I knew I didn't belong here – that I came from the stars in another place and always wanted to know what God was and where I came from.

I was sad and very alone as a child. I used to walk with my dog along the creek and lie on the ground, look up at the sky and want to go home. Then I asked, "When I get old enough, I want a teacher to come and tell me what God is and where I come from." These beings told me long ago that all would be revealed to me.

Finally, in my thirties I was in Edmonton, Alberta, in a store called Ascendant Books, and I spotted a video called *Super Consciousness.* It was a video of Ramtha the Enlightened One. I rented it and was spellbound. I watched as many videos as I could get my hands on and then went to his school in Yelm, Washington in 1988. Much to my delight, all my questions and more have been and are being answered.

My dad always told me that knowledge was the most important thing you can get, because material things can be taken away from you, but what's in your mind can never be taken away from you. I honor my dad. I am living his dream.

J.RENI STORM
New Hampshire, USA

LOOK! THERE IS A GOD IN MY BACKYARD

E veryone has a story to tell. Some of those stories can be fascinating, as witnessed by the books on library shelves and those made into movies. What I didn't realize until 1992, when I happened upon a storyteller's group at Vassar College, is that there is an art to storytelling. How do I describe my own journey?

A gifted few have talent for this and fewer still can give their story a twist of humor. Robin Williams I am not. To say that I lived the first forty years of my life adrift in an average middle class consciousness and steeped in the crowded East coast corridor mentality is an understatement. Think of the movie *Moonstruck* and that describes my Italian Catholic family upbringing with a Jewish mother who didn't know she was until she was forty. She came into a family inheritance only to discover she was adopted out at birth to Doc and Shirley Diddle. They lived in 'Mothman' town of Point Pleasant, West Virginia. Her family was a very wealthy and well-known Jewish family from Cleveland. Her father was born in Chile and she was an illegitimate baby. No wonder I was confused.

Since I was ten years old, I had a "calling" to God that I now refer to as the voiceless inclination. The nuns misinformed us students, claiming that the 'calling' was a privileged

---

151

religious vocation to be one of *them*. Fortunately, I learned in my tender, innocent youth that it was not. Is it any wonder when I decided to follow the voiceless inclination after turning forty, I pointed my headlights west and never looked back? I was headed for New Mexico. I had no idea where New Mexico was except that it sat above Mexico on a map and if I got to a place where they asked me for a passport, I had gone too far.

I was halfway "there." It only took me another fifteen years to get me the rest of the way. Thank God the Ram has infinite patience.

The struggle to follow this voiceless inclination began early but I lost my faith when the parish priest grabbed my bottom and my best friend's boob once too many times. I had a horrific experience, shaking and stammering in a dark confessional chamber one Lent afternoon. I was afraid of this man. There I was in the dark, kneeling on a hard board so close to the face behind the screen with this misdirected man who reeked of wine. All I could do was remember those times his hands groped my buttocks and her breast. In my sheer terror, I forgot the words to the Act of Contrition, for which he humiliated me unmercifully, refusing to forgive my trivial sins. I withdrew from that tomb-like closet still shaking and thought to myself, "How dare he act like that, the old fart. What sins do I have to confess that are any worse than what he liked to do to girls at school?" I never went back. At thirteen, that inclination told me I didn't need the Catholic Church, although I never told my Italian family. Who needed the hassle? I would find God elsewhere.

Years later, I was introduced to Lama Norhla Rinpoche, who headed up a monastery not far from my home city. I thought that he would be my sage and only teacher. I took refuge in Buddhism, which didn't cut it for me either. I stuck that out for a while, thinking it was better than Catholicism, until I noticed a similarity in the litany and practices. The ani's (nuns) and monks all looked alike - bald, red robed, androgynous. Lama Norhla didn't speak much English so what was I learning from all of this? The old man did a divination for me when I decided to leave the east and asked what I thought I would be gaining by leaving. I responded that I wanted to create. I wanted to paint again and be an artist. I wanted to go where art flourished. His response hit me to the core. He said in broken English, "Hmph. Art is for ego. Nursing is noble calling, service noble work.

You do that." Bullroar, I was confused and conflicted again.

I finally decided I needed big change. A series of lucid dreams followed that decision, including experiences with light appearing in my room at 3:00 a.m., filling me with awe and imbuing me with a trance-like state of bliss for three days. During that period, I walked through a zippered veil into my future; all of these experiences were leading me to an unknown destiny. It was worth leaving my family and childhood friends behind on the East coast for; a valorous effort to rid myself of the past. Life was passing me by and I needed to live. I came alive in New Mexico for thirteen years, before I had that restlessness again.

I happily experimented with "New Age" everything, thinking it would salve this inner hunger for God. My first band-aid for the soul came with shamanism after a trip to Bolivia and Peru for an 11:11 adventure. I came close to getting kidnapped and shot on that trip. Many fire ceremonies later, I gave it up knowing this just "wasn't it." My soul hunger was hemorrhaging in a gaping wound and all I had was a band-aid. I began to reflect about a master teacher and wondered if that would come in the form of another Buddhist monk. The concept intrigued me and I wondered why I hadn't found one yet. I was actually creating the search and not finding what I needed.

In Crestone, Colorado in a Zen retreat center high up in the Rockies, I had mystical adventures with a psychologist and self-professed shaman named Alberto. I thought he had potential to be a teacher. The contention between us ran high however, and the gamut ran from excursions with cactus needles to naked offerings at a fire ceremony. The tension began to ease a bit when I stepped outside of the sweat lodge ceremony into a cactus patch and had to be carried on Alberto's back down the mountain to a bathtub at the retreat. It ended a week later after a fire ceremony under a full moon fraught with chaos. Zen monks and retreat-goers singed their eyebrows and nearly fell into the coals. My "natural attire" presentation to the fire stopped the crowd and brought calm, frozen stares, and mystery. I spent the night in a teepee meditating while Alberto looked for me. We eventually reconciled our deep differences and I never went back to his workshops. I ruled him out as a potential teacher.

Next came Native American church "meetin's" in New Mexico and Arizona. I was invited to these by an aged Pawnee elder whose cragged, beautiful face I immortalized in copper. I soon discovered he just needed a chauffeur and why not have a comely woman to drive him around? He was not a stupid man.

The peyote never affected me anyway, nor did iayawaska. While the ceremonial congregants barfed all around me, I sat wondering what all the mystery was with these nasty tasting plants. My insatiable hunger for God reached beyond the scope of substance hallucinogens, priests, shamans, and Buddhist lamas. It was time to research another angle. That is when a beautiful man with long black hair, beard, coal black eyes, soft lips, and cinnamon colored skin came into my life.

I was attracted to him for reasons I could not explain. He was a Sikh. He played beautiful tablas and took me often to his temple in Espanola, New Mexico where I enjoyed listening to him play those drums. I also took a good gander at women dressed all in white with turbans and veils on. Humble as they were, they seemed so impressed with their own images. Imagine that.

Tradition stultified these people, this culture, and their lives. They actually worship, of all things, a *Book!* I watched them get the book up in the morning and put it to bed at night. To them, the book contained the history and teachings of the great Guru Nanak, founder of Punjabi Sikhism. They did not eat beef or smoke, and prided themselves on their symbols of a metal bracelet and the sword. I made a mental note to go to India one day to the Golden Temple to see the Big Book of the Nanak. It must have contained something spectacular for it to be treated like a human. My Sikh friend told me recently that a God they called the Ram was at the root of his religion in the great text. Well, the Ram doesn't need to be put to bed. This was all a great runner.

Then one day as I walked into Whole Foods in Santa Fe, I saw a poster with what looked to me like a Sikh staring back. The face looked strangely familiar. I attended a beginning workshop to find out more about this guy, Sant Thakar Singh and his teachings. I was sure he had the answer, particularly due to a dream I had a year before and a painting I did that was him! I did not know at the time that I remote viewed this man and painted him for my future. How could I? I did not know Ramtha or his teachings.

The initiation into Sant Thakar Singh's teachings involved a meditation and visualization of a blue light that resonated with me, although I was turned off by the white clothes, vegetarian proclivities, and many worshipers adoring *him*. However, I decided I had to go to India someday to find out about the man. Nothing else in my life was satisfying this growing hunger to be more than what I was becoming.

For ten years, I experienced multitudes of premonitions I now know from Ram's teachings as runners. These pushed me to go West, to pursue knowledge, to create, to become, and they made me restless. I followed that call diligently only to be disappointed in the end because I felt unsatisfied and lost. One such runner was at a workshop in Phoenix for my work, where brochures for Master Degrees and continuing education were on display. I picked up one in particular for a Master's Degree in Law and Ethics and bingo! I saw a flash in my mind that this was what I needed to pursue. I researched the Baltimore University Law School, looked at my finances and schedule, and enrolled. Two years later, I graduated cum laude with a Masters Degree, and a school loan for the next twenty years but I was still unfulfilled. I survived my law professors, final exams and serial killers shooting innocent bystanders outside and around my dorm the last semester in school. Some mysterious person nominated me for and I was accepted into *Who's Who in America 60th Diamond Edition* after graduation. Yet with the acknowledgment of my accomplishments, I still felt empty.

My hunger could not be satisfied, my burning desire to find a master teacher grew stronger, and my frustration at not finding either put me in an emergency room face down on all fours, unable to breathe from the stomach pain. I eventually had surgery and recovered. I know the root of its cause now.

The best adventure was the restlessness driving me to search the web for a trip around the world. I needed to find an itinerary that would take me to all the countries where I might find a master teacher, in whatever temple I could enter. I decided to go alone, with a backpack and a map. I packed as light as possible, buying disposable under-wear to reduce the clothes in my pack. I made sure to have a water filter to purify my water in the third world countries I was traveling to on my trip. As a nurse, I made sure to bring along anticipated remedies for any conceivable malady. I ran out of Pepto Bismol in Nepal.

To my horror, I could not find any during the remainder of my trip. It wasn't my worst problem; I had other matters to concern me. At a time when Americans were beginning to disappear in Pakistan, I was fifteen minutes away from that border visiting the Gold-en Temple. I found myself grabbing the roped railing, pushing back 1000 sweaty, hot, and pushy Punjabi worshipers on my trek down the bridge into the temple, which saved a demure, fragile old Indian grandma in front of me from being crushed. She returned the kind favor by making me drink five times from the moat water around the temple. Apparently, to her it was spiritually significant. The last of my Pepto Bismol saved me from whatever amoeba was swimming around. Tradition had it that worshipers bathed in the moat after offering prashad to the Guru Nanak who was supposedly present in the form of a very large Book.

Mystical as the events seemed, no master teacher came forward after that day. I sat in front of a book wondering what the heck I was doing thousands of miles from home, alone, grimy, tired, and unsatisfied. I was running low on rupees too.

Instead, a small, turbaned, and swarthy looking cab driver came forward to drive me across northern India to Dharamsala. As a per diem (as needed) Buddhist, I figured the Dalai Lama might offer me some succor. In Dalai's village, I got taken by the cabbie, who also tried to dial up my nipples like changing music stations on a boom box before I threw him fifty feet and ran to find the authorities. He regretted that day for a long time. In the meantime, I set about to search for Sant Thakar Singh's ashram. To my dismay, I discovered later that he had more than one. I kept missing him by minutes. However, I caught up with him outside of Delhi in the middle of nowhere. He agreed to have an audience with me and offered me tea and cookies.

There I was, half way around the world, with thousands waiting outside for this saint to speak with them and bless their lives, and *I was granted* a private audience! Wow. He came in, sat down and stared into my face. I handed him a photo of the painting I did of him. He was unimpressed. I looked up into his eyes waiting for the shivers of recognition. Nothing came. Nothing for him either. He patted me on the head, blessed my life and went back out to his balcony and his thousands of admirers. I finished my tea and cookies and left. I left India with a handful of rupees and no master teacher.

In neither Nepal's Himalayas nor Thailand's reclining Buddha temples did a master teacher come forward. I was left flat inspirationally in Israel's holy lands where Jesus taught and was baptized. The waters of the river Jordan only left my sneakers wet for days. I had to come home to find Him.

Desperate for succor and spiritual awakening, I lived in a Buddhist Dharma center for nearly two years after my return from traveling around the globe. I became personal nurse and health advisor to the Ven. Lama Dorje when he fell seriously ill. It was peaceful there and for want of anything better to come my way, I convinced myself I was satisfied. I saw many monks and teachers come and go but none impressed me enough to call them "master teacher." I reconciled myself to spending my years in Tibetan chants of compassion, devotion, and calm abiding. I was becoming the "nun" of my youth. My calling descended upon me, until my best friend rescued me from myself.

To this day, I am deeply grateful for her presence in my life. She was even present to comfort me when my mother passed over on my sister's living room sofa. I have always felt "related" to her, like a sister. So, when she left my life to travel to the state of Washington, I felt abandoned as though my own flesh was leaving. I loaded her up with Buddhist prayer books to chant away at some local dharma center if she found one. Lama Dorje gave her his blessings; he was very fond of her and hell bent on getting her to be his "student" too. The two of us were determined to convert her to the path.

Joyce returned to Santa Fe a year or so, later. By that time, I had moved into my own condominium and was settling in for the long haul. I asked her about dharma centers in

Washington, to which she replied half-heartedly that she wasn't led to any. Instead, she found "The Teacher." I was amazed. *She* found her teacher in one trip when I traveled tens of thousands of miles up and down and all around the globe coming back home empty handed. I wanted to scream, to cry, to beat my chest and render my garments asunder like a Sanhedrin in a trial.

"This is it. You have to read his teachings and watch his video tapes. He is the One. That's all I can say. I can't tell you much because I am unable to describe Him. You just have to see for yourself." She handed me the *White Book* of Ramtha the Enlightened One. I was dumbfounded. I wondered if he wore a turban and spoke English.

Who could possibly be better than the Buddha, or Jesus (or, as Ramtha would say, 'Chief Chicken Feather')? I thought I had seen them all. I went to every crystal banger within a thousand miles of Santa Fe including Sedona, AZ, the Yucatan, and Colorado. I thought I had listened to every channeler, psychic, shaman, medicine man, religious whatever, I could imagine. I just could not take one more snake oil salesman. I was skeptical, frustrated, stubborn, and downright jealous that Joyce looked, behaved, and believed as if she found a Master Teacher. She did not care how I reacted because she knew in her heart of hearts this was the answer. She left me to my ruminations and the *White Book.*

I opened it up one evening and did not put it down until it was finished. I read Truth in this man's words. My soul cried out to me. My inner Self or shall I say, my Voice screamed at me, "Hey, are you having a moment or what? What took you so long to get to this point? Do you need a two-by-four to get you actually following truth when you see it? How many snake oil salesmen do you have to give your power to in order to get it?" Silly me; but look at all the adventures I enjoyed in the process. Why, I almost was killed a few times too; now that's an initiation.

After reading the *White Book,* my need turned insatiable for more of this man's teachings. I then watched an introductory video and fell back on my sofa as I saw a dainty but very attractive blonde woman speak, when I thought Ramtha was supposed to be a man. It took me a short while to wrap my mind around the concept of JZ Knight's channeling and the truth of Ramtha's words. I had no problem adjusting to the teachings presented this way; going beyond my personality to actually hear what I really needed to hear. I was convinced I had found my teacher.

I enrolled in my first Beginner's Retreat and drove north 1900 miles to Washington State and a little town called Yelm. It was not Santa Fe, New Mexico but I got over that quickly. I did not come for the ambience; I came for the Ram, the teachings, and the truth. Heck, I lived in West "by God" Virginny for a while as a child, so Yelm felt a bit familiar. The rest is history.

Choosing to accept the Truth I heard from these beautiful teachings never made me feel different or special. My family distanced themselves from my life, except for my lovely granddaughter who came to see me in Yelm. I also detached from them and their insistence that life revolves around electronics, pleasure, and normal, average living. My daughter grew jealous that I found peace here and traveled less to the East coast to visit. Her rebuttal to my commitment for personal and spiritual growth was to call me "Ramtha Reni." She intended it to be an insult, when actually I was flattered that I found that to be an association with a Master Teacher.

That is my past. When I look in the mirror, I can say to my reflection, "I love you. I love me," and mean it. I did not join a cult, or sell my soul to a preachin' devil and grow horns, or give my life savings to a charismatic leader. Just the opposite happened. I discovered that I could register in a school of legitimate scientific learning and I could stop when and if I wanted any time, no questions asked. It was just like any other school in which I registered. I soon discovered that I gained more from this humble but great school than any law curriculum or Master's degree from the University of Baltimore.

My life is changed and remarkably alive as a direct result of applying the Great Work and Ramtha's teachings daily. I built a lovely home in this bucolic, beautiful countryside. I continue to serve my community in surgery, and health care. I have an esteemed profession. My peers regard me highly, and I love that I see the God in them. I work in

Tacoma, Washington and travel extensively to inspect other surgery centers for quality improvement. I have written a book and am beginning a second one. I have a cartoon strip online and I continue to paint. I love my art. I am very busy; my life is full and enriched with wonderful experiences. I love my dreams. I shall never stop dreaming and creating my future as I have been taught and encouraged to do by my Master Teacher, Ramtha. You know, the one I went around the world to find? He was in my backyard all the time, waiting for me to arrive.

DR. ROBERT P. BECKFORD
Jamaica

THE JOURNEY TO KNOW MYSELF

"Father, I thank you for his life. Bless my baby and use him for your service." Words to this effect were spoken by my mother years later when she recounted to me the circumstances of my birth. She had miscarried a beautiful baby boy prior to my birth. Thus when I was born, these words were very meaningful to her. My lighthearted surmising of the situation is that the beautiful baby boy was me, but I decided I wanted a body with green eyes so I waited until her next pregnancy. Throughout my childhood, she continued to hope that I would serve God in some way. In fact, at various times during my childhood, I remember my mother asking me the question as to whether or not I'd like to be a Minister. Growing up on the Caribbean isle of Jamaica I remember being a little confused as to why she wanted me to go into politics; Minister of Finance, Minister of Tourism, no, it was never a consideration for me. However, I found out that she was referring to being a Minister of Religion - still not a consideration for me.

My journey was one of a typical middle class upbringing in Jamaica, the son of an intelligent and well-respected father and a devoted mother. My father had little use for religion but believed his children should go to church and allowed my Methodist mother to see to that. **I believe that Jamaica at one stage had the honorable distinction of be-**

ing one of the most Christian islands, having one of the largest number of churches per square mile of almost anywhere in the world and certainly the Caribbean.

What I learned about God came from observing my grandmother, who with great faith would tune into evangelical broadcasts by Oral Roberts in the wee hours of the morning. When I was a child, she shared a room with me when she stayed with us. With one hand on the radio she would summon me: "Come child, lay beside me," and would place her other hand on me to receive the blessings that were being broadcast. What a resounding faith. Through church and involvement in I.S.C.F. (Inter School Christian Fellowship) at my boarding high school, I too learned that I was a sinner and that Jesus died for me. I was never really comfortable with that approach but thought it better than the alternative of burning in Hell.

I did, however, have a deep abiding love for the Master Jesus and many years later when I found out how his life was misrepresented and what his true message was, I understood why.

At an early age, I was exposed to the idea that the future could be known, through tasseology (tea leaf reading), palmistry (the markings of the palms of the hand) and cartomancy (tarot or playing cards). I was always fascinated by one of my older aunts (actually a family friend) who had some of these abilities and would listen to or overhear conversations about her exploits. She, however, would always put off reading for us, as we were too young.

I did my fair share of the circuit of visiting the local psychics both in Jamaica and then upon my return to Canada. I desperately wanted to know what the future held in store for me. Somehow, I knew that if I could just have an idea of what was going to happen then it would make any present challenges more bearable.

Fast forward to 1994, a pivotal year for me; it was the year of my graduation from Chiropractic College and also the year of my father's death. My father passed away on my birthday after a short but observably painful illness. **One of his most poignant mes-**

sages to me prior to his passing while he transitioned between two worlds was 'Son, let me tell you something, believe in God, believe in God.' The impact was tremendous. My resolve has been to move beyond belief, into knowing God. My father as he transitioned had begun to discover a great truth about the existence of God, hence his words to me.

Interestingly, although it was very upsetting for my mother that my father passed on my birthday, I had a different take on it. In many ways because of earlier circumstances to do with my father's health, I had put my life on hold. This was a teaching of the cycle of birth and death and the permission to get on with my life; and so I did. Sitting in my basement apartment, I contemplated my efforts thus far in making it through chiropractic school and pondered my bright future.

Something strange happened, in retrospect. Every time I considered a point of accomplishment, a voice somewhere inside my head, or so it seemed, would resound "And then what?" At first I thought, 'What an interesting question and how curious that it keeps repeating itself.' Then it became annoying. I kept answering until I had projected myself to my retirement and beyond and then my final answer was "And then I die?!" This I vocalized loudly, got up and a bit flustered said, "There seems to be a Cosmic Joke going on and I don't intend to be the brunt of it!" You see, in that moment the realization hit me that after a life of achieving all these things, that if death was the reward, something was very, VERY wrong. I resolved to search for the Truth, whatever that meant.

I read more, visited more psychics, and explored my own abilities in tea leaf reading, palmistry, card reading and dream interpretation. The advent of my career as a chiropractor saw me making the decision to do locums (relieving other chiropractors on vacation or other leaves from their practice) and this landed me in Thunder Bay, Ontario, Canada in October of 1994. Originally determined to spend three months at the most, I have now spent almost fourteen years here.

The interesting side to this story was that two masters, a chiropractor with whom I worked and his wife, were long time members of Ramtha's School of Enlightenment. Although I didn't know much about the school, what I did know is that they had fabulous music there because they would return with such. I also knew that the Ramtha group in Thunder Bay met in a 'secret' place in the clinic basement and did 'whatever it was that they did.' I remember asking my colleague what he had learned at one particular event and he shared his excitement at knowing that God lived in the synapses of the brain. A bit deep for me at the time; I continued with my self-taught meditations and other local workshops. I was doing just fine, thank you, delving into the mysterious world of spirit and the mind.

I did, however, end up in receipt of a 1986 Beginner's Workshop on cassette tape which was loaned to me by these masters. Intrigued, I decided to listen to it one night after supper and within a short time promptly turned it off as I felt extremely fearful and a bit unsettled. I thought to myself, well it was night and I may have been tired; however the spooked feeling was a bit odd.

The next day was my half day at work. On my return to my apartment, I decide to give it another try. It was bright, the sun was out and there was no chance of being spooked. I turned on the cassette and to my best recollection, words were spoken by this voice to the effect of 'You know entity, you are loved or you are God.' The exact words escape me but the remembered effect never has. I instantly burst into uncontrollable tears. It was as if someone had said in a few words something that I knew to be true, but never knew how to articulate. Unable to stop crying, I immediately assumed my best meditative posture and sternly, but silently told myself to just breathe and be calm. The crying continued. I went to the phone, called the loaners of the tapes and said to them, "I am not sure what was on these tapes that you gave me but I can't stop crying." One or both of them chuckled in a comforting way and said, "Oh, your buttons are being pushed," - whatever that was supposed to mean, I thought at the time.

I determined that anything that had such an impact and unexpected effect on me had to be explored. I entered Ramtha's School of Enlightenment in August of 1996 and am honored and humbled to have the opportunity to study under my beloved Hierophant and Master Teacher.

My journey continues.

ELEANORA FRANIC
Croatia

You Make Me Shine

On the 19th of May, 1966, I arrived in the country that was once called Yugoslavia, in the town of Osijek, the capital of the northeast region of Croatia. Once one of the six republics of Tito's Yugoslavia, it was now an independent country. Tito, its president, had unified different nationalities and religions to create one country in the Balkans, an area in the middle of Europe between the east and west blocks, completely independent and free.

I arrived in a house with a yard and garden, where my parents already lived. They were of an age to be grandparents through their children from their first marriages. It was the second marriage for both, and my mother always called the situation "yours, mine, ours." The "our" was me. In the house lived a beautiful German shepherd, Dick, who wasn't very happy when I arrived. But one afternoon my father took me in his arm and with the other arm he petted Dick and explained to him that I had arrived, that they loved me, they loved him too, and that he should also love me. From that moment, no one could come near my stroller, and when I was crying, Dick was crying too.

My parents loved to travel. My dad bought a new car, a Peugeot 404, and I traveled with them. From very early, I started to see beautiful places, towns and things. When

I was five, my dad sold the house and my sister and two brothers started their independent lives. I moved with my parents to a flat in the center of town. They gave Dick away to someone and it was never completely clear what happened to him. Eventually I didn't think about him anymore. I had a tendency not to think about the things that hurt me throughout my life.

When I was six, my parents didn't know if it was the right time for me to go to school, so they decided that it was alright if I played for one more year. But when I was five, I started to take private English lessons, and when I was six, French. I didn't like French and I was angry with my dad about having to leave my friends outside and go home for lessons. I was always outside and we were playing a lot until I was fourteen years old, when I started my first relationship.

My desire as a child was to learn ballet and play piano, but my dad said that would be too much and that with a knowledge of language I could go anywhere in the world. I went to elementary school for eight years. I sang in the school's chorus, I danced in the school's folklore group (the typical dances of that region) and I played basketball for the school.

When I was in 5th grade, the professors asked my parents and me if we would agree to an experiment – that I would go directly, after that class to the 7th grade, and take all of the exams for 6th grade that summer. I did it.

When I was eleven, my grandmother, the one who was with me from the moment I was born and who I loved even more than my mother, passed away. At her funeral, I wanted to jump into the grave, but afterwards, as I did with Dick, I never talked about her. I didn't like it when my mother talked about her and I never wanted to go to the cemetery.

Regarding religion and God, from an early age I had a feeling that I was here to do something important for the world. I never had the feeling that my parents were my parents. I never went to them when I was sad; I just handled it alone. Even when I was crying and my mother would ask me what happened, I said nothing. I felt different from others – I was different. My mother went to church every day, but my dad taught me that I could pray to God in the bathroom, too. I was baptized in two churches, one Catholic and one Orthodox.

When I was ten, I asked my parents if I could go to church since one of my best friends was going there for afternoon lessons, and they said yes. I went only once, because I didn't like it. I was going to church when I felt like it, usually when it was empty. Every night I would pray. I always felt protected and I thought that I was special because the others around me were not like me.

I was always happy. I woke up in the morning happy. People were always drawn to me, and there was a light shining inside of me. I could listen to people, really listen. I would understand their situation and say something that gave them hope. I was fifteen when I started to go to the disco, and I was sure that I would go there forever. I didn't think about anything when I was dancing, and swimming in the sea gave me the same sensation.

My high school was in the old part of town (with Turkish ruins – this was their dominion for a period) and I loved to walk to and from the school on a beautiful, huge boulevard lined with magnificent aristocratic houses and old trees. The climate had all four seasons: hot and dry summers; beautiful autumns with colorful falling leaves; cold and dry winters with icy winds coming from Russia and snow, and with it lots of opportunities for children and adults to play; and then spring, time to go to the park and pick the first violets.

The town is situated on the right side of the river Drava, which comes from Austria and after 30 km joins the Danube River as it flows from Germany to Romania. On the left side of the town there is a zoo, a little forest, and a Copacabana, a recreational center with open swimming pools and Drava's sandy beach. There are three bridges that connect the two banks. One of them is like the Golden Gate Bridge in San Francisco, but smaller. Along the river is a promenade that usually was very crowded. If it was raining, cold and windy or snowy, I loved to visit it because it was deserted.

When I was sixteen, my dad sent me to a college in Grenoble, France for one month to improve my French. The first two days I didn't say a word. Then the language just started to flow from inside of me after all those years of private lessons that I didn't like. I phoned my dad and said, "Thank you." I was always with the Italians there. I loved their language, music, and their disposition. Even before that month, I had a desire to go to Italy; I thought the man of my dreams was there. I was always dreaming about the man of my dreams.

After the first two years of high school, we had to choose a direction for the last two. I chose mathematics and information because I was preparing to study medicine at the university. In the summer of 1984, I passed the entrance exam for the university. It was a great achievement. I never completed my education there, though, because I didn't like to study by heart for hours every day. I transferred to the University of Economics and after two years, I didn't want to study anymore, so I took a different set of exams and finally I finished the first degree of university. In Yugoslavia, lots of people went to universities because under socialism, schools were free and parents had working security. That's why the young people had the opportunity to study.

While I was studying, I was giving lessons in English and French to children. In the spring of 1991, I was working as a translator and a tour guide to an expedition of Jacques Cousteau's, the great oceanic explorer. They were filming in a protected national reserve, Kopacki Rit. It was the home of different kinds of birds, animals, and flora. Ten kilometers from Osijek, it was once Tito's private residence.

In the summer of 1991, major change was about to happen. I could smell it in the air. After fifty years of different nationalities and religions living together, celebrating each other's religious holidays, it was over. In three months, the powerful tools of television, radio and newspapers completely changed the situation. People were first bombarded with the news twenty-four hours a day, and after that, the bombs came.

When the first bomb fell, I was afraid and very sad. I went with my girlfriends to Hungary (Osijek is only 50 km from the border), thinking that we would stay one week. That became five months. When I came back to town and I saw my mom, she looked ten years older. There, in that small Hungarian summer tourist village that November, I lost my faith. I lost the connection that I had always had. I sank to a new low.

When I came back after five months of life in Hungary, to Osijek, I didn't want to sleep in the underground until one night pieces of the bomb entered my house. I was in the bathroom with my mom. I was shocked, because I was sure that nothing could happen to me. From that moment on, I went to sleep underground. During that period, the last four months of war in Osijek, I went to Austria with my sister to see her children that were living there. They were staying in one small, beautiful Austrian village, with a little river and ducks. There were family houses where happy families lived. I wanted to remain there in that fairy tale forever.

In May, 1992, after nine months, the war ceased in Osijek with the arrival of the United Nations Peacekeeping Forces. I was happy. I was awaiting their arrival and hoping that both sides would respect them. And so it was. I started to work in a Duty Free shop which opened in a hotel for soldiers.

After six months, the shops were closed and I started to work in the office of the hotel, but I was waiting to go away. I was waiting for my mom to be better. I wasn't happy; I didn't belong there anymore. In April, 1993, I asked for one month holiday plus another month, without salary, to go to Italy. I informed my boss that if I stayed there beyond two months, I would fire myself by phone. I remained in Italy and my mom and my friends knew that I would never come back.

I lived for the first five months in Rimini, a town on the Adriatic coast. It is a town with two faces – one, a tourist town with long sandy beaches, discos, shops, restaurants and pizzerias. Then there is the other Rimini, with Roman ruins and Renaissance ca-thedral, where life is lived all year long. In September that year, I went to Tuscany, where I lived for ten months. I got a job as a bartender in a disco, but the following summer, I was again in Rimini.

After two years, tired of jobs as bartender and waitress, I found a job in an office in the center of town with an American time-share company. They sent me to London for two weeks of training. I thought that I was dreaming. Everything was great with that job, but after six months, I started to be bored. I was worried about that. I asked myself, "What will I do with my life?" After one year and half the company decided to close the office in Rimini and open one in Milan, and I was the only one happy with that decision.

From that moment, I did different jobs with working hours and a salary that were comfortable for me. I was not searching any more for a job. From the experience in the office, I understood that I was spending all of the money that I was earning, that I wasn't any happier, and that I didn't have enough time for myself. I decided that I would work less and have less money but more time.

During that time, in 1995 – 96, I had started to go to a yoga class, even before I started to read "new age" books. I was searching. The state of falling that had started that November in the small summer village in Hungary continued, and I couldn't forget how I was always feeling. I couldn't forget how it had felt to be in the state of joy, to be light, to love and understand people, that treasure that couldn't be forgotten. I was drinking Bach Flower remedy, doing a little bit of aura soma, a little bit of homeopathy, some shiatsu, and attending different conferences. In my life were present Angels, American Indians through the cards of the tribe of Lakota), runas (stones with signs on them) and several times I played the Game of Transformation. I would visit a medium for a short period, and visit a woman who had contact with people who had passed on, etc. Wherever I was attracted to go and do, I went and did, but I never remained anywhere. I took something from everything. And I was reading. A book arrived in my hands: *Ramtha*.

When I read the book, for me it was enough. He became one of my Masters, instantaneously, immediately part of my life. But how? I didn't feel a desire to read every one of his books, to see all of his video tapes. For me, the wind was enough. I have always loved nature, all parts of nature – on the earth and in the sky above us, all flora and all fauna, and every expression of weather. The wind was with me, and I was glad about that. The wind would blow, sometimes just a gentle breeze touching my face and playing with my hair, sometimes wild, strong, cold wind, but always beautiful. That, for me, was Ramtha, for years. He was one of my Masters, as I was feeling for myself. The others were St. Germain and Yeshua Ben-Joseph, more commonly known as Jesus Christ. Those were and are my ideals.

I was at a crossroad in my life, with the opportunity to be born again in the same lifetime. In the summer of 2001, I decided to go to the Italian Alps for two months. I wanted to get away from Rimini during the hot, humid summer full of tourists and to meet and know the mountain. I arrived in a small mountain village surrounded with high peaks. It was like paradise, absolutely silent with green, green grass, flowers, butterflies and Bambies. When I saw it for the first time, I started to cry. Things went differently from how I had planned. I stayed for almost one year.

I met a boy, a stranger to the village. To say everything about that period and that experience would take too long and even now, I don't know all the layers of it. I entered into a state that was the opposite of wellness. I saw myself as evil and had pain inside. I don't know if I can call it depression. I was aware of everything, but it was like having surgery without anesthetic. I was scared that he would die, on his bicycle or by falling from the mountain. I became pregnant but I aborted it because I didn't see a future with him and I wasn't well. I couldn't take responsibility for a child in that state. I understood women who hurt children; I understood how it was for someone to decide to commit suicide.

I left the mountain at the end of April 2002. I went to Rimini for only three weeks. I couldn't remain there because I couldn't work, which meant I couldn't earn money to live. At the same time, I had to go to Croatia to solve the situation with my dad and the lady who was taking care of him. I stayed in Osijek for almost six months. My blood cycle stopped and I was sleeping only from midnight to 3:00 in the morning (I know what insomnia means). I was walking from before sunrise until dark. My dad, my sister, my friends, they all wanted to help me, but none could. My Italian cell phone stopped functioning and my only contact with Italy was from my friend Roberta, who knew my dad's phone number. I couldn't move. When you are well, you can do anything. But if you are not well, you have difficulty taking a bus, talking with people, going to the shop.

Someone who was already a student of Ramtha sent me a letter, and inside was a photo of Ramtha. The words under the photo were Ramtha's words, Ramtha's instructions. He said to look into his face, into his eyes, because his training deep inside of me was more powerful than anything else. I believed it. I walked with that photo and I watched Ramtha's face. I prayed to him and to Madonna. At the end, nothing remained of that photo. It had lost its color because of how much I had kept it in my hands.

In November, finally, I was ready to go back to Rimini, to Roberta's house. She talked with her two sons and explained my situation to them, and that it would not be easy, and the boys accepted. The trip was difficult. I was taking trains to go back to Croatia, and then again trains towards Rimini until, finally I entered one train that I knew that would not stop until Rimini. I arrived.

During the first month, I only went out to buy bread. One evening in the beginning of December, I called the hotel where I had worked in the mountain and they told me that a strange boy was dead. He had fallen that summer from the mountain. That was the first night that I slept. I knew that when my blood cycle came again, it would be a sign that that experience was over. On the first of February, 2003, my blood cycle came back and after two days, I started to work in a warehouse of books. I moved to a cute little flat that belonged to my friend who was leaving it because she was getting married.

And then, one Sunday afternoon in Spring, 2003, I went to Sportilia, the chosen place for the Italian retreats of Ramtha's School of Enlightenment, to buy a book and I was curious to see and feel the place. Immediately, I felt a power in the air and when one newly pregnant student said that her baby would be born before a retreat in August, I asked her if she would need a babysitter. We remained in contact, and at the end of July, she phoned to say that the baby would be born later and that she would not be coming; but at the same moment, the Italian coordinator of Ramtha events was asking for a babysitter for the children of beginning and advanced students, and I said okay. That was one of the most beautiful experiences of my life. I was a mother, not a babysitter. I was surprised by how I was feeling and who I was. I didn't know that before.

Only two months after that experience, I went to Croatia because my dad didn't want to eat and I knew that I had to go immediately. I arrived on Thursday and he passed away on Friday afternoon. I was there. When it happened, it was so deep. I just kissed his hand and frontal lobe and I was so grateful to him for everything that he did for me. Then I started to prepare everything that needed to be done.

Those were two very intensive weeks. I came back to Italy, to my job in a warehouse of books. After only two days, I hurt my feet and needed to stay home for three weeks. I needed that rest; I couldn't walk, but I was okay. I read, listened to music, and created a collage for my friend. I called one lady that was preparing Bach Flower remedies and told her to prepare something for me that would move my "guide" inside me to direct me to my road. I was tired of searching. I would do every step of the way, but I wanted to know what the way was, to see it in front of me and finally put my feet on the path.

After two months, in January, 2004, there was another retreat in Sportilia and I went again to be the babysitter. Almost all of the children from the previous August were there, but five months older. We hadn't forgotten each other and they hadn't forgotten each other. In the evening, I was sitting and talking with the students, and more than once they told me to come to the School, but I didn't feel like it. I didn't think I needed to go to the School. On the last day of the third time as babysitter, May 2003, the day of my birthday, the retreat was finishing and my moment arrived. I knew in that moment that I was coming in August for my Beginner's Retreat with Ramtha.

I went back the same day to Rimini in the afternoon, to a cute little flat where I was living alone. Even when I was only going out to the shop, I was always checking if the gas and water were off. When I was leaving for several days, I would always check that everything was off, including the TV and stereo.

Almost every night for months I was listening to Ramtha's subliminal CD on low volume, and in the morning when I woke up I turned the volume up high and sometimes I was able to hear a voice in the distance, far away, speaking an archaic language. When I entered the flat that afternoon after my trip, I saw that the stereo was on. It had been on for ten days, twenty-four hours a day. I hadn't left it on and nobody had come in the flat.

That afternoon, my friend Roberta gave me a gift for my birthday. It was *A Course in Miracles*, inspiration for lots of writers of "new age" books. I did exercises from that book every day for one year and one month. In August, 2004 I went to my Beginner's Retreat with Ramtha.

I became a Student of Ramtha's School of Enlightenment.

I became a Student of the Great Work.

I became a Student of The Greatest School of Wisdom that has ever existed on This Wonderful Planet, on This Beautiful Earth, on This Emerald of the Universe.

And now, this story that is a Journey to my Beloved Master Teacher, The Lord of The Wind, Ramtha The Enlightened One finishes, but a Journey continues, and there is a New Story to be written.

FABRICIO LOCONTE
Argentina

How the School Arrived in My Life

My history began after reading the book called *The Ninth Revelation* by James Redfield. The same author wrote another book where he describes how he wrote his story and tells what he did to find the path or solution he was looking for. He went to a bookshop in the USA and simply stopped to see which one of the books seemed to be the illuminated or enlightened one. Delighted with his story, one day I decided to go to a bookshop of my city, Mendoza, and predisposed myself to do the same thing James did. So I stood in the middle of the bookshop and began to look everywhere all around until I lowered my sight and there it was! THE BLUE BOOK.

It caught my attention for I always had unanswered questions about death and reincarnation. I continued looking around at little more, but while I did, I could only think about the book below me. I tried to walk around a bit and continue looking for another book, but my head was thinking about *The Blue Book*. I returned to the sector, took it, I read the back cover and there was no turning back! Very excited, I bought it and took it with me on a trip. Up to this point, I had no clue about who Ramtha was. I began to read it in Spain and I took about two months. As I was reading it, I started getting more passionate and I felt a connection and an understanding that I never had before regarding birth, death and reincarnation. I fell in love with Ramtha and his teachings.

Reading this book was a really shocking experience. When I finished it, I immediately I went online to search more information about Ramtha. I found the RSE official web-page and it was a great surprise to see there was a contact in Argentina, a gentleman called Aníbal Kravetz. I sent him an email that he answered and, when I returned to Argentina, I took a trip to Buenos Aires and I called him. Then I went to his house and we talked a lot. I was astonished to be able to talk about these issues with someone like I never did before! Certainly, I bought many other books that I read one after another.

After a few months, my wife and I attended the two-day Creating Personal Reality workshop. Some months after that, we arranged everything to facilitate the first CPR in Mendoza and then we continued doing that up to the present day.

This is a "one-way ticket trip" for me. To have known Ramtha meant everything for me and today I have many things to solve, but I'm certain of one thing: I love his teachings and I'll follow them forever.

EVA LETH
Sweden

How I met my teacher Ramtha

The meeting with Ramtha.
My meeting with Ramtha.
I found it to be a line, more than a point.
I see the line made up of many episodes of which a few I choose to mention here.
This line has no beginning and no end.
This line is like a thread in the vibrating weave of life, of which I, myself, am as important as the weaver, who is also me.

How I met my teacher Ramtha

Episode One

At the age of two.
Sitting in an elevated child's chair.
The chair and I falling backwards.
I see my grandfather at the far end of the table.
I see fear in his face.
I, myself, have no fear.

I am fully occupied by looking at his expression.
I observe.

This is how I met, in me, the knowledge of my teacher Ramtha.

Episode Two

Out on a stroll, with my father, in a park.
Coming back, telling my mother about our adventure.
 "Feed bird, squirrel come. Balloon"
I remember my father being proud of me
. . . and I remember me being proud of me!

That is when, in me, I met the knowledge of my teacher Ramtha.

Episode Three

Around six years old.
Making a deal with a friend.
Trying to throw a heavy brick stone
to the other side of the road.
Being in the moment, fully concentrated on throwing that heavy stone.
Crash!
I hit a car, the stone goes right through the window.
I ran. ran.ran.
Ran away to hide – forever.
My only memory after that is being found.
Found by my parents.
No guilt, no blame.
Being found.
Being brought back by loving parents.

This is how, through my parents, I met the knowledge of my teacher Ramtha

Episode Four

A long awaited Sunday.
A picnic, planned since long, with many families involved.
On the morning of that day I woke up with prickles all over my body.
It was decided I could not go.

My father stayed home with me that day.
My mother and brother were to go without our special picnic blanket.
That blanket, my father said, was to be left for us.
Picnic with my father, in front of the fireplace.
Sitting on the magic blanket, on the floor in our living room.
The most memorable picnic I ever had.

That was when, in me, through my father, I met the knowledge of my teacher Ramtha.

Episode Five

My father coming home after a long journey.
He brought a gift for me
A small metallic toy car.
I heard my mother say that maybe I would have preferred something else.
Between the lines I understood that little metallic cars was really meant for boys.
This I did not understand.
I was very, very happy with the gift in my hand.

That is when, in me, I met the teachings of my teacher Ramtha.

Episode Six

On Saturday night we used to have a family gathering with sweets and lighted candles.
The candle light in the dark room made shadows on the ceiling.
I loved to watch those multiple shadows.
Fascination.
Magic.
I called them Balloons of Pascal.

That is when, in me, through the shadows, I met the knowledge of my teacher Ramtha.

Episode Seven

Two pictures – one being somewhat the reflection of the other.

Fantasy.
It was said I had too much fantasy for my age.

Will.
It was said I had an extreme will.

Yes, I remember long inner journeys and immense creativity.
and
Yes I remember me literally stamping my feet to get my will through.
Fantasy and Will.
Ready to Create!

That is when, in me, I met the knowledge of my teacher Ramtha.

Episode Eight

My father crafted me a wooden cupboard.

It had a lock and a key, a precious key that was my own.

For some reason my father put the lock upside down.

To open the door the key, then, had to be turned in "opposite direction."

That is how early in life I learned that what is experienced as a child leaves huge imprints.

I still have to think every time I turn a key.

That is when in me, as a young child I met the insights of my teacher Ramtha.

Also it taught me, on a more symbolic level that, in order to open a door the key might have to be turned in the opposite direction.

Episode Nine

I always loved to draw and paint.

I always loved colors and forms.

For a long time I was fascinated by triangles.

Hundreds of pictures I made with thousands of triangles.

I can still see those pictures.

I can feel the intensity with which I made all those triangles.

Many, many on the same piece of paper.

Brightly, boldly, beautiful – in all colours.

Great fun.

Great fascination.

That is when in me, through geometry, I met the knowledge of my teacher Ramtha.

Episode Ten

I had learned a song about the stars.

A child song, about climbing up there on a ladder.

This song stayed with me for years.

I sung it to myself.

I kept it as a secret jewel, for only me to look upon.
I would watch the sky at night and sing to the stars.

That is when in me, and with the stars, I met the knowledge of my teacher Ramtha.

Still I carry with me this beautiful tune.

Episode Eleven

Each winter my family took us to the high mountains of either Sweden or Norway.
Above tree level. All snow, all white.
Vast white landscape where no man had yet made a footprint.
Visuals of eternity I found in me there.
Such peace in my mind.
Such joy in my chest.
Beautiful!
One week up there was worth more than a month of summer.

That is when, in me, through nature, I met the knowledge of my teacher Ramtha.

Episode Twelve

Pre-puberty.
Everyone wore a new model of elastic pants.
I did not.
Someone teased me for being out of place.
It did not bother me.
I continued to wear my out-of-date pants.
No more was I teased.

That is, when in me, I met the knowledge of my teacher Ramtha.

Episode Thirteen

My parents have many friends.
Within their group, as in all groups, there was a certain expectancy of conformity.
I remember my mother wore no make-up although everyone else did.
I remember her wearing the color of clothes she liked, sometimes totally out of fashion.

I learned to be unique.

That is when in me, through my mother, I met the knowledge of my teacher Ramtha.

Episode Fourteen

An assignment in high school.
We were to write an essay on life.
I wrote a long story about death.
A train on tracks, and a tunnel.
My teacher was shocked.
She hardly let me pass, although she did say the writing, in itself, was excellent.

That is when, in me, I met the knowledge of my teacher Ramtha.

Episode Fifteen

My brother passed on after many years of struggling between life and death.
Thanks to him I learned that life is a choice.

And from my parents I learned that being fully alive is also a choice.
I saw them live and do things they had never done before.

That is when in me, through my brother and my parents, I met the knowledge of my teacher Ramtha.

Episode Sixteen

I had an absolute compassion for life, in all of its forms.
In teen years I very actively engaged myself in practical work connecting thought with action
On this earth, for this earth and all life.
Before the age of twenty I was speaking to large groups, at university and other places
about the importance of taking the future in our own hands.
Today I am stunned by the courage, the passion and the insight I showed at such
young age.

That is when I acted upon knowledge in me, that I met in the knowledge of my teacher
Ramtha.

Episode Seventeen

I went to university.
I choose work in a field new and not yet established inside medicine.
I had many years of experience there, followed later by more studies.
In cooperation with a college I presented a working model on time.
This was not only a paper, but a tool meant for practical use.
I hardly passed the critics, who thought the topic was out of place and not useful.
(Time however, showed it to be useful and it is still in use up to this day).

After many years of experience I went on into what at that time was way out comple-
mentary medicine.
Today it could be called quantum physics applied in medicine.

I was ahead of time.
This has given me many opportunities to experience doubt and questions from others.
. . . and still continue on.

That is how I met, in me, proudly, the knowledge of Ramtha.

Episode Eighteen

When my grandmother got sick, in old age my family and I went to say goodbye to her.
It was a beautiful and happy moment.
Our youngest son crawling on the bed where she was lying.
I was pregnant and told her there was still another child to come.
She joked with me and asked how many we would end up with.

After this happy meeting I did not see her much.
I did not attend the funeral.
I choose to stay home with the life of the newly born son.

That is when in me, through my grandmother, I met the knowledge of my teacher Ramtha.

Episode Nineteen

On a windy day a ladder fell on my neck.
The circumstances of this I can not determine.
I know I had an experience meeting immense light.

Again
I learned that life,
as well as death
is a choice.

That is when, in me, profoundly, indeed, I met the knowledge of my teacher Ramtha.

Episode Twenty

I wrote a book
Poetry and paintings.

About life, my life, all life
About power of self.
Sold it beyond all expectation.

That is when, through me, I expressed the knowledge that I met when I met my teacher Ramtha.

Episode Twenty-one

The youngest son sitting by me in the car. He was still a baby, in his second year.
Even beyond his vocabulary he said, "It smells like someone is in the ditch."
One minute ahead was a crashed car, lying in the ditch.

That is when, through a child I met in me, the teachings of my teacher Ramtha.

Episode Twenty-two

Driving a car.
A truck pulls up to overtake.
Another truck simultaneously does the same, on the opposite side of the road.
I find myself in the midst of this, squeezed in a minimal space in between two heavy vehicles.

First thought: "This is not gonna work"
Second thought: "I have to make this work"

. . . and so
There was a stretching of time and space, like a rubber band.
Allowing me to gently slide in behind the truck in front of me.
Very smooth, very natural – very unexplainable.

No emotion at all.

I just continued on.

After a while, however, I had to pull aside, and rest for a long time before I could continue.

That is when in me, I met the knowledge of my teacher Ramtha.

Episode Twenty-three

A group of people gathered for the weekend.

We decide to watch a video. I don´t know much about it.

The device is turned on and before the actual film starts there is a still picture shown on the screen.

That is when I knew.

In my head I hear myself say: "I´m going there to find out."

At that time I did not know where there was, and I did not know what there was to find out.

But I knew!

The video was with Ramtha.

I remember him walking around answering questions.

To me this was immediately and fully real.

The topics I don´t recall.

Only that still picture and "I´m going there to find out."

That is in me, how I found my teacher Ramtha.

Episode Twenty-four

I found a woman in a small book store who helped me to search for anything readable of Ramtha.

This was before ordering from the net was an accessible tool.

Book by book were shipped over the sea.

Sometimes it took months for them to get here.

I read them thoroughly like few other books.
The book in one hand, a dictionary and a pen in the other.
Most of them were read aloud, taking turns with my partner.
Rereading, discussing, sharing.
Many are the underlines in books from these intense studies.
For years they were all thoroughly read and contemplated.

That is, through the books, how I met my teacher Ramtha.

Episode Twenty-five

I had an opportunity to see the create-reality videos that were in use at that time.
That is where I learned the breath, the C&E.

A week later I took off to Yelm, USA.

That is how, through the breath, I met the knowledge of my teacher Ramtha.

Episode Twenty-six

Coming to Ramtha´s own school in Yelm, Washington, USA.
Huge challenge. All in a foreign language.
I attended a beginner's first learning group, then stayed and continued to learn in other groups.
I remember smiling.
Through the teachings I did meet my teacher Ramtha.
I remember I smiled.
. . . and I smiled!

That is how through smiling, I met my teacher Ramtha.

Episode Twenty-seven

At one event Ramtha asks that I share with my partner what is the most important thing I have learned so far, from coming to his school.
I find myself saying: "To say no. To say no, also to Ramtha."
I, myself, was surprised at what I said.
But it is true.
Through Ramtha I have learned the importance of trusting myself.
Also I have discovered that being a student of Ramtha is not as much meeting Ramtha as it is meeting myself.

That is how, through my own answer, I met the knowledge of my teacher Ramtha.

Episode Twenty-eight

During an event in Yelm.
I am engaged in walking the field together with hundreds of other students.
At some point I stop at the end of the field, I turn around and look at this moving sea of people, each one doing their work on this field.
A stillness comes over me.
I am absolutely observing.
I get the sense of fully knowing.
I stand there for a while, I bow to myself in thanks, and then continue on with my work.

That is when, in being still with myself, I met the knowledge of my teacher Ramtha.

Episode Twenty-nine

I am sitting in the arena and Ramtha is walking the aisles.
He grabs my hair, and lets it fall. No words.
I sense the power of God Woman Realized.

That is how, in me as Woman God, I met the knowledge of my teacher Ramtha.

Episode Thirty
I talk with my friend the white-haired lady.
I meet with the little girl of no age
In communicating we reach beyond words.

That is how through old and young, I met the knowledge of my teacher Ramtha.

Episode Thirty-one

This very day.
I am going to catch a train.
Some stranger passenger turns to me and asks where the train is heading.

I look up, and find myself looking into the eyes of God.
Jubilant is my heart at that moment!

That is how, in me, I continually meet the knowledge of my teacher Ramtha.

And was that not a question worthy of any God.
What is the destination of my train!

Episode Thirty-two

And when the storm
was raging
and change
was inevitable
and I knew
exactly what to do
and where to be

That is how
in future now
through me – in me
not only did I meet
but also fully did I own
the knowledge
of my teacher Ramtha

Episode Thirty-three

And when all is over
and the time is new
All from past that I recall
the knowingness
of a child
the knowingness
from when I
myself, was a child

Whatever happened I used to say to myself:

"No matter what happens it always turns out well in the end"

That is how
in me
I met myself
that was my teacher
that was Ramtha
that was my teacher.

Episode Forever

I know who I am
the knowingness
that I have
Always Known

That is how in me I grew in the knowledge of my teacher Ramtha.

With thanks to my parents who gave me life
With thanks to my partner and my children and the gift of adding to giving life
With thanks to my teacher Ramtha who made me remember
With thanks to myself for being unique
. . . and one with the all

JEAN CAVALLARA (A.K.A. JEANNA)
New York, USA

THE QUEEN OF ANCIENT FLOWERS

I begin to fly. I am flying over the golden grasses. For miles, as far as I can see there are only golden grasses, grasses, grasses. Now, off in the distance I see what looks like a town. As I get closer, I can see that it is only the remains of a town from ages ago. Only the foundation stones are showing. I land on one of the streets. It is very muddy. The mud is about four inches deep and very sticky. It is the kind of mud that pulls at your shoe when you try to move forward. I walk to a doorway and go into a space that was once a home. After a moment, I am attracted to a spot on the floor and I begin to dig. I dig down below the mud into the earth, deeper and deeper. Suddenly, my shovel hits something. I dig around it and I see that it is a large treasure chest, ornately detailed. I bring it up to the surface, then open it. It is completely filled with ancient jewelry and flowers. I pick up a few of these beautiful artifacts then look deeper inside this chest. I pull back what I can to dig deeper, and then, I find the queen. The queen was buried in this chest. It is her coffin. I don't know what to do; but, I feel I must return her to her burying place for now. I am not ready to understand what to do with her.

After reburying the queen, I walk out to the muddy street and make my way to the top end of the street. There, still standing is "The Temple of Ancient Wisdom." It is a beautiful wall of candles burning from floor to ceiling. But there are some candles still unlit. I pick up a match and using the flame from another candle I light my candle and look for a moment at the beauty of the lights.

Then, in a move uncharacteristic for me, I put my two hands together and deeply and respectfully, I bow. Then I pick up my shovel and leave. I return to fly over the grasses and come back to wakeful consciousness and my friends from the dream group who are holding the space for this "shamanic journey."

Helen, who is in the dream group, told me that she saw my face as the queen when I said "queen." I accepted what she said but I hadn't seen my face as the queen; I saw a face covered with jewels. Richard, the shamanic trainer, asked me, "What did it mean?" I answered, "I don't know; but, I guess I need to find Ancient Wisdom."

And so began a journey that ended up in Ramtha's School of Ancient Wisdom in 2005. The date I arrived at Ramtha's School was exactly twelve and a half years from the day of that journey.

That was not the beginning of the journey to my Master's House. It started in my youth and progressed through many ordinary experiences.

My family is a religious one, recently populated by born-again Christians. The genetic strain is filled with preachers and philosophers. But it is also made up of people who were pioneers, and the family history is peppered with stories of runaways and elopements. I guess all of that is why I chose them. I wanted a strong spiritual environment but one with a history of independent characters. It probably "saved" me many times to have my close family members know of relatives who did independent and outrageous things within recent memory!

So, I survived the first forty-five years of being a scientist and a compulsive experimenter, using the only thing I felt completely free to use, my own life. I recall, at age forty-five, sitting on the floor in my quiet space and asking out loud, "How is it that I have spent most of my life expectancy and only now I am getting to a point of relative wisdom and experience? It seems to be in the wrong proportion. I have nearly used up my time and I am only beginning to be aware." Soon after asking this question, I organized a dream group to seek the answers from myself along with others of like mind.

For many years I had studied a work called *Toward the Light* as well as the writings of Djwahl Kuhl, a master from Tibet who wrote many volumes with the help of Alice Bailey.

I continued with these, but when I had the journey that instructed me to find Ancient Wisdom, I understood that this was not enough. From then on, I studied anything that had even the appearance of ancient-ness to it.

I studied astrology because the ancients did.

I learned to calculate daily time as well as long time by the use of the Stonehenge stones. I even had moments of understanding. For instance, one day while contemplating time, I was interrupted with an image of the ancient astronauts saying goodbye to the humans and telling them to keep time until they returned, then seeing them take off from the Stonehenge area. Fanciful, perhaps, but it added to my understanding, nonetheless.

I read all of Zecharia Sitchin's books. *Toward the Light* describes the formation and creation of humans from a spiritual point of view. Sitchin describes this same creation, but from a purely physical perspective using cuneiform tables as his reference library. This was stunning corroboration of information which I believed to be true.

I read everything I could find about the pyramid. I even retrieved the patent that Edwin Kunkel received that used a copy of the lower chambers of the pyramid as a two stroke ram pump (a pump that uses no external power source other than gravity and air pressure with an occasional spark to move enormous amounts of water to a high level).

I found it was easy to move around in time to ancient times. I did not know this was called remote view.

I particularly liked to think about "The Void." There were only two references to it in my life. *Toward the Light* described it and Djwahl Kuhl spoke of it from time to time. I would think about The Beginning a lot. I did this alone. I did not know anyone who wanted to talk about this with me. I loved to think about Primal Thought and Primal Will considering all the possibilities. I knew that somehow, I was a part of that and the part that has a body and experiences it; but, without anyone to talk about this with me, I did not get much beyond that initial step. *Toward the Light* also described the various spheres where we go between lives to contemplate, rest and plan a new life. I also liked to think about this but no one ever joined me. I gave up bothering to bring it up in conversation.

One day, I was with a group of people who met for spiritual meditation, and I was told that they were all going to see a movie. At first, I didn't want to go because anything with the word "bleep" in the title must be about news or other stupid modern stuff. No one knew anything about the movie, but someone had heard about some interesting water experiments that were described in it. "C'mon, Jeanna, let's just go!" they begged. So, I went.

And then I saw a picture of The Void looking much as I had pictured it, and, I knew I was going home!

Everyone I knew loved the movie. I desperately wanted more. I especially liked that brilliant woman with the interesting accent. I looked for more but didn't find it for many months. You see, I had been avoiding Ramtha for twenty-four years.

I need to tell another story here. I saw the movie, *What the Bleep Do We Know?* twice. Both times I sat in one of the first four rows. I liked it up close. The credits filled the screen and to read the whole credit I needed to move my head. But when Ramtha's credit came up, I couldn't move my head fast enough. I didn't get to read it all and never knew this brilliant woman was channeling Ramtha!

Finally, a friend told me to go to the Ramtha website which I did. And only on an inner page did I see the words "School of Ancient Wisdom." I was stunned. Was Ramtha the head of the school of "Ancient Wisdom" that I had been looking for all along? And was I looking for a teacher of that "Ancient Wisdom"?

So, I signed up for a Beginning retreat. While there in the fall of 2005, I became convinced that Ramtha is who he says he is. My long search had shown me and taught me many things that were taught in that beginning retreat that I, because I am a compulsive experimenter, had tried out and knew to be correct.

Helen was right. I am the queen. The queen is now out of her coffin. She represents the wisdom of my Being. I am allowing that queen to live again in my life, as me.

So, yes, Ramtha is my teacher of ancient wisdom and it is he is who I had been looking for all along. I am very grateful to him for doing the work he is doing.

AMANDINE ONGOTHA RUSSELL
Gabon

DROPPING THE LAYERS BEFORE MEETING MY MASTER TEACHER

My story has nothing to do with the fact that I am an African woman, and that I was born there. Maybe I do not like to be put in a box. It just so happened that I met my master teacher, Ramtha the Enlightened One, through his book while there. During that time, we lived in Johannesburg in South Africa.

I was born in Gabon, a French-speaking country in central Africa. I never fit in there. I felt like I did not fit in anywhere. The experience of being in Africa at that time just happened because my husband's posting was there. My husband is from Canada, and our two children are of mixed race. We have been traveling for so many years now because he works for an international organization. We stay in one place for two or three years, and the four of us have a wonderful ability to adjust and adapt. It is a beautiful quality, necessary for this kind of life.

In 2001, my family was in Pretoria. I used to drive regularly to Johannesburg, which was an hour away. It had everything you could ever look for. I had a driver at that time, because there were certain places in Johannesburg that I could not take the risk of driving to. Carjackings and kidnappings were commonplace. So, with my driver, I went to this small, esoteric bookshop. I had so many books.

I had been looking around for some time. When I saw the *White Book,* I thought, "Strange. Ramtha – what is this?" I took it with me. Not far away there was a video. One was about the ultimate change in religion in the quantum age, by Dr. Miceal Ledwith. I also saw one about the brain, *Where Science and Spirit Meet,* by Dr. Joe Dispenza. "Now this is what I'm talking about: real stuff," I thought to myself.

At the time, I had no knowledge that these three were related in any way. I went back to Pretoria and went through the *White Book* but nothing really interested me. It was like reading a fairy tale, especially when it referred to ascension. Miceal's video did nothing for me either. I knew that he knew more than I did, but I also felt great resentment towards Mother Church coming from him. I didn't want to go there. I had enough to do with churches, so I didn't finish the tapes.

I moved on to the brain tape. Dr. Joe's video, now that captured my interest. The way he explained the brain made me want to go deeper. His video had so much information. I kept rewinding it again and again, without going all the way to the end. I still had no idea that he, the *White Book*, and Miceal were connected in any way.

I moved on with my life. Dr. Joe was the only one I'd listen to. I was really taken aback by his understanding of the brain. He was trying to pass the information on so that you could understand it better. He was really an excellent teacher, and I got a lot from listening to him. Like many people, I then forgot about it.

Three years later, I had a major accident. I was at home playing with my dog, Shadow. He pushed me accidentally. I hit my head really hard on the cement, with the biggest noise I have ever heard. For thirty minutes I could not move. Then I managed to go inside my house. My husband was on a business trip outside of the country, but my children were there.

I was in the garden, so no one saw me fall. I don't know why, but I did not go to the hospital. Instead, I called my husband, who suggested that I should not go to sleep. I was so afraid that if I did, I would not wake up. So I stayed up all night until the morning and then went to the hospital. My children were so afraid for me that none of us slept that night. It was terrible. I seemed to be okay, so I moved on with my day-to-day activities.

At the time of the fall, I heard a voice asking, "Do you want to stay or go?" I said, "Hell, no, I want to stay. I want to live."

All went well physically. It was as if nothing had happened. After a month passed, I began having awful headaches. I was screaming like an animal. I finally had to go back to the hospital. They asked me the usual questions: What happened today? Did anything happen yesterday? I kept saying, "Nothing." The same voice that I'd heard when I was falling said, "You didn't mention the fall." I thought, "Which fall?" I didn't even remember it. Finally, I did remember it and mentioned it to the doctor. They rushed me to have an x-ray right away. The results came back and, oh my God. My brain was full of blood. They would have to drain the blood right away.

I was immediately admitted for surgery. My husband, who was abroad, returned right away. My hair was all cut off, and for six or seven hours I was operated on. The surgery went well, but after a few days, I became paralyzed. The doctor did not know or understand why it happened; it was as if I'd had a mini-stroke. Even then, I did not want to give up on me. I kept having that visitor, the one that no one could see except me. I was able to see and hear him, and I was also able to see the dead. I had to choose again and again whether to live or die. I could have died so many times. It was as if everything that I had repressed in my life was alive. Everything was on the loose.

I am a quiet person by nature, but I started to abuse the neurosurgeon that had saved my life. I would also abuse those who kept telling me, "Mrs. Russell, be strong. It will be okay." I rejected all of the nurses' kindness. Somehow, I could see their fears and insecurities. I didn't want to be a part of their game any longer.

From my bed in that hospital I could leave my body, travel through walls, and talk to my visitor that I called God. I could go anywhere and be aware of it.

When the surgeon would come to see me, I could read his fear and his doubts. My brain was open, sensitive and intuitive. I just knew. Everyone was afraid to approach me or to come into my room. The neurosurgeon that did the surgery didn't have a choice. The strangest thing was that I didn't get any medication to keep me from going crazy or help me sleep. The doctor gave the instruction that nothing was to be done to me and to just let me abuse the staff. I was a nightmare for him, for he was treated as a god in that hospital. I asked him many questions about that particular part of my brain. I wanted to know everything he wanted to do to me. I was never the same woman again.

I had to relearn to do everything – to walk, to talk, everything. Through it all, I kept rewinding the movie with Dr. Joe in my head. It helped me to not give up on myself. After many weeks, I came home. Our posting in South Africa was finished. We moved to Amman, in Jordan. I stayed in touch with the doctor who let me be, who didn't try to suppress me.

One day, he told me that he had been so afraid of not doing a good job on my surgery. He said that it felt like someone was there with him, making sure that he repaired my brain correctly. He said that he could not shut me down – he couldn't do it. That was why he let me do everything, without any medication or sleeping aids. I was so grateful to him. He told me he'd never had a patient like me, one who was so strong and determined and who saw the truth on his face. We were both laughing when I told him that if I'd been a black woman in the time of apartheid, I would have had no chance. They would have killed me. He was happy to see I was getting better.

I kept having powerful experiences while awake and remembering them. One day on a mountain, I had a dream of being in a place where someone was teaching me how to use my thoughts to fight. I started to question myself about my life. Then a voice clearly said to me, "Go to the white book." What white book? I didn't even remember having a white book.

It took me three days to go through all of my books. Most of them were still in boxes because we had only been in Amman for six months. At last, I found it. I thought, "No, not this one about the man who ascended." The voice said, "Read it. Your answers are inside. The book is about all your questions." I decided to read it.

By this time, we were getting near to Christmas. My husband brought home a video called *What the Bleep Do We Know?* I stopped reading my white book and watched it with the whole family. Then I saw Dr. Joe and I told my husband Michael that I knew him. Then, later during the video who appears but the RAM, Ramtha being channeled through a woman, JZ Knight. I didn't know about this, and I passed over the Ram again without awareness.

Then Dr. Joe started talking about Ramtha's school. He mentioned the Ram. Was this the same Ram in my white book? I had so many questions. Later, I finished the movie on the brain by Dr. Joe and I finished watching Miceal's DVD. I could not believe they were both talking about the same school. I finished the White Book, and what was at the end of it? The same information… so the three of them were from the same school with the same master teacher, Ramtha? That was the biggest shock ever.

If it was not for Dr. Joe Dispenza and his wonderful way of explaining things, I would not have found my beautiful master teacher. He was there all the time, but I didn't see or recognize him for some reason. Through his soulful way of teaching and passing on the message of the Ram, Dr. Joe brought me to him. I thank you, Dr. Joe. He was there with me through that video. Without his information, God knows where I would be today.

Now that I have found my master teacher, I follow him and his teachings wherever he goes. Thank you Ram for waiting, and for coming back for me. And thank you, JZ, for dedicating your life as an example for us all. Thank you both.

****

I came from a country where 95% of the population was Catholic. My father was a

Protestant and my mother a non-practicing Catholic. My father loved to read the Bible but was always questioning it. He could not let go of the idea that there were too many contradictions in the Bible and he was not afraid to point them out. Going to Church was not an obligation in our household. He was really convinced that God was not in the church but everywhere else. He taught us through stories about life and people and I guess set examples for us. Even today, I do not understand who taught him about those values with so much determination. I was always looking for clues, and how to make good use of them.

The obligation coming from the Catholic school was to go to Church every Sunday. I did not mind because I felt at the time that it was my way to God, and I loved God so much. My brothers and sisters were interested in others things, but I was really addicted to my love for God. At an early age I knew I was very intuitive, because I could feel things. I felt like a presence was always with me. In the beginning, I thought the whole world was like that but through my brother and sisters I discovered that I was alone on that matter. To joke about it, they used to say that maybe I was chosen by God. Sometimes I felt guilty, so I would share what I knew, through the powerful dreams that I used to have. I wanted God to send them the kind of dreams I had to help them, so at a very young age I decided to save them. I also felt that God was going to be happy with me, and my work, to save my family. That decision made me interested in social work and later on psychology.

Because I could feel presences around me, I knew I was not alone. When I was around nine years old, I decided to work very closely with my friends, the angels. Whenever we would go outside, I always sent my friends the angels ahead wherever I was going, just to clear the way. Going to school was hard, because I did not like or understand what they were teaching me, but I liked having my angels with me. I always felt secure when I would put them around the house, in my bedroom or in our car or taxicab. Sometimes I would send the angels to help my brother and sisters without them knowing it.

One day when I was around nine years old, I really discovered the power in me, especially the power of my thoughts. I was not a difficult child but sometimes when I did not want to do something, I would pretend that I was sick. That particular day, I lied so well that right away I got really, really sick. I was also afraid that if they took me to the doctor, he would find out that I was lying or I was not that sick. I was in such pain, but I decided to change it. I closed my eyes and called God to confess. At that moment, a voice was talking to me from the inside: why don't you tell the truth? You know you can get better if you tell the truth! So I did. Right then I felt better. Everything was gone, so I knew not to play with my thoughts. I promised myself to remember not to play that game anymore. Yeah right! I was nine years old! Until the next lie!!!

That same evening my father was telling us a story about the fact that if we do something, good or bad, that thing would come back to us. Of course, back then we saw it as a punishment from God. That story traumatized me so that I tried my best not to lie and always to do and be good.

This other experience happened when I was 18 years old, after I had left the Catholic Church. I was part of a branch of Christianity, and we were studying the Holy Bible. I had so many questions (I remember my father telling me in our discussion to go and search for my own answers, because he could not help me any longer). Even in that group study, my questions were not answered properly, so I was not happy. In that congregation they liked to use the Old Testament and the minister used to talk about the impurity of women during their time of monthly menstruation, adultery, going straight to hell, and so on. After a long while during which I was not getting anywhere with them, I turned to my unseen world for help. One day, I saw the same evangelist touching and kissing another woman on her private part, when his wife did not know what was going on. He was going against everything that he was preaching. I was so angry with him I left for good.

That evening, before going to bed, I asked for guidance. I sat on the floor, lit a candle, and questioned the Holy Bible. I remembered that time much earlier when I was so determined to become a nun. My father objected and asked me why, "To find God, of course." I was still thinking that maybe God was in the church. My father said no, he was not near there. He said God was in me. I knew I had some abilities to feel, know and hear that inner voice, that I had powerful dreams precognitive dreams, but still I could not see God. I needed more, needed Him so much, I cried so hard. Then the voice said, 'maybe the answer is not inside the Bible.' I thought, what? No! So in that state, I found myself sleeping on the floor with my Bible in my hand.

Later, the unimaginable happened. When I woke up, it was late. I smelled burning and felt heat. When I opened my eyes, the whole Bible was completely burnt, consumed by the candle. My nightdress, well! Nothing happened to it, nothing happened to me, but the Bible was all gone.

I knew in my heart it was time to move on, to leave the whole Catholic Church and everything related to it forever, and go on searching for my God and what was there for me to discover.

After the whole situation with the burning Bible, I started to listen more to that inner presence or feeling, and my life took another turn. I was establishing some kind of trust with that inner knowing. It took me many years to finally find the missing pieces to my puzzle.

I kept on crying for God's help. Then the biggest Challenge came. There were no other choices: I had to awake. An opportunity came, the last chance for me to see and experience what I had always wanted, My INNER GOD.

I was in Gabon. Every night when I would go to bed, whenever I had a question or needed to understand something, I would use my old technique of writing the question or my desire on a piece of paper, putting it under my pillow and going to sleep, trusting that I would have the outcome. I would concentrate with all of my trust and faith, and wait for the response in my dream. It always worked. Still, I was always amazed.
The more I grew up, the more I could not stay in Gabon any longer. It was like I could not learn anymore, or the environment could not provide for me. I was on a mission to learn more, so I decided to go and find it outside.

I had a strong knowledge that someone was waiting for me outside of Gabon. I had to go to that ONE, the Spiritual teacher, and I knew I was the one who had to go to Him. I was so sure that He was waiting for me in United States of America to teach me something very important about my soul and God. That sense of knowing was rooted in me. I started to plan a six month trip to the US and Asia.

Time has passed. I was now twenty-four years old. Sure enough, I met my present husband, Tom, during that trip in 1985. Tom is Canadian. I thought, oh no Canada! But where am I going to meet the ONE? After many moons had passed, my father passed away. When He did, I left Gabon. My family respected my decision. Later on, Tom and I got married. Married life was another discovery, another challenge, but that by itself is another book. We had two beautiful children, both of them very sensitive and intuitive.

Back in Canada, I went back to school. It was natural to go and study social work and later on psychology. When I was going to school, I had the opportunity to work for six years on the Palliatif Care Unit (with dying people). I had a lot of experiences with people dying in my arms. Other times, I was just there with them, taking someone's hand, until one day it was time for me to experience something new.

A time came when I was interested in exploring the breath, in learning how to breathe properly. I found myself with very different teachers from India. I learned a great deal about meditation and Pranyamas, which are different breathing techniques. I traveled to India, went to the Himalayas and stayed there for a month in silence. I stayed with a particular group that was very well known worldwide. The Guru made me one of his teachers, to go everywhere and spread his teachings. All went well for years. Then one day, I got bored again. I felt like I was losing myself. Everything was focused on the Guru. He was our God. Because we could not face every adversity and challenge alone, we always had to go to our Guru. The credit was given to him. I also felt that I was really moving away from my inner space. I was missing the fact that I was not in charge of my life anymore, or my decisions and choices. I was missing my life.

One day, another teacher told me that in privacy, our Guru had told someone that the best chance to gain enlightenment was to be born in India, to be a man, and to practice

Indian philosophy. I was really hurt. This was telling me that as a woman I had no chance to be enlightened one day. A part of me was happy to leave and move on. How dare he decide my realization? I left and never went back. I did not care even if I was one of his teachers. I did not turn back.

I took my life back. I realized that I had given many parts of myself away to him and his teachings. I worked hard to bring it back home inside of me. I was now ready to experience something else.

Meanwhile, my husband got an offer to go and work overseas with an international organization. We all agreed to go as a family. I was already traveling even before I met my husband, so I was looking forward to the moment we left Canada.

Our first posting was New Delhi, India in 1998. Our first night was calm and relaxed. That night before going to sleep, I felt like writing my letter to God. It had been a long time since I had done it. In my letter, I was just looking for a sign just to tell me that I was okay, even without having an outside teacher, and that God was still with me. I put it under my pillow and slept. At some point, I woke up. I was half asleep and half awake. It was 2:30 in the morning. Then I saw an eye, one big EYE occupying the room, just looking at me, just staring at me, no judgment, no emotion, nothing - just looking. Not two eyes, only ONE. I opened my eyes; I was still able to see it.

I thought, oh my God, is it God's EYE? I did not go and search for the answer. I was happy that I got my sign. Then slowly, slowly, the image started to fade . . . then nothing more was left. For a long time, weeks to come, I could just sense the presence of that EYE. Then I remembered my search, to look for the ONE in the USA.
I did not know the meaning of that EYE in my bedroom, only that GOD was responding to me, and that I was not alone.

Now, we were living in South Africa after Ethiopia. South Africa is a beautiful country. The only situation is the security issue. I let people tell us about all the bad side of that country, not realizing that I was inviting the situation to become more real. Our first two weeks were awful, full of fears for the children and me. Erica's French school was all the way in Johannesburg, while we were in Pretoria. She had to travel every day by bus for an hour there, and an hour back. With traffic, it took longer. I was afraid for them. I did not feel safe. Tom was always going outside of South Africa for his work. He was responsible for seven countries, including South Africa, so most of the time we were alone. The fear that I was creating was really getting strong. One evening, I wrote my letter to God asking for help. I put it under the pillow.

Sure enough, the dream came. In my dream, some men, thieves, got inside the house. They wanted to steal all our stuff. I was trying to find a way to protect my children. At that moment, a very tall, giant-like being appeared from nowhere and said to me, "What are you doing?" Surprised by his question, I said, "Can't you see, I am trying to hide from those thieves who are inside our house!" He laughed!!! And laughed!! So hard. I didn't like that. He finally said, "But you have invited them! You have called them!" I defended myself. "No, how can I have invited thieves to my own house?" He said, "But what have you been doing since you got here? What is your mental state? Which kind of thinking have you been entertaining?"

Ah, that !! I recognized that it was true, that he was right! I admitted all the fears. Then he said, "It is all up to you to change your mind right now!" I replied, "Just change my mind and all will be ok?" He said, "You used to do that in the past, remember?" I said, "Yes, I did." Then I asked, "Do I know you?" He disappeared, just vanished. I thought to myself, I can do this! In my dream, I closed my eyes, and all those people disappeared from my house. I said, "It works!!" Then I woke up.

From that moment, I took control of my fears and insecurities. Being in South Africa became joyful and exciting, because I never let anyone tell me bad things about the awful security issues.

****

I have no regrets about my accident, because it made me strong. It was preparing me to meet my Master teacher face to face. Nobody can meet a Master like Ram without any preparation. Meeting Ram has been the most powerful and challenging moment of my entire life. It has been such a journey to finally meet a true master, who knows that it is alright to want more out of life, and to keep creating a new life as we go along.

Back in South Africa, after the hospital I came back home. Even though I was afraid to stay alone, life was still moving on. My children still needed to go to school, and Tom was doing his work. I was back in my bedroom upstairs. The telephone was there just in case of any emergency, and I knew that the housekeeper was downstairs and was keeping an eye on me. After all the effort, my legs were not taking me places yet, not even around the house. I decided to develop a mental program for myself and make use of it every day, including the video of Dr. Joe about the Brain. In my imagination, I was able to see myself walking. I knew it would happen but, when? When?

I knew I could not stay too long in a depressive inner state, so I took everything under control again. I closed my eyes, and asked for help from the unseen world. I put myself in one place, one state of mind. I surrendered myself – I needed all the support I could get. At that moment, I heard the sound of the wind outside, and I felt like it was a message for me. Just that gave me enough courage to know that no matter what, I would be okay (In 2006 I discovered that the Ram was called "the lord of the wind").

Back in Jordan, after watching *What the Bleep Do We Know,* I finally put all the pieces of the puzzle together: that Dr. Joe and Father Miceal were all from the same school and that Ram was their teacher. I started to look around to see if there were other people interested or practicing the Ram's knowledge, but really nobody was. My biggest joy was waiting for all my tapes, cds, dvds and books from Yelm. Then one day my husband Tom was looking on the internet and discovered one contact for me, the coordinator of the Israel Ramtha events.

Our first experience in Yelm, Washington for our first Beginner's retreat was amazing. I was ready, because before coming, I had all those dreams with Ram. I was so happy . . . and afraid. Somehow, I knew it was the end of my past and the beginning of a new me.

It was like my whole body was shaking just before Ram got inside the Great Hall and when I looked up, Erica was standing there with all the young people. I realized Ram was talking to her, to my baby Erica... I was so happy for her.

At that point, I did not remember my name, or what I was doing there. My body could not move - it was like meeting God face to face. My whole being wanted so much to go where my baby Erica was, but I could not move. I closed my eyes and put myself in that state, where there is nothing else. I said, God please help me! I came all this way just to be with Him. I want Him to see me, make Him see me. I surrendered myself completely to the moment, let go of every tiny detail. All was ready to just be. Then out of the blue, someone was pushing me to go to the front. I looked. It was Anita, our host at the bed and breakfast where we were staying. I said, "What are you doing?" She replied, "You came all this way - just go!"

By the time I realized it, I was in the circle facing the Ram. At that moment I wanted to say something to Him, He turned His face away from me and went to someone else. I thought, oh my God, what do I do? Do I take it as a rejection or just be patient? The voice said, Just wait! I decided to wait for my turn. When I looked, Ram was talking to a little girl. I remembered Jesus saying that the Kingdom of heaven belongs to little children. I closed my eyes and waited with trust and confidence. I was determined to wait for my turn. I joined my two hands together in a praying position. When I opened my eyes, he was kissing my hands. He removed my hat to see my eyes, and I said to Him, "I came to see you. I answered your call. Here I am!"

He hugged me and all that was remaining of the old me just vanished. I was Home and ready to write a new page of my new life. I showed Him my card from Field Work on my chest. It was so cool! He said in my ear, "I will help you to have everything." I knew what He meant, because everything that I always wanted was to know God and know myself, and more recently to master my thoughts and my focus, to understand and know my brain. In the past, I had always looked at the brain with interest but thought that it could only be studied by certain people. Now I know even better. It is my duty to study my own brain, because it is where my God resides.

Now, getting back to Ramtha, the Enlightened One. Since my childhood, I was always hoping that one day I would maybe see or be able to put a face to my spiritual friend, to that voice, to that knowing, to the one who guided me from when I was a child, up to now. I recognized Him through the similarity of some aspects of his knowledge that I used to practice.

I now know it was Ramtha the Enlightened One that I was looking and waiting for. The One that I was supposed to meet in the United States of America, and I did meet him.

Now that I'd met him I kept thinking, now what? He is teaching me to get rid of all the layers, to redefine everything, especially the old thinking about God. I questioned the whole thing, because I realized that Ram was not IT. There was more, but what? Then I got it: He has been guiding me from childhood. He had been some kind of a bridge to help me cross to the unknown God, to help me reunite with my God, the Big Mind.

Ram has been helping me to get ready to re-connect with my beloved, my God that I loved so dearly since I was a child.

Ram is the one who had helped me not to forget the unknown God, but au contraire, to always remember.

God bless your Being, RAMTHA the ENLIGHTENED ONE for helping all of us.
I LOVE YOU.

SABINE PALINCKX
Netherlands

SAILS OF DESTINY

At the age of six, I often questioned why we were on earth, and how I could learn about the other endless part that we cannot see, smell or breathe. I can bring back my feeling and remember clearly how I viewed the world when I was really young. In a way, I felt lonely about that, because I never discussed these things with my friends. They did not understand what I was talking about. The only person who understood partly was my sister Judith. She is two years older, and we often discussed what a fourth, fifth or even sixth dimension would look like and how we possibly could experience these parallel worlds. Sometimes we tried to synchronize our dreams and meet up somewhere. We never succeeded. We had two other sisters, but we never discussed these things with them.

My sister and I have more in common, like this little brain dysfunction called synesthesia. Only a small percent of the population has this. How it works is that you see colours and shapes for numbers, words and taste. Also calendars and weeks have certain shapes. For Judith and me this was a most common thing, and we were around eighteen years old when we found that this is not something all the people have. When we were kids and I could not recall a name, I told my sister that it was a 'red' name, and she understood immediately and started guessing. It is the connection between the left and right brain that causes it.

When I was in school and was bored, I started mirror writing. This calmed me and made me focus easily. I still use it to calm down thoughts and be focused. Also mind-mapping is a natural thing to me. I had a hard time learning vocabularies of other languages until I visualized them; then I can remember them well. Anyway, I always felt a 'stranger,' but in a positive way. I really believed I could achieve a whole lot, and everything went very well. I had many talents, and used them actively. I was good in almost every sport, school was easy; I made nice pictures and had a good sense of humor and nice friends.

The years went by and I did my thing, and passed my exams easily. I accepted the fact that I was lonely and that ninety percent of the population were 'unaware' and just spending their lives the way their parents, grandparents and so on did, until they die. Maybe to solve a bit of the loneliness, I started praying. I have never been a very strict Catholic (although I was a server in church for years), but felt by taking the time every evening to run through my day and prepare for the next one that it kept me focused and balanced. I prayed to a God that I made up myself. Not the 'guy with the beard,' but someone with unconditional love for life and nature. I also saw God as someone who always understood me.

Sometimes I asked God for things to happen. Not very often; only when I really wanted something did I pray for it. It almost always became reality. This was satisfying and made my life easy. In general, however, I found the world stupid and life nothing but a game, which I happened to play pretty well. Life was not such a big thing to me.

When I started studying at the University, I met my first friend with whom I could level. Her name is Sandra, and she still is my best friend. We spent so much time together those years. Night after night, we kept on talking about our feelings, about the unlimited possibilities of this world, and had a lot of fun. We also did many dangerous and stupid things, which resulted in both of us saving each other's lives once. We had a great friendship. Sandra helped me to open up and be more in the moment. She pushed me to do things now, and turn ideas in reality immediately. She was also the one who lent me several thousand guilders to free me from any guilt so that we could travel for four months through South East Asia after our graduation, a wonderful experience that made me hungry for more. That was when I started realizing that I was indeed special and my capacity to change anything in this world was within my own reach.

At a certain point Sandra's father got really ill, and died within a few months. This was my first real confrontation with death, and triggered a turnaround in my life. I decided to take life in my hands and create something beautiful. I was twenty-five years old.

Sandra and I owned a sailing boat together; her name was 'Goede Waar.' She was a little over seven meters long, and had space to sleep four people. This was really cool and we were very proud. Almost every weekend we went out and had a lot of fun. One day I was sailing and Sandra was reading the magazine *Ode,* a new magazine in the Netherlands that wrote about spirituality, culture and healthcare. She found an article about the book *The Field,* and was totally absorbed by it. She tried to convince me this was really something and started reading the article out loud. It touched me, though I was not as enthusiastic as Sandra. She decided to buy the book, which made her enthusiasm grow. She got really into the quantum physics, googled a lot about the topic, and found the site of Ramtha's School of Enlightenment. She decided to go the Beginner's Retreat and see if this school could teach her more. At the end of the first day, she called me and told me: "Stop looking any further Sabine, I found the answer to all our questions." That was my first meeting with Ramtha.

Sandra told me extensively about her experience with the school and gave me the White Book to become further acquainted with the concept. I loved it. It indeed explained what I had always thought, and it made me feel even stronger than I was before. I decided to go to the Italian Beginner's Retreat. I lived in the US at that point, so it was quite a journey to get there. That trip turned out to be a complete disaster. On my way to the airport, my bag that included everything you need to travel - my passport, wallet, Ipod, computer and so on - got stolen.

It was 5:00 p.m. I canceled my flight and drove to the office to borrow some money from my colleagues. Then I went to the police station and called the Dutch embassy to ask how fast they could get me a new passport. The answer was not satisfying: it would take three days and a drive to Los Angeles.

I called Sandra, who was waiting for me in Italy, to tell her that I would not make it. She was really calm, and told me that my bag would come back to me, because my bag wanted to be with me. I thought she was crazy, but it helped me and I focused on my bag coming back to me. When I was in my apartment that evening, being sad about the canceled trip, the phone rang. It was an agent from United Airlines who gave me the number of a woman who had called earlier that evening about a bag that was found. I called the lady, and she explained that her husband, who was a taxi driver, found my bag in the street and took it with him. Once they were home, they realized that the owner of this bag must be extremely sad to lose all of this, and that made them decide to start the search for the legal owner: me.

I made the hour drive to their place, gave them $200 and a big hug. Nothing was missing: unbelievable! When I got home, I confirmed my rescheduled flight for the next day and bought a new ticket to get to Italy. I also bought a big bouquet of flowers to send to the couple that returned my bag. I then called Sandra to tell her the bag found me, and I was on my way… my first event could not have started better.

The event was really inspiring and it was so great to meet all these loving people together. The teachings were impressive. They indeed did answer questions I had, and reconfirmed my view on the world and on people.

I was a bit disappointed however, two days later when Ramtha was teaching the beginner's. I found him arrogant and not inspiring. And looking at all the people who really adored him and prayed and made toasts, I felt I was in the wrong place. The next morning I left the event and went to Bologna. I don't know what exactly happened to me, but I felt I made the right decision. When Sandra followed me after the event was finished, we had a great time in Bologna and we talked about the event and why I left.

I explained to her that nothing changed with regards to my view on the school and the teachings that we got. I decided to move forward with the disciplines and teachings of the school; however, I was not sure if I wanted to visit the school again.

Sandra moved to Yelm to be closer to the school. I got an offer for a new job in the Netherlands, and decided to relocate back to Europe. When I was planning one of my visits to Sandra, an unexpected 'catch up' event was scheduled for exactly those days. This could not be a coincidence, so I decided to register again and go back to the school. This was an amazing experience and re-energized me completely. Ramtha was in Italy at the time, but we got amazing teachings on DVD. I feel like I am really back.

I am still crafting my fairytale, and things are working out really well. I have gained more and more self-confidence, lost a lot of fear during the past years and created a beautiful situation. I live in a very nice houseboat, make lots of money in a really fun job and travel around the world a lot. I meet many different people, see different cultures and have lots of energy to further explore. Ramtha is and will always be my guide and mentor on my journey that actually has just begun.

NATASHA ARTHURS
United Kingdom

UNEARTHING SELF

I was born in the early hours of a wintry December morning in 1967 in a quaint English village maternity hospital. With a choking cry, this blonde-haired, blue-eyed girl stared into her new environment, much to the disappointment of my parents who were hoping for a boy. They adjusted to my arrival and loved me as best they could, but it soon became clear that I had a wild untamable spirit in me.

My baby sister arrived just before I was three years old. Her arrival gave me the freedom of space to explore this curious world I was living in. I was quick to learn and as soon as I could string sentences together, out reeled continuous questions that would leave my mother speechless with a disconcerted look on her face. You know, normal questions like 'mummy, why don't you hear my thoughts?' or 'Mummy, why can't I see all the things that are in the air, like in the space between you and me?' Or 'Mummy, why in my dreams do I speak a strange language?' My head was filled with unanswered questions so it was not surprising that when I walked past a church with my mum one sunny afternoon and heard it was a place for God who created this world, I instantly thought God was the one to answer all my burning questions. My mum didn't seem all that keen on my new idea to knock on God's front door, and scurried me away; I knew in that moment I would have to meet this God secretly.

Early the following Sunday morning, at the tender age of four and a half I crept down the stairs dressed in my smartest clothes and snuck out of the house whilst my parents still slept. I hid behind a large yew tree next to the medieval church for what seemed like hours before I saw people arriving. I watched for a while before mustering up the courage to open the huge impressive wooden doors. A friendly hand touched mine and led me to another room where the children attended Sunday school. I was somewhat disenchanted when I didn't find God sitting in this magnificent ancient building.

Several weeks passed and my disappointment grew because God still hadn't showed up, which was somewhat rude seeing as his followers had all come to witness him. I listened intently to the teacher who read from a very old and holy book written in a time when God did make appearances but not today, it seemed; so I left.

A very poignant moment happened in my life when I was seven and a half years old. My parents, unknown to me, decided to divorce. Oblivious to this information, I believed my mother, sister and I were just having a long summer holiday with my grandparents who lived in a quaint little country village. Several days into our 'holiday', my grand-mother sent me on an errand to purchase potatoes from the village greengrocers a quarter of a mile down the main road. I was given a penny for my labor and merrily skipped towards the shops imagining in my head and mouth what sweeties I would buy, toffees or chocolate…. Mmm? In a blink, the reality of the village completely changed; I was no longer skipping along a tarmac path but a dusty track! Old buildings had miraculously appeared, a pub, a coal merchant's house with a wooden cart loaded with coal; somehow I had stepped back in time! I scuffed the dust up with my shoes in disbelief; it was eerily silent and not a soul was around. I didn't have the courage to knock on a door and ask what was going on.

I began to panic; my grandmother would be angry with me for not returning with the potatoes for dinner and I was so looking forward to the toffees. I began to run down the dusty road, willing the village shops to be there when I turned the corner - in a blink, thankfully, reality switched back to normal and my feet were once again on tarmac. This experience affected me profoundly. Reality was not solid, as I had been taught to believe. My mother tried to convince me I had been daydreaming but I knew otherwise - what had happened was very, very real to the touch.

After this I became 'sensitive,' aware of many things others did not see. I would spend hours on the playground swings staring into the starlit sky; I felt a strong distant remembrance that somewhere up there was Home. At night instead of being tucked in bed, I would stare out of my bedroom window and demand the starry sky to reveal itself to me. Then one night a small UFO appeared. It did a high-speed zigzag dance in the sky, shining a bright torch light before landing in a neighbor's field. Now I knew for certain life existed up there. It was the talk of the village the next day but my mother never told me, trying to convince me I had dreamt it. I see now that I spooked her with my strange observations that perpetuated my curiosity and deep longing within my soul. A school project at the age of twelve at least brought some answers through old black and white photographs of the village taken fifty years previously - it was exactly as I had experienced it.

I was clever at school but the lessons really bored me; they never came close to answering the greater mysteries about life. Back in the seventies, the only place for such answers was the Church; so back I went, spending my early teens learning about the Christian God. I was classed as an awkward pupil asking uncomfortable questions. I just couldn't understand how this loving God could be so wrathful, punishing and final. The story of creation never made sense. And then there was the 'Rapture' for the 'chosen.' Why would Mother Teresa, after dedicating her entire life serving God, be turned away because she chose to speak to Jesus via his mother? Why would a dead newborn baby in Africa be refused bliss simply because it had yet to hear of Jesus' message - yet... an absolute scoundrel a moment before death could recognize Jesus as his savior, repent, and (hey! presto) be welcomed into Heaven? Huh? God had so many peculiar rules; you know 'conditions' that are supposed to be expressing 'Unconditional' Love?' I scratched my head many a night trying to understand; all I got was eczema in my scalp (ahhh). Still....matters got worse....

I made the mistake of telling my Christian leader about the apparitions I regularly saw.

For the next few months, I was subjected to exorcisms and prayers to release me from Satan's clutches but nothing changed . . . I still remained sensitive to unseen things. AND, I had discovered something else, a curious thing that the church would certainly disapprove of and label witchcraft; I've never owned up to this childhood secret. I noticed that if I thought about something hard enough it would happen in my reality! I tested it out many times, sometimes shamefully (*I squirm now*). My experiments even led me to read horoscopes and if it said I would find something on Wednesday, I did! It didn't even have to be my star sign; I just had to believe it, for it to happen! I had magical fun for a month, that is, until something went awry and I suspected I was cursed with my tinkering in 'devils play'; I got frightened and stopped (*If only I knew then what I know now*). Anyway, I loved my Christian friends but I had to face tough facts - I wouldn't accept that my extra sight was Satan. It was time to leave. Their Christian God was not my yearning.

At sixteen, life became extremely challenging what with leaving school, becoming homeless, starting work, living in a rat-infested bed-sit and falling madly in love. Childhood instantly died as I struggled with life's demands and responsibilities. If that wasn't enough, I kept having a particular premonition that haunted me; I so desperately tried to either ignore or change it. On my seventeenth birthday, I became engaged with my head filled with dreams of growing blissfully old together. Three months before my eighteenth birthday after a silly misunderstanding, my fiancé tragically committed suicide - I had failed to stop the premonition. For a short while I hated God for not allowing me to change the destiny of my sweetheart; I felt cheated, numb, lost, betrayed and dead inside. Village life can be cruel and ignorant; I was blamed for his death, ostracized, refused permission to attend his funeral, stalked and at times I feared for my life.

What made things really unbearable is that my fiancé kept visiting me, either making his presence known in the daytime or in my dreams at night. Having your loved one so near yet being unable to dive into their arms was an unbearable torture. A week after his suicide I planned my own; I wanted nothing else than to be with him. Destiny decided to say 'no' to my willful intentions. I swallowed one hundred painkillers and fifty sleeping tablets. It wasn't discovered until the next day, when I collapsed after break-fast whilst swearing at the village vicar.

After three days of coma I miraculously awoke in hospital with no side effects, de-manding a 'Big Mac' burger, much to the surprise of the doctors. I can't say I was overjoyed to be alive yet I slowly began to understand that something bigger than what I knew had prevented my death. Over a two-year period during sleep, I some-how spontaneously visited my fiancé in the astral realm, seeing where he lived and all the things he did there. I so wanted to stay but I always returned by morning. My fiancé had changed so much each time I saw him; he was studying and helping other suicides and was so happy and content within himself, so different from his earthly self. Finally, the moment arrived to say our farewells as he had chosen to move on. He didn't say where to, yet I intuitively knew this involved somehow dissolving the personality I recognized and one day incarnating again in a different body. At least in the Astral I could hug him goodbye.

Life sped on for me and at twenty, I was married with a beautiful baby daughter. Being a mother was certainly a shock to the system yet I soon began to love my new role. I cher-ished my daughter Tessa, and she became my world. Once nap times were harmonized between the two of us, I began to read and seek again. Spiritualism answered many of my experiences with the Astral but I didn't need convincing that there was life after death because I had experienced it personally. It did not answer my other questions about God, and reality's purpose. My husband tried to discourage my search as such subjects frightened him. Well, as you probably guessed the marriage only lasted four years and in leaving my husband, I became excommunicated from my birth family.

It was then that life finally took a wonderful turn for the better (thank god), where I met my lifelong partner Pete who cherished my daughter as his own. For the first time in my life I felt supported and encouraged to find myself. Sixteen months later my second daughter, Alannah, was born, looking uncannily like me with big blue eyes and a beam-ing smile that would make me go all 'love sick gooey' inside.

It was at this juncture in my life that I joined a development circle and learnt how to willfully still my mind. Our teacher was a gentle soul and each week would lead us into guided meditations. I would have the most fantastic experiences during meditation time. The only trouble was what I experienced had nothing to do with the guided mediation the group was following - I would somehow in trance spontaneously arrive somewhere else. It was because of these experiences that I pondered 'Time' and came to a wild conclusion that somehow All Time had to be happening Now! This was the only way I could reason how reality was so flexible (*In hindsight, this understanding of all moments past, present and future existing Now opened up doors within my brain*). The development group only lasted for three months, so I continued silently on my own at home, going deeper into the secret world that was within me.

Over the years, I wrote many journals, logging strange experiences and wild theories of how reality possibly worked, just like a scientist would study a lab rat. For instance, all my life I desired to understand the mechanics of 'premonitions.' Contemplation brought me to a very wild concept: What if a 'premonition' was actually remembering my Past! Could an incarnation be repeated many times over just like in the film *Groundhog Day*, where 'I' the 'player' keep forgetting and repeat and repeat rather than doing something new to move on? This might explain why during childhood I wanted fancy ice creams on a stick that wouldn't be invented for another twenty years. So could 'premonitions' actually be a 'remembrance' of repeating a timeline that is warning me 'I've been here before, change!' Thankfully I was wise enough to only share some of my experiences with close friends as such behavior in today's society would get me locked up in a mental institution, diagnosed with schizophrenia!

Motherhood taught me so much about my own childhood and humbled me to understand the struggles my mother had gone through. My children would come out with breathtaking comments, describing their lives before this incarnation or seeing bright lights in the atmosphere; I couldn't answer their questions, yet encouraged their unique observations to grow.

In 1996, something out of this world happened that I will never forget. In brief, it had been a very busy day preparing the house and cooking a lavish meal for relatives arriving in the late afternoon. Everything had gone perfectly and after dinner, the family sat down with a glass of beer. Later that evening after the kids were in bed, the subject of extraterrestrial life was discussed and was frankly ridiculed by my relatives as 'impossible nonsense.' This closed mindset upset me, so I decided to retire for the night having my last hot drink and smoke on the porch, gazing up into the stars, enjoying my own company.

I had nearly finished my drink when a strange low vibrational sound filled the still night air. I waited for the neighbor's curtains to twitch - but nothing moved; that is (and this was freaky) the starry sky above me was disappearing, or should I say blocked out, by an enormous space craft that just hovered above my neighbor's house, looking at me! I instinctively knew (somehow) this was a Mothership that held huge cities within its glistening craft that shimmered with a strange blackness that was liken to liquid mercury; this craft was a live intelligence and could change shape at will, and it too was looking at me. This awesome Mothership sat motionless in the sky where I could see what looked like windows and on its underside was a huge circular wheel-type thing that slowly turned.

Then... (oh boy!)...this Mothership began to communicate with me by displaying colored lights and numbers on the front of the craft that fired images in my brain. I was shown a huge blackness of space bursting forth with Light/Creation, diving into its ongoingness through evolution all the way up to this present moment in Time - and then *way on* into the future! I was transfixed, as these holograms in my head were more than just pictures - I was there, being a part of all that I saw, living and breathing it! It was a real awe-inspiring head rush!

There is much more I could write on this subject but typing space does not permit. So I will quickly summarize and mention that six weeks later I awoke not myself and automatically grabbed my kids' colored pencils and filled a blank piece of paper with symbols similar in nature to hieroglyphs into a mandala formation. That day I remember very little except by the time evening was approaching I had a picture like nothing I had seen before that charted the history of creation in this particular journey/fractal we are all exploring in the Mind of God. This mandala at times has a life of its own, with random symbols projecting outwards in 3D. Years on it is still bigger than my understanding yet it has given me many joys when another piece of wisdom is gleamed.

Over the following year while I slept at night, I would spontaneously find myself inside a massive school that I reasoned had to be either somewhere in the future or off-planet because there were many different types of humanoids but few humans. It was a huge arena type place filled with thousands of beings. We were taught via the mind by one great teacher who would send downloads of vast quantities of information into our brain within a nano-second (and similar to how the Mothership communicated) I was living and breathing the information. I was taught, for instance, how reality changed in its atomic appearance by tweaking frequency just like changing the station on a radio. The frustration in the morning when I awoke would be remembering so little of what I had been clearly taught the night before. My greatest desire was to hear these teachings in this reality so I could remember its entirety.

Time kept ticking and my surprise third pregnancy took me into a state of awareness where I could literally sense/feel the wings of a butterfly flapping in my garden or be aware of the worms under the grass I walked on. Everything was full of Life and celebration. This heightened state of awareness sadly left me shortly after my daughter Breze was born in 1997. Experiencing this wonderful connection to nature and now the loss of it spurred me on in my search.

In the summer of 1997, a voice in my head told me to go to Egypt the next year and spend the night in the Great Pyramid during the Spring Equinox. They were very specific instructions, something I didn't normally receive. The idea sounded impossible, but I kept telling myself I was going and purchased a special bum bag (fanny bag) for the trip. Then out of the blue the following February, I received a letter from a total stranger who was organizing a trip to Egypt spending a private night in the Pyramid on the Spring Equinox! She had written to me because she intuitively knew I had to be there. The money manifested and I packed myself off to foreign lands with complete strangers, knowing nothing of the trip's relevance or Egypt's ancient history. Two fantastic experiences in Egypt were part of the lead-up to finding Ramtha.

The first Egyptian Temple I visited was Karnack, which is guarded by many stone statues of rams leading to giant stone columns that tower in the azure blue sky. I surprisingly felt very familiar and at peace in this place. Our group was told to form a circle for a stand up meditation - this was a first for me; still, I'm willing to explore anything once. Suddenly I found myself high in the sky; I can't explain how I got there but right below me was the most magnificent golden phoenix I had ever seen. Its wings were vast and each feather glittered, individually catching the sun's rays. Next, I was looking through the eyes of this magnificent bird and I could zoom in my vision with great precision right down to a grain of sand. Then I was hovering over a group of people down below when I suddenly realized I was looking at myself - *whoooosh* - I was now standing in the group circle again.

What happened to me was nothing the group did in meditation - I immediately looked up into the sky, surprised not to see the bird. I had never felt such freedom and exhilaration before. I couldn't explain what had just happened, but happen it did and it was really majestic! Also, near the giant columns I kept seeing a particular hieroglyph, a small triangle sitting within a bigger triangle. Our very educated Egyptian guide had never seen this hieroglyph before; I just knew it was important (*Many years later I found out this part of Karnack Temple was dedicated to Ramtha and the statues of rams were encoded to awaken the soul memory of Ramtha and his teachings of 35,000 years ago. The triangle sitting within the triangle is the symbol of the Void contemplating itself. Maybe this goes part way to explain what happened to me here*).

My second puzzling experience occurred on the Spring Equinox inside the Great Pyramid. I was very excited, as this was the main reason that had brought me to Egypt. All lights were switched off inside the pyramid. Upon entering the King's Chamber, we saw a solitary candle lit, which we sat around. One by one, we each made our way to the sarcophagus for our ten minutes of enlightenment. I lay there with great anticipation - I waited and waited but nothing happened. I calmed myself more - still nothing. By the end of my ten minutes, I was raging with anger inside (actually off the scale pissed off) – I hadn't felt even an inkling of anything! I wanted to scream out my frustrations but couldn't destroy it for others, so I quietly stepped out and walked over to where I was previously sitting. It was then that a loud commanding voice in my ear said 'Lie down now!' It was the sort of voice you didn't question, so I hastily began to lie down just outside the group circle on the sandy floor.

Before my shoulders and head even touched the floor, I found myself standing in front of a being of dazzling light that was holding out their hand towards me. There was a deafening, pulsing, roaring wind sound and I saw a huge vortex of energy spinning with incredible speed in the center of the King's Chamber! I moved my hand up and held this being's hand. I was then gracefully led into this vortex of energy. Inside this vortex, I was weightless and floating and I could see it was made up of minute colored light particles, except it was now spinning the other way. Huh? I decided to ask 'where am I going?' 'To the Light City,' this radiant being telepathically replied as we continued to effortlessly float downwards inside the pyramid.

The next thing I remember was jolting back in my body, wide-awake with adrenaline pumping throughout my being and three and a half hours had passed. Seconds later, instructions were now spoken to the group to move down into the Queen's Chamber. Shakily I followed them and no sooner had I sat down in the Queen's Chamber I was gone again - to awake with a jolt one hour later; again conveniently seconds before the group were told it was time to leave.

Immediately upon reaching our hotel, I ordered a pint of beer for breakfast! I was shaken and dazed; something incredible had just happened. It was wonderful to experience that lightness of being, a serendipity of freedom and adventure. One thing troubled me, though - during this experience I didn't remember my loving family, not even my daughters I so cherish - how could I have forgotten them? What happened must have been bigger than my maternal love; this astonished me. I contemplated this, because it weighed heavy in my heart that I could walk into a strange beautiful vortex knowing not where I was going, with no desire/concern about ever returning. The only way I could reason this experience was the possibility I was another 'I' somehow.

This question of what makes up 'Self' was huge and I knew instinctively I would not find my answers in New Age teachings. They were too airy-fairy; I had to have tangibility. I wanted to know the truth and how I could learn to control such experiences, to invite them at *my will* rather than being taken by surprise and afterwards left with confusion. I wanted to understand this unseen world that I sometimes glimpsed - I wanted to be a part of it.

So much more happened in Egypt and I returned home war-torn and shell-shocked; reality had turned itself inside out, and upside down (well certainly in my world) and I could not voice it to anyone, let alone begin to explain it. For the first time in my life I was terrified to go to sleep. I felt so alone; there was no one who could help me out of this hell. I had gone too far to go back to the comfort blanket of Christianity. I flicked through numerous books on my shelf from Buddhism, Hinduism, Witchcraft, Spiritual-ism, and New Age but nothing brought me answers or eased my troubled mind.

It was then at my lowest ebb that I pulled out a book from my shelf that I had intuitively purchased two years beforehand and had somehow missed reading. The book cover was plain grey with the simple title *Ramtha (This is now republished as the White Book)*. What can I say other than this book literally saved my sanity and life? As I turned each page tears welled up in my eyes. My heart pounded as the words on the page sang to my soul of the loving God of creation I had so long searched for; this book to me was about HOME. I read this book over, and over and wished with all my heart to learn more from this amazing being Ramtha. It was not until I plugged into the internet in 2000 that my wish came true and I discovered there was a school! Oh my god, did I jump up and down for joy!

In 2001, I attended my first Beginner's Event in Cadeques, Spain. Ramtha marched on stage – oh, words are just inadequate to describe his presence and the rush I felt inside my being as I looked upon this awesome god that smiled lovingly back at me. His teachings profoundly touched and enriched my mind, soul and spirit. Finally . . .

at long last I was hearing REAL answers of TRUTH that made absolute pure sense. Ramtha teaches to empower and inspire his students to reach for their greatness and to consciously create wonderful magical realities, which pales Harry Potter's 'Hogwarts' to extreme dullness. Why undermine ourselves into dreaming of fantasy wizards when we really are alive, conscious-creator-gods! I realized I had spent my life trying to fit in with society, to be 'normal' and in doing so dumbed-down, which only led to doubting myself. I had never celebrated my uniqueness, which ultimately leads to embracing my god. Ramtha has created amazing disciplines, which promote students to experience firsthand the magic and empowerment of uniting with one's god. It was the strangest thing the first time I was blindfolded in the Name Field with 700 other blindfolded students and told to 'FOCUS' and find my two cards somewhere amongst 1400 cards posted around the edge of the field. It is an 'onement of peace'; 'magical' then 'exhilarating' finding one's cards. Ramtha's teaching methods absolutely convinced me they worked – I found my four cards! My beginner's event was a complete liberation. His beautiful loving message is for all humanity, conveying we have a choice to wake up and remember what we so long ago forgot, so we can wrap it up and go HOME - into Fantastic Elsewhere.

It is an understatement to say that I returned home buzzing from the event, I was ecstatic. The excitement was multiplied by joining JZ's new Zebra chat room on the internet. She taught the most profound teaching on 'out of body experiences' and I learnt the most thrilling news - they could be controlled at will! For the next month, I willfully and adamantly refused to go to sleep until I had a 'controlled' OBE. Many times I did slide off into sleep yet I succeeded in consciously peeling out of my body seven times during that first month – I was learning to unshackle myself so lift-off could begin! It is out of this world to defy gravity and float around my bedroom, hovering over my sleeping body and then flying off on an adventure. This was the start of many fantastic journeys that taught me so much about the unseen realms. I am now in my seventh year as a student and absolutely loving it! Life is so much bigger with a great sense of purpose and my family has grown alongside me. Why choose the 'norm' when we can be unique gods!

My dear beloved Future, I have seen sweet glimpses of you in the brave new world. These words of mine are old history from an old fading timeline where creator gods forgot themselves, lost in our own possessions, consuming our planet without a care. We got possessed in owning the world – when it was all about 'owning ourselves.' It's hard to convey just how sluggish this dimension is and how easy to slide and forget over, and over again. It is like waking out of a long amnesia. The smell of great change has arrived in the breeze and we humans now have to make another courageous change with our lifestyle and rekindle our relationship with Mother Nature. I have lived in an era that promotes a technological lifestyle without responsibility and consequence. The irony is those who choose to live simply, growing their own food whilst living sustainably and in harmony with Earth, are classed as a backward move towards being natives again. These simple folk deemed outcasts to society's 'norm' are in fact aligning with the future - your wonderful future. A future of outrageous freethinkers, creating fantastic adventures in the Mind of God.

At present I'm involved in educating myself on how to build a cozy hobbit home amongst a community of students, intent on aligning ourselves with Nature's natural rhythms celebrating Life; and preparing for the ride of our lives! If I am reading these words in the brave new world, it means I applied the teachings that I was so lovingly taught over the years by my beloved Master Teachers Ramtha and JZ Knight. A big kiss I blow to you Intrepid Future! I will join you soon to clink goblets in a celebratory toast. So Be It!

BIG P.S. Ramtha and JZ you have literally rocked my world into a greater orbit! I love you both dearly! Sending lots of Love & Hugs on the glittering Grid.

MARION LANCASTER
Massachusetts, USA

HOW I CAME TO KNOW THE RAM AND ATTEND THE GREAT SCHOOL OF THE MIND

There were a series of events that led me to the Ram; but in all earnestness, my journey to this teacher really began the day that I was born and perhaps before that day. I will venture to say that I was born to come to this place to learn and apply these teachings and there could have been nothing else more important in my life.

From the youngest age I can remember myself as a child, everything I did didn't seem to fulfill me. I always had some deep ache and longing desire deep within me for something. I didn't yet know what it was, but knew I was going to know, some day, and just kind of happen into it. My quest to know pressed me for a greater knowledge, experience and understanding beyond what I saw and learned from the news media, television, public education, religion, college studies, and people, places, and events.

And it wasn't that I lived a sheltered, uneducated, inexperienced existence or an unadventurous life. Not at all. In 1975, at age twenty-nine, I began a journey of self-discovery. I was leaving family, friends, and a revealing and inspiring intimate relationship with a man, to travel and explore life in other areas of my country. This venture was begun after a very exciting, life-changing, and challenging five years of college at the University of Massachusetts in Amherst, which included anti-war protests and the liberated sex life of the 60's. I left thinking it was all to find myself and what other options and opportunities I might find in other places, if not even perhaps an altogether different lifestyle.

I had bought a camper van that I could stand up in, completely outfitted with sink, stove, built-in cooler, bed, closet, beautiful red and purple curtains, lots of storage and a super great sounding stereo system.

With the money I saved for the trip, what started out as a month or so long venture turned into a couple of years. I was mostly on my own, except for my amazing cat, who had made it very clear he wanted to come. I lived sometimes just off the land, camping out and meeting new people all the time and doing things differently every day in my travels. This journey came after having worked as a social worker, teacher, childcare worker, artist-dancer, waitress, store clerk and cashier, and research assistant to a college professor. I'd also had a very intense, often disturbing but extremely rewarding job supervising activities with "mentally retarded" populations in an institutional setting in the last days of the existence of that institution.

One day at the institution, with no forewarning, a resident pulled me by my hair and dragged me across the entire floor of a very large gymnasium before he released his grip. I was too in shock to feel any pain. When I recovered, I asked if I could work with my "attacker" individually to devise ways to give him opportunity to express himself more and where he would be able to do so without losing control. I would help him find some ways to release emotion without bringing harm to anyone.

I had NO idea what I would do with him. Something in me just directed me to do it. Up against everyone's resistance and disbelief, I just wouldn't accept "No" for an answer. Finally, I was granted the opportunity, though they warned I was putting myself at risk and I must be very careful. But to me, after the first hair-pulling, body-dragging event, the rest seemed very easy and in fact enjoyable. All I did was talk and listen to him. I found out he was quite an extraordinary pool player and brilliant in his ability to manipulate energy and talk about it in a way I never had heard before. Prior to that, no one knew about his mind and his skill at pool and other things. I brought this to everyone's attention and everyone enjoyed the challenge of pitting his or her skill against his. He would always win. He also began to share his unique ideas with other staff who became impressed, intrigued and humbled by what they learned from him. I accomplished a beautiful, productive, and safe relationship with that man that allowed him an opportunity to be seen in a different light by everyone and to have the possibility of being released from the institution to an almost normal life.

It was experiences like that that made me want to know more and find more resources within myself to do more, especially to change the way people, including myself, see and think and do in our world that affects other people, nature, and all of life.

I also had ideas that no one I knew seemed to understand and I felt quite alone sometimes because of that, no matter how many "friends " I had, until I met the man in my college years that I fell deeply in love with. This was one of the many experiences that I really understood better once I heard or read some of Ram's teachings.

While everyone else was dating, I had not one date my entire four years of high school; I fantasized every single day about the kind of man I would meet and love, the kind of conversations we would have and how we would think about life and each other and what else we would do together. I even acted it all out and rehearsed our imaginary encounter daily. Then out of nowhere, one day this young man DID appear in my "REAL" life and fell immediately in love with ME.

It took me months, however, to wake up and realize my own feelings and until then I refused any notion of romance with him. One day in our long friendship, I suddenly shifted from seeing him as a friend to feelings more intimate and romantic, but without even knowing it until the words just snuck out of my mouth and surprised even me. He laughed and told me he knew that day what I was going to tell him. How do some people know us and know something about us like what we are going to say, before WE know it? I still didn't realize until years after that, that this was the man and the relationship I had dreamed and fantasized about every day as a teen and NEVER believed it would actually happen.

After those years of travel, I settled in Tuscon, Arizona for no reason I was consciously aware of (my camper van broke down and what I intended as a temporary stay turned into almost fifteen years). There, I pursued a lot of interests that I thought might lead me to greater understandings. I studied Astrology, Yoga, meditation, religion, Dance, Art, psychology, different spiritual philosophies, a bit of science, dance, mind and body therapies, and anything that I thought might open my mind to understanding myself and other human beings and the world…and life itself.

Then a series of very unusual circumstances brought me closer to the Ram. These experiences also helped me to see and get more serious about doing what most excited and inspired me, such as dance, art, self-expression, and music. But even more than those inspirations and understanding them, I began to sense and even experience that there was something kind of transcendent or transcendental that appealed even more to me than anything else; it was an understanding of realms that we don't see and the places and the dimensions that we came from that we don't remember and where we go after we die.

Religion seemed farthest away from the truth or the real knowledge I was seeking. I loved talking to and about God. I loved hearing people talk about God. But I didn't like the Bible (I thought the God described and the people were absolutely cruel and absurd in many or most accounts, particularly before the time of Jesus - and I was raised JEWISH!!!) I didn't like the ministers or rabbis who claimed to KNOW the word of God better than the rest of us and claimed they were chosen representatives of God to us. There were, however, some ministers or other religious leaders who I loved and adored.

One of these was at a church called St. Francis in the Foothills. I spent many Sundays at what was called the "Sunday celebration." He never lectured to us; he only shared his experiences and what he believed God and spirit and soul were and how he would use his experiences to grow and change and encourage us to do the same. He would on occasion read something from the Bible but never as though he were an expert on the inherent message, meaning or application of the words he quoted. He inspired self-discovery, and cultivating one's own contemplation and understanding, self-awareness and one's own relationship and interpretation of 'God' and spirit and life. Rather than preying on people's desire and need to find contact and connection with the Divine only to uphold his own self-image, he empowered and inspired others that EVERYONE can talk to and listen to God.

****

One day, I woke up and tried to get up but I couldn't stand. I thought I must have just pulled something. But three weeks later still couldn't put any weight on my foot and it was getting worse. When I couldn't even walk anymore I went to the hospital and after that to excellent doctors, sports specialists and then to lots of alternative health prac-titioners. At the hospital, four doctors conferred with each other about what to do with me. Every physician and specialist told me I had a bone disease and would never walk again. They all wanted to give me a medication which I refused to take because of the side effects and my aversion to medicine. They all told me I would never walk again if I didn't do what they told me to and take the medication.

I suffered much pain, physical and emotional, and four to five more months on crutches. I missed dancing more than walking and couldn't bear a life without dancing. I decided I wouldn't let this stop me: if I had to dance sitting down, I would do it - and I did. I also danced on one leg a lot. I visited a church daily when no one was in it . . . and walked down the aisle with my crutches, in agonizing pain, and talked in my mind to Jesus. I was not feeling religious and sometimes I really thought I was losing my mind, but I just wanted to talk to Jesus, so I did. I also imagined that I was able to toss my crutches and just walk . . . and I did that every day.

Now that I had a lot more time in solitude, some spontaneous, and what I thought of as out-of-body and transcendent experiences directed me in my self-healing to total re-covery when none of the best physicians or specialists in sports medicine or alternative medicines could help me. I know this experience not only recovered my ability to walk again but also saved my life and changed my future in more ways than I can explain here. During this transformational period, time seemed to be in super slow motion and more like I lived through five lifetimes in five months.

Upon recovery, I was really much more driven to find some book, some teacher, some place, some people, where I could learn more about these things. Everything I could get my hands on (Rosicrucian studies, Theosophy, Rudolph Steiner, Science of Mind, Yoga, Meditation, healing, natural healing, self healing, Tai chi, Chi Kong, dance therapy, etc.), every book, every course/class/workshop, every independent study, every person, teacher, every way I would attempt to learn more would lead me only so far and never as far as I wanted to go. It seemed as though the way was blocked or barred. Maybe it was just "God" I was looking for. I certainly didn't believe that I was unworthy of knowing or unworthy of any kind of closer, more intimate experience of God, whatever God was, So I could not figure why I hadn't found what I was looking for YET but I wasn't ready to give up.

One day, I did stop looking. I didn't give up. I just decided I wasn't going to find it or God or whatever it was, in any way I knew. I stopped studying astrology and going to spiritual, philosophical classes and listening to psychics. For awhile something inside me told me to just live and learn from life now because somehow that all I had learned and I was 'using' to arrive at a better understanding of life actually barred me from a true and real understanding.

I got much more involved then in just listening to my own thoughts, following my own inner impulses and discovering what I could do and know on my own. I found myself capable of knowing and doing far more than what I had believed. I seemed to be developing a somewhat more heightened inner awareness just by paying more attention to everything I was thinking and feeling and experiencing, and being in a sense more present with everything, every day. I retreated somewhat from more activity and yet put more of myself and especially more of my **mind** (attention) in whatever activity I was engaged in.

This unfolded even more powerful and rather outstanding experiences alone and with nature, and with dance, with some major and very unexpected and profound healings.

A few examples of these are:

1. A woman who had an implanted back brace of some sort, so she couldn't stand upright due to a spinal imperfection at birth had never had any feeling in her entire back, her whole life. During a two-hour workshop I conducted in movement and movement awareness, during an attunement to one's body's responses to music, she felt sensation in her back for the first time and continued to, during and after the workshop.

2. There was a woman with Down Syndrome, who for at least the last eight years of her life had shown no emotion, hadn't spoken, and had no expressions: no smile, no tears, etc. During the 6th weekend, during a one to two hour session with her, she cried, smiled, and laughed for the first time in at least eight years or more.

3. A man also in his thirties, also developmentally disabled, with a mental age of about six, based on behavior and communication abilities, had an extreme sensitivity and fear of being touched on his head. His parents, who still physically cared for him, could not wash his hair without him screaming loudly and fighting them off, every time. After two movement sessions, he came home from that session touching his head and laughing and smiling and they were, for the very first time since birth, able to wash his hair with no screaming - and have been able to ever since (these and more, except for #1 are well documented and can be verified).

All of these just whetted my appetite even more to understand what happened in these incidents of extraordinary, unpredictable and almost impossible healings and perhaps even more important, if these occurred, why not more often? WHAT MADE THEM HAPPEN WHEN THEY DID BUT NOT ALL THE TIME?

Then, in addition to the unusual experiences above, one day things took another significant turn.

I went to a friend's house, just intending to make a very short "stopping by to say hello" visit on my way somewhere else. This was a friend I was very close too for many years. When I knocked on his door, a stranger answered, a very beautiful, blond, blue eyed and wonderfully friendly younger man.

I had no idea someone else had moved in; OR that he had gone away for awhile; and I was usually pretty informed of goings on in his life. I was so shocked and disappointed that my friend wasn't there. I just sort of stood there with my mouth open and finally the man who was there house-sitting for a while…invited me in. This man was going to be my first introduction to RAMTHA.

But I resisted the introduction to Ramtha, wholly, for I had given up all sorts of those "kind of things," thinking that I was never going to learn any more from anything or anyone now, but my own life and paying more attention to my own thoughts, my own experiences and my own mind, and not anyone else's, whether they were a great teacher or not. I had given up teachers!

This man didn't tell me about Ramtha the first night I met him. He just talked to me. It was very soon though, probably even by our second meeting, that he brought up the name of Ramtha. And I must say Ramtha's name did not have any impact on me like it has on some people, but maybe because I was so totally resistant.

But my friend persisted, not offensively or to the point of alienating me, but just to give me a little bit of information each time we met. He really believed that from what he knew about me that I would only LOVE the information that came from Ramtha, once I heard it. But I wouldn't hear of it. I was totally against it, and told him that every time and told him to give it up.

Weeks of regular contact turned into months and into many years. I found this person to be like a long lost friend. Like a brother, a real buddy and also a very inspiring man. We also were able to be very intimate, without sex. It wasn't that he wasn't attractive. He was gorgeous and manly and yet very understanding and gentle with women and kind and patient. But most of all I loved his mind. Every meeting was an adventure into new perceptions, whether about something in nature I never thought to observe before or something about the body I hadn't known or paid attention to, or a new outlook on people or events.

I began to notice as the months went by that my friend, who all this time was always attending Ramtha events, was changing immensely. He seemed to come back from each dialogue almost a whole different person. At the same time, he never lost what I loved about him, but it grew and **got better;** and what limited him, he grew out of. His confidence grew so much and his ability to communicate was becoming greater than I could have imagined it would. I wondered how this could be. **I never saw anyone change that much that fast.** He would also come back from events able to under-stand things that he hadn't before and able to explain it clearly to me. He was changing in ways that I had perhaps seen happen before in people over a time period of five to ten years …but for him this much change came in ONE event.

That made me more curious and had some impact and influence on me, leaving me thinking maybe I should give a little bit more consideration to the opportunity he offered to me to hear Ramtha speak on something, at least on a cassette, or to read some of the material.

Though in my thinking I reasoned that way, I still refrained and withdrew from that op-tion for a long time. I reasoned away my opportunity. This went on for YEARS! Mean-while my friend was changing not only now in how well he could communicate and how much his confidence was raised and how explicitly and fluently he responded to my questions : answering them so completely, calmly, and undisturbed by my challenging and sometimes very confrontational nature.

It wasn't just his mind that was so obviously changing, and his personality that was growing and becoming very different from month to month and event to event; but physically he was also changing profoundly.

One day I was at his place and there was a tape already playing in the other room. I didn't notice at first that the tape was on. We talked and a pause came, and he left the room for something and I noticed the tape and listened. I heard one sentence and it just blew my mind! It was like the most extraordinary perfect explanation I had ever heard of anything… anywhere. This was an understanding of womanhood that no psychology books could have given (and I studied enough psychology in college and after graduation many more years of human behavior studies and books, written by both men and women, to know the potentials for insight into human behavior that offered). NOTHING explained anything about anything like Ram did.

And it wasn't within the boundaries and the confines and the language of anything that exists in anything that I knew of in any form of study. He didn't talk about women in the way WOMEN talk about women, but from a whole different perspective that just made my mind light up with understanding about my whole life and all the feelings I ever had in any situation where I really identified myself with the fact that I was a female and what goes along with that. No one could understand what I felt like… at least not unless they'd also heard those tapes!

So here I was, listening for the first time to Ram. I heard a sentence and then another, and another, and when my friend returned I said, "sh …sh…sh…I want to hear this." I listened to almost one whole side of one tape and said, "I HAVE TO BORROW THESE." He just got the biggest smile, like he was saying "I just knew this day would come." He said, "Of course, take them home.**" WHILE I WAS THINKING, "HOW DID HE HAVE THE PATIENCE TO WAIT SO LONG FOR ME TO LISTEN TO THIS AND HE KNEW THE IMPACT IT WOULD HAVE ON ME?!"**

So I took the tapes home and I listened to them not once, but over and over again all night long. And kept learning more and understanding more each time I listened. I never got bored with what I heard.

By the morning, and without having any sleep time, I called friends to **hurry** over to hear these, informing them that it was important information and worth dropping almost anything to hear it NOW! They came and stayed all day to hear them over, and over also! We were all deeply moved and changed.

After that I asked my friend for more tapes. I asked him to give me as many as he could possibly spare. I also watched videos that were shown at people's homes.

I listened to Ramtha tapes for the following two or three years, regularly, on every subject I could get that he had talked about, almost daily, before ever even considering attending an event. It wasn't that I didn't WANT to. It was that I felt so fulfilled with listening to the tapes, I felt, probably as a lot of people do who have not ever seen Ramtha, that that's all you NEED because there is so much IN them. The information alone and listening to them over and over was seemingly taking me so far in my life and in my understanding of things and in my changing and in how I dealt with things.

I was loving myself and loving who I was becoming and never in my life had I had that much success in changing and loving who I was and who I HAD been, while at the same time always wanting to be even greater.

I was never against the idea of attending an event, I just felt I had enough...and one of my limitations was thinking that I could never AFFORD IT, which postponed it even longer once I did know I wanted to.

Now it was time to change that thinking. Once I made the decision and was committed to it, it was a matter of a couple of months before I actually did it. I thought I didn't make enough money to go for even one week or one weekend. I couldn't even imagine taking it out of one paycheck. I did not earn much money working for a program that relied on grants every year and paid very low teachers' salaries and no benefits (health insurance, leave with pay, etc.). Unless money would come out of thin air, which was the only way at first **I thought** I would have the means to go, I would not be able to attend.

So, I decided to put to use some of things I heard on these tapes and I also started to talk to Ramtha in my mind. I said: "Look, I want to see you. I really, really want to see you." And as I said it, the desire to do it built up in me every day (once I admitted it to myself). And it got so big it grew to mean more to me. I said: "Ramtha, I want to see you almost more than anything else. NOW! I just want to know what it is like to be face to face with you, to look into your eyes, and to see you and to hear you in person."

One day the idea came to ask: "Couldn't you just come to where I am, or **closer** to where I am, maybe not more than an hour's drive away?" (he hadn't ever been to where I lived) and I added: "...and perhaps just for a day and maybe it could just cost $100? (I could **manage** that) just so I could SEE you?"

Once I got really passionate about that, there it was, within a week or two on the schedule: JZ channeling Ramtha, in PHOENIX, ARIZONA, for the price I could pay. I lived in Tucson at the time. And was I happy. I felt like he was eavesdropping.

So I went with my friend to my very first in person event with Ramtha. And I was ecstatic for the entire two weeks before that and at the Hotel the night before. We were not going to risk not getting there on time in the morning so we were there the night before. I could hardly contain myself.

The next morning we were at the event. From the first breath until the very last moment, it was as though I was hanging on every word as though they were the first words I'd ever heard in my whole life and the last words I would ever hear in my whole life. I didn't MOVE at all in my seat. I was so mesmerized, NOT by Ram's charisma, though he does have it, or because I was entranced, though I was, but by the WORDS - THE TRUTH BEING SPOKEN, THE KNOWLEDGE THAT HAD WAY SURPASSED ANYTHING I HAD HEARD ON TAPE. Awe silenced all my thinking. I could just follow him along as though I was journeying through lifetimes of self-discovery missed and now getting caught up on.

There were hundreds of people in the large hall there and I was at the back of the room. After approaching and speaking to about four or five people, he came around to the back, came right up to me, and looked into my eyes and I stood right up out of my chair and looked back into his. Those were the eyes of JZ Knight's **body,** but I was looking into HIS eyes and I knew I was. I knew it was not JZ there, but him and I can't tell you HOW I knew that but boy, did I know. It was just amazing. I know I was looking into a man's eyes and they were his, while I was looking at this woman and I never thought for a moment that I was looking at a woman.

I was just so taken by what I was feeling. I just never had any encounter like that one. It was really clear that there was something behind those eyes that was bigger than human. And then without thinking, I said, "I have been wanting to see you for a long time." And then I cried - burst into tears. In that moment I realized I HAD been wanting to see him since the day I was born, or perhaps even lifetimes. And I had just realized it sometime AFTER I said those words…it was as though they came right up from my subconscious.

When I first said that, I thought at first that I meant for weeks or months since I first listened to tapes, but then realized no, it went back much farther than that and much deeper and that was why I cried.

The whole day was so beyond what I can describe in words in what I felt and how it moved me. I was not anyone I was before, and it was as though you could have ended my life then and it would have all been worth that moment.

What he talked about that day was of huge importance to me. Ram's talk covered everything imaginable, and even what troubled me that I couldn't formulate into words to even ask the question …and yet I was given the information I needed to resolve it. I will never forget the transformation that took place. I went back to my home, and my work a different person.

I returned to Phoenix about six months later for the next time Ramtha appeared there. That time was for a two or three day event (this time I had no problem earning the extra money). It was at that event he announced the intent to form a school. I made the decision right there and then that I would be in that school and would have the money to go no matter what the cost financially or otherwise.

I was there at the formation of the school, beginning with an event in Snow Mountain that summer, followed by Estes Park later that year, where consciousness and energy and the breath was taught. I have been in the school ever since (about twenty years), never missed any of the required events since, and have attended every year, much more than what is required to remain current in the school.

Every one of these events was worth more to me than all the money and all the time spent not only for the knowledge that is nowhere else so detailed, simplified and easy to understand on so many subjects, but also for the **opportunity to actually experience what we learn in tangible results and changes.**

It is truly the school of the future, the kind of education / learning/ and teacher I always dreamed about and always wanted and will always be grateful for and richer because of. Now I am finding my self - long lost to lifetimes of not knowing the truth of what I was and where I came from and why I am here.

I know now what I never knew from any philosophy, any religion, or any person. Knowledge from a being that was human and transcended that life is the only true and whole knowledge that can add what I need to know to be finished with a past and to move into a truly unlimited future. Now, I can remember what I forgot and reconnect to the real me. This is worth more to me even than the most amazing accomplishments, healings, miracles, manifesting matter, mind over matter, unplugging addictions, reversing age, and all the other actual and witnessed accomplishments by students which are the side effects of the real accomplishments of the purpose and reason for my study and training here - some of which can and some of which cannot, at least not yet, be put into words. It is an awakening.

AMANDA GIFFORD
South Africa

ARRIVING . . . A NON-LINEAR JOURNEY

I stared. Ramtha was on stage in Scotland. It was my first event. The music pounded in my heart, the drums of Scotland played. I stared harder.

What could I see? Something I was sure I had never seen before.

A part of me woke up. The sleeping god awoke.

The sight of Ramtha was extraordinary, illuminating, exquisite, unexplainable, hard to capture and hard to hold on to.

My journey had begun.

The journey to my master teacher has been non-linear. It feels like it is happening forward and backwards in time. It's a multidimensional journey... a hidden, invisible and mysterious becoming, although the Observer Effect in quantum physics has done much to help my understanding of this mystery.

A childhood friend asked me once, "So what happens. Are you just going to float away one day?" She was referring to my study at the school. In contrast, I often wonder how this journey can seem so dense and heavy at times. It's almost impossible to explain to others. Where do I start? "I am just in the middle of it right now! It's not what you think…" I say. I try and search for the best explanation but I have just arrived back from a month long trip to Yelm for my event. I am more disoriented than ever.

It takes me months to find my feet after an event. Everything seems out of place. You could call it 'Past Reality Unplugged!'

Nothing is as it was.
I am looking through a new window.

My mother was a seeker until she met Ramtha. This was the end of seeking and the beginning of truth. She has always been an inspiration to me. I, too, have a passion for truth.

I knew more about the Hindu religions and mediation before I knew multiplication. I accepted reincarnation. I knew about cause and effect of my thoughts.

I did not attend any religious ceremonies that I can remember growing up so when I was asked if I was Jewish or Christian at school when I was young, I said that I was not sure. My mother loves to tell this story. Her daughter did not know whether to go to Carols by Candlelight or Hanukah!

I was never sure why I was afraid of Christianity when I was younger until I understood more about the missing gospels of Thomas and Mary Magdalene, the violent history of the church, the role of Constantine, the Council of Nicea and the use of religion as a tool for power.

I always felt judged.

I am happy that my choice was to grow up with an understanding of meditation and enlightenment.

I remember when I was ten, my mother was going to be initiated with her Saint Matt Master in the Satsangi path and I was allowed to ask one question.

My question was: "Why are there no female masters?"
Apparently Maharaja Sharan Shingh just laughed! My interpretation of that was "One day I will understand!"

I think that day has come.

I first heard of Ramtha's teachings in the early 1990's. I do not remember who introduced to me to them. I just remember listening over and over to them ~ like rain onto parched earth. The one that I loved and remember listening to in Cape Town, which was particularly intriguing to me, was one on Emotion! I remember the gist of the message. I loved it.

My journey to Ramtha led me to anything that was connected to enlightenment, masters with extraordinary abilities, visitors from the future and the concept of ascension.

When I was very young I remember writing, "In this life I will ascend to the 5th Plane." I had no idea what that meant. I now know it that means mastering my thoughts and learning to hold my focus to attain a different level of consciousness, and the journey is one step at a time.

I visited Sai Baba in 1997. I was fascinated about this idea of enlightenment. What did it mean?

I remember reading some Melchizadeck initiation statement and promising myself to go to the future that would take me towards my mastery.

I used to practice bilocating to Mount Shasta from Cape Town with a guided tape by a teacher who said I should say, "I am now in Mount Shasta!" and imagine being there. I practiced every night.

I loved all of these things. They all brought me joy and this knowledge of my destiny – mastery of my mind.

Finally, after many years of these different influences, my mother went to see Ramtha in South Africa in February, 1999, on the world tour. When she arrived back, she said to me, "You are coming with me to Scotland." We booked for Scotland in July, 1999, and that was my first event with the Ram. Thanks mom! I cannot ever thank you enough for that.

My journey of the Great Work is my life's work. I will never give up and one day in the not too distant future. I will arrive. That will be that fine morning of the magicians, when I have arrived at the doorstep to my master teacher's house and I can say I have arrived as an equal.

LAURENT MOURIER
France

My Journey to Ramtha

I tell this story with great enthusiasm. But how to tell something that is so old and done with that remembering it requires a lot of concentration? And how will I tell this narrative through the eyes of today, as it is three years since I came to the school? What is the start of this story: my birth, the birth of the universe? It may take time to tell!

The path that led me to Ramtha? It is LOVE! Love of my beautiful wife Catherine, my daughter Anaëlle, my friends Vincent and Valerie, and the many people I met on my way. Those have been the mirror of myself, giving me messages that allowed me to move forward step by step on the road to what I can now call my Great Work. The love I am talking about is a state of mind that can be chosen. This story describes how this energy guided me.

****

This is it! We are now arrived at Sportilia, Italy. I am not really sure what this seminar is about. Vincent and Valerie welcome us with big hugs full of fraternity and love. Catherine and I have mostly followed their enthusiasm to this teaching. We saw a video of the introduction weekend. The discipline of C & E made the biggest impression on me, and almost shocked me. But we feel that we are going to live great moments.

The journey brought great excitement and questions. We started at 3:00 a.m. and we arrived after ten hours of driving. We crossed the Alps, and part of Italy. Anaëlle is six months old and we are going to attend the beginners retreat with her. Everything has proceeded smoothly since we decided to come: Although we have registered at the last moment, our friends found a very convenient place for the baby: a nursing center housed in a bedroom! That was one of our concerns, but a light heart gave us the answers.

Coming to this seminar has been an adventure. First, the price was high for us. We really wanted to come, but it was too expensive. We distrust "money pumps" that we know exist in various personal development seminars. French culture mistrusts gurus and groups, which can insidiously deprive us of our freedom. Both my path and Catherine's have exposed us to these kinds of groups. I don't think I have ever been a victim of a guru, but I know people who have found philosophy, psychology or religion more comfortable than exploring on their own. In France, there is a mistrust of most things coming from the US. Influenced by our culture, we at first decided not to go; however, that decision quickly made us depressed. When we observed that, we changed our minds: we would go to Sportilia.

And here we are! I am very happy to experience this retreat with Catherine, my dear wife and Anaëlle, my wonderful little girl.

****

During the last few years, I have changed, profoundly changed. I am no longer the same. I'd rather say I don't give voice to the same potential of myself I used to. I have never been so close to my true self.

Only four years ago, I lived through a cruel separation with my ex-wife Lydie. We had no children, and I did not want them. I had never wanted them. I felt unable to give something consistent to a child. I had very low self-confidence. This world was so chaotic that how could anyone raise a child with any consistency?

What made me change? Chosen love. Not love of a woman, but love as a state of mind. *Conversations With God,* a book wrote by Neale Donald Walsch, made me aware of this fundamental choice that every moment of my life gives me, the choice between the two states of mind on which our lives are based: Fear and Love. All other feelings result from that choice. And that is my actual experience.

In January 2001, I chose to change my life. Not that I had changed nothing before, but I had built security, stability. I am a teacher of construction techniques. I am well paid, with a lot of holidays. I also assigned myself a recognized role as a facilitator and mediator in a team of teachers. But at the deepest level, I knew that security means death.

Parisian friends came to visit us on a weekend. Jean-luc and Christophe are friends with whom I have worked to learn the profession of psychotherapist. Discussions are usually intense and true. We seek the truth in us. How can we liberate ourselves from our psychological conditioning, how can we integrate spirituality in our daily life, and what is the meaning of our life were issues that the four of us usually discussed. Suddenly, a sense of urgency came up intensely.

What would Love do in this situation? Love wants the flowering of my soul, my spirit. In my heart, I was making a decision for profound change. I would start with my work: take a sabbatical, devote myself to painting and artistic creation. I was sure that this would bring me to open my consciousness even more. I didn't know where it would lead me, but I had to go.

At the end of the weekend, our friends left and I spoke to Lydie about my realization. I did not want to upset our relationship. I was convinced that this would be positive for us. But six months later, she was gone. She found a man who offered her the security she needed. Even though I let her go, a few months later she sought unsuccessfully to return. I lived very badly during these times. The feeling of abandonment was very powerful. I found support from some friends, especially Valérie and Vincent.

During this time, I was aware of this choice between Love and Fear that Neale Donald Walsch spoke of in *Conversations With God*. Thus, I focused my thoughts as often as possible towards Love. I also understood that if I remained in that state of mind, the organization of my life would arise spontaneously in the most fair way for me. Objectives that are too specific are often linked to the intentions of my Ego.

As Christmas, 2001 approached, there I was on December 19th, at the Paris airport CDG, departing for India. My friend Jean organized this trip. He is an artist and philosopher who reads and translates Sanskrit. I attended a creative arts training in France with him. Through him, and especially his first seminar, it was revealed to me that I have an artist's soul. Now, he was returning to India, and he organized tours whose theme was Indian spirituality with visits to spiritual places. He was also our guide, and we learned about India, its history, religions, and his state of mind.

I felt confident with him on the trip. I would not have embarked on such a trip otherwise. My intention for this trip was to learn more about myself and to recharge my spirituality. I remained present to Love and I trusted this state of mind. It would help me to express my highest aspirations.

I arrived at the airport and the small group of passengers was already gathered. I saw Catherine for the first time. I said a quick hi to everyone, with apologies for my lateness. On the plane, I was seated next to Catherine although we had obtained our boarding passes at different times! A chance out of 250! Since then, we have been together and never separate, we got married, we had two girls, and Anaëlle and Cristale journey together with us on the trails of the expression of the Gods that we are!

But let's return to the trip to India. The start of this love story took place in spite of us. I experienced no 'love at first sight.' But after a few days, we shared with each other everything that we had experienced. I sought her presence. It was friendship with great joy. I had the feeling of being in a state of love. My Love choice was working! But I was not looking for any love affair: I had found a girlfriend two months before this trip and I was doing it for self-development.

For western tourists, India can reveal some psychological disorders. A young woman in our group began to behave weirdly, and the assistance of everyone was required for the rest of the trip. This experience impressed us all. The initiation aspect of the trip had been strengthened. My discussions with Catherine became deeper.

After a few days, we were at Hampi, a wonderful and magical place. A temple was abandoned on a hilltop. I decided to spend a night under the stars. Catherine decided to come along with me. We climbed barefoot, as is done in India in temples, with a few blankets. The roof of the temple offered us a magical night view with the full moon that illuminated the surroundings perfectly. Our unique Indian night of love was in this quiet temple. We talked about our best intentions for our lives and what we wanted to achieve. I wanted to devote my life to the service of mankind. I wanted to live with Catherine. I felt a spirit of love for the whole of creation, for the magnificence of humanity that is a real promise of transcendence.

****

That night reminded me of my first spiritual experience. It was twenty-six years earlier at a retreat weekend to prepare for the Catholic sacrament. I was with my childhood friend Laurent. As we belonged to Catholic families, we had to attend catechism. We learned that being nice, wise and obedient was to be good to Jesus. Despite this indoctrination, those three days of prayer, speaking of faith and being outside of our families led us to raise our state of mind toward life. Walking in the forest, I felt something beautiful in me, a kind of power. I wanted to bring knowledge to the world, to create goodness and beauty. It was like the force of certainty. No out-of-body experience or flash of light, or voice in my head - only certainty, obvious and strong.

****

From the roof of our temple, Catherine and I talked about profound things. It was obvious: she was the one! I did not ask the question of what love would do in this case: I was love and embraced the whole of creation. During the remainder of our journey, we built a deep and chaste love for one another.

Back in France, Catherine and I spent a few days at Vincent and Valerie's. They had a friend who wrote books and channelled divine entities. We met her, and Michelle dedicated her book to me. She said that the message she received comes from Jean. She asked me if I knew someone called Jean. I did not believe it, but I thought it was my father who had died in 1995. She wrote, "Go Your Way. Do not return. Everything is Joy. Enlightened children are waiting for their parents." Upon leaving this interview, I did not think. I asked Catherine if we could have a child together! That was exactly the clear message that I had just heard. In that moment, I was not looking backwards. I didn't even ask what Love would do: I was Love!

But to clarify why, let us look a little backwards. I was thirty-eight years old and I had always considered my life as one that would be without children. Or rather, I had always refused to see it any other way. I saw the world as committed to dehumanization, the generalization of a warrior state of mind. I did not want to create people who need thirty or forty years to get rid of their education. And I did not feel able to be a father. In that moment with Catherine, the past didn't exist, only this clear idea. The choice of Love allows that.

Anaëlle was born three years later in February, 2005. We were longing to welcome her! When Catherine became pregnant, we celebrated it in a gourmet restaurant. It's incredible, how eating such a good meal gave me the impression of beauty and magnificence. Even eating and drinking are perhaps an ecstatic experience! Catherine and I were in intense joy. Our happiness had created the feast!

And what would love do now? Take responsibility and autonomy for the birth of Anaëlle and create this event by ourselves, to go even further in the process of knowing ourselves.

The hospital is necessary for emergencies. But knowing the psychological consequences of some unnecessary care, and the risks of the conventional position of delivery, we decided on a birth at home with a midwife. Our goal was to experience the power of the mother and how her self-confidence could make it. Physicians usually use fear of any risk for the baby to take power over women. Their lack of psychology skills can't help women to manage their own emotional responses. Childbirth at home was a spiritual initiation for us, and an ecologic act to preserve mankind!

We researched all of the information we could find about birth and delivery, from books, internet, midwives, physicians, mothers who did childbirth at home, and people for whom childbirth is still natural. We got informed about the legal aspects, physiological aspects, psychological aspects, and what non-conventional medicine said.

The ultrasound had been done to verify the proper physiological process of pregnancy. We had been practicing haptonomie, which is an approach created in France to "talk" through touch with the baby in the belly of the mother. Its aim is to give self-confidence to the baby. All that was necessary to raise our self-confidence. Catherine had done a wonderful job of transcending her fears and her past. So had I, because for someone who did not want to engage with children, I chose a challenge!

My preparation for the first birth was to help restore confidence to Catherine. Secondly, it was to ensure that at the birth, I would not myself be panicked. I examined my own birth. It was something that I had done in psychotherapy, but it just had to be updated. Even though the days following my birth had been very stressful, the effects of trauma had faded and at the birth of Anaëlle, I was now fully aware and peaceful.

Anaëlle was born. I welcomed her in my hands. The midwife arrived after the birth! I experienced something intense and wonderful. The Past no longer existed, only the Now and the attention to this being who trusted us, who relied on us to preserve her potential. The first breath occurred after long seconds, quietly, with no cry ... Now, Anaëlle, you were there in my arms! I was now forty-one. It was amazing! It was impossible for me to have done so only a few years earlier. It's nice to see a birth. It's nice to be born. Since that day, I started to feel more tenderness, more love for myself. I saw myself in the mirror of this event. The path of my daily spirituality was made of moments of preparation and moments of shifts. And when I shifted, I rarely felt welcomed. I understood that I was the only one who could welcome myself, recognize myself and give myself any tenderness. So I welcomed Anaëlle with all my love, as I would like to do for myself!

I discovered every day the path of love: caring, responsibility, accepting change in myself, expressing the best of who I am.

Vincent had again played an important role. He had graduated recently with a degree in osteopathy (a kind of chiropracty), and the subject of his doctoral thesis was birth! Three years before the birth of Anaëlle, Vincent that suggested we listen to the presentation of its argument, to help him prepare. Thus we heard a detailed course about the physiological process of childbirth before I thought I might even need it! It's amazing the work babies have to do to get born! I retained much of this data which helped me to understand the problems of childbirth, including the supine position.

A few days before the birth, he gave me some tips to better help the mother. After the birth, Vincent and Valerie came to our home and he took care of Anaëlle in order to limit the consequences of the deformity of the skull imposed by the passage.

I have a long history of heart connection with Vincent and Valerie. Vincent and I became close friends during several personal development seminars. His parents followed the same psychotherapist training as I did. I started learning about psychotherapy while undergoing my own therapy in 1992. At that time, I lived in Paris and my job was very stressful. I was responsible for building sites. I felt like I was in jail and I didn't even know how to escape. My soul suffered. A suicidal impulse led me to undertake psychotherapy. I was fed up with suffering. I was convinced that what happens to me comes from me. But how to change?

First, I understood that the expression of my emotions was almost non-existent. Within a few years, I was able to express emotions such as simple joy, anger, sadness. This restored some common sense in me and calmed my thoughts.

Then I discovered and applied the "mirror effect." It is the capacity to understand that what I see in the others is me. I then taught techniques of building construction. I worked with young people from sixteen to twenty-two years old. When the atmosphere of the class is one of conflict and disorder, it is difficult to work. I felt uncomfortable and I was angry about it. Thinking of the mirror effect at the time allowed me to see my internal state of mind! I then shifted my thoughts: I decided to see my students as young and beautiful, filled with magnificent potential! Actually, I was sincere; I believed it because I knew it was true! The change was immediate. Calm returned, relations improved and the work could continue. I noticed that in relationships, the fact of seeing each other as someone wonderful helps to create wonder in this person. Relations become excellent, and exist in a higher register than social relationships. This is the mirror effect. I resumed acquiring power over myself step by step.

I spent another important phase when Nicole discovered *Conversations with God* by Neale Donald Walsh. I found something so complete, so encouraging, so empowering, and so frequency specific with my conscience at the time, with the psychological work and the knowledge of myself that I had before. For the first time, I saw God, who seems to be outside of this man, as a positive. It gave me a perspective on my life, and my future. I felt a great release.

I felt something similar at the age of seventeen when I discovered a group of spiritual searchers. This group had a holistic approach to being: physical, mental, spiritual. They had no dogma or ritual, but were very inspired by the future. The themes of survival, futuristic architecture, reincarnation, symbols, technologies, and so on were developed. Relations with these people were very fluid and generally affected the essence of being. They created also wonderful performances.

The consistency of this new approach was a lifeline, in the context of the inconsistency of the Catholic religion with "the mysteries of God" as the answer to any uncomfortable questions. The meeting of the group has ended years of malaise since my first spiritual experience.

In *Conversations With God*, a message that I put the most into effect was the idea of "I want." As long as "I want an interesting job," for example, I experience the fact of wanting, but never having! That means thinking: "I have" or "I am" to succeed in being so. That is how I changed the course of my life. I thought as often as possible "I am Love" to be imbued with love. And Love does come to me! I think of love as universal creative energy. I do not know what it is. But by putting it in my thoughts, I am sure to attract greater things. And it works!

This was how I decided to change in 2001, and how I met Catherine, my first daughter Anaëlle, and Ramtha. Everything was chained in a logical manner, going towards a broader knowledge of the world and knowledge of myself.

I also thank my fears, my conditioning, the Catholic religion, materialism. These impasses have helped me find the Way.

KAREN DITCHEY
Montana, USA

MY PATH TO RAMTHA'S SCHOOL

I remember as a little girl looking at my hands and wondering what made me - me? If everyone had the same "parts" . . . blood vessels, bones, fingers, eyes, etc., what made me who I was?

At the end of my senior year in high school, I read the *Life and Teachings of the Masters of the Far East.* I wondered how I could find a school or teachers such as those without having to travel so far away. I knew, however, that if some people could do those things, others could as well. The question was how.

When I turned twenty-one, my parents decided it was time for me to experience Las Vegas. I was a newlywed and had a new baby. I didn't have a lot of money, didn't know how to gamble and wasn't too interested. A high school girlfriend was attending college in southern California and offered to drive up to Las Vegas to have a brief visit. We met at the Dunes, where my family had booked our stay. My parents went golfing for the day and my girlfriend and I looked for a comfortable place where we could sit and visit. That, of course, was the Keno area. Nice chairs, no interruptions, relaxing, etc. We ran keno tickets all afternoon, one at a time, and of course, every game we played, we were going to win! By the end of the afternoon however, I was broke and she had to leave to return home for school the next day. I walked her outside, gave her a hug and told her that I had had a most wonderful day (in spite of losing all my money)!

My parents had come back from golfing and were up in our room getting ready for a dinner show they had booked at another casino. As I walked back into the Dunes, heading for the elevator, four numbers became very clear to me. They just seemed to "pop" into my mind: 15-17-27-41. They were so clear to me, clear in a way that I "knew" beyond any doubt, they would be winning numbers if I played them. I hurried up to the room, walked in and (excitedly) announced to my dad that if he were to lend me forty dollars, I would double his money back!! He chuckled a bit, as he knew how this gambling thing worked, but lent me the money anyway.

We left for the dinner show across the street and walked into that casino. I looked at the keno board and two of my four numbers were on the board. We were waiting in line to be escorted to our table and I jetted over to the keno area. I placed the minimum bet and waited. All four numbers came up and I won $120!! I was ecstatic! I paid him back and we went to the show. When it was over, we caught a cab down to another casino and walked in the door. Two of my numbers were on the board. My mom and I played a ticket . . . we both won $560!!

We did this for the next two days. I could walk into a casino, look at the board and know whether we'd win or not. After awhile, we were in our room doing the classic tossing of bills into the air all over the hotel room!

The feeling that I had, though, was that I couldn't explain my "absolute knowingness" about those numbers to anyone. Every time I tried, someone would say that my biorhythms were up or my horoscope said I was lucky or some other such thing that I knew wasn't the explanation. I lost interest in those ideas and explanations from others and gave up trying to have anyone understand how absolute this knowingness was. What I did know was that there was more "out there" - that there was something greater that I just hadn't grasped – yet.

A few years later, I had a meltdown with a friend. She was speaking about God's judgments and, as this was a difficult period in my life, she was directing an unfavorable view of what my judgment was going to be. When I hung up the phone, I was crying uncontrollably and said (out loud) to myself, "God would never judge me because (he) knows my heart, (he) is inside of me; I have done nothing wrong. I am not a bad person."

The following weekend I was in our local bookstore and found *The White Book*. There was only one copy of it in the store (I have since looked for it in our community and haven't found it). Anyway, I read it; ordered the introductory tape and, with my husband, attended a beginning class in February of 1989. We came home and manifested our dream property.

I now know that all of this has been a journey that I asked for and found. When I look back on these events, I know they were the stepping stones, my path, if you will. My school is right here and just as I couldn't find the words to explain the knowingness, words cannot convey how grateful I am for Ramtha's teachings, JZ's sacrifices and this school.

F. PAUL MARKIN
Canada

FIRST LOVE

I was in the middle of the most emotionally rendering period my young life had yet to offer: I no longer knew who I was. It was during this time that the opportunity to visit Ramtha's school would present itself; however, in order to get to there I would have to travel down with someone I both feared and hated – the very person whom I deemed the cause of it all.

My journey to the school began in June, 2005. I was seventeen and had just graduated from high school. I loved literature and hiking, and would meditate from time to time. My peers didn't share these interests, so I would often just do my own thing. Partying wasn't exactly my idea of a good time, but on one particularly warm summer night, my cousin Zach mentioned to me that a house party was going on up the Pass Creek valley, near his place. Zach was older than I – he was studying physics at the local college and had let his curly hair grow shaggy. I agreed to go and we left, complete with booze and another friend we'd picked up. The party was for a girl in my grad class whom I wasn't very familiar with. She was moving to Calgary and wanted to go out with a bang.

It was a short drive from Zach's, and it didn't take long to find our destination. The property outside the house was alive with music, sound and people. There was a bonfire and a live DJ. I had a few drinks, said hi to people, and moved from group to group. After a while though, I began to feel bored, which was pretty much the norm for me. Unless some other soul was up for a philosophical conversation about the nature of Something, I decided I was ready to cut out and head for home. On the patio, the DJ was doing his thing, and I was half-heartedly paying attention. Not my cup of tea. From inside the house approached a girl, an acquaintance back from high school, someone a year younger than I. She was small in stature but strong in presence. I didn't know her very well, except that we had talked about hiking once. She called me by name and gave me a hug. I remembered: her name was Jade, an unusual name. Being the social creature that she was, or perhaps groping for conversational topics in order not to appear awkward, she asked me to tell her something that she'd never heard before. Interesting request. I thought for a moment, and recalled a cryptic piece of advice that my mom had mentioned once. For some reason, it had stuck.

We create our own reality, I said.

Back then, I wasn't aware of that statement's magnitude. When Jade heard this, her eyes lit up and suddenly we were engaged in a lively conversation. She demanded to know where I had heard this. I told her I didn't really know, and Jade proceeded to tell me everything about herself. She mentioned somebody called Ramtha. She even ran through the party into the house to grab her notebook of poetry when I said I liked to write. You see, Jade was living with Kriya, the girl who was throwing the party. The two weren't sisters – rather, Jade had struck a deal with Kriya's mother, Christine, and so had found a new place to live, a place to run away to. This was Jade's home.

Jade had learned about Ramtha from Christine. Christine was her legal guardian, and loved nothing more than to share her wisdom. Now, amid droves of drunken teenagers and a DJ who catered to improv rap, I found myself listening to the story of a 35,000-year-old enlightened master. This was turning out to be a pretty good party! Jade and I continued to talk unceasingly until the crowd thinned, and Zach said that he wanted to leave. The girl who held my attention was bubbling over with energy, but had yet to spill her wine. This was fantastic. I left with a phone number in my pocket and a date to go hiking next week.

Jade proved to be a fascinating friend. Since I wasn't on the hunt for girlfriends or sex, our conversations remained unfettered by games and ulterior motives. Next week came fast and soon I was having another rapid-fire conversation with this strange girl, breathing hard as we made our way to the base of Mt. Gimli – an enormous dark granite spire which holds the imagination like a fly in honey. At the top of the hike, near the spire's base, I read Jade some of my poetry. The rock and snow were shining in the afternoon sun. She had my head spinning: here was a girl who likes to read poetry on mountaintops! Her eyes were the colour of warm, rich earth, and just as difficult to escape. We talked about spirituality and she asked if I believed in fairies. I said that fairies are probably the same thing as orbs (those lights that appear in photographs from time to time). We talked all the way back down to the car, and all the way down the dirt road, and all the way down through the green valley bottoms until I dropped her off at Christine's. I flew passed Zach's house on the way home, flipping through the details of our next hike in my head.

A friend was organizing a group for an overnight trip to Old Glory, a peak visible from the local ski hill. It was the highest mass of earth in its range. I asked Jade if she was up for it – and of course, she was. We were part of a six-person party heading up through densely forested trail. It would take about an hour or two until the sub alpine revealed itself. In our tent that night I learned the details about Jade's past – how she can't stand living with her mother, and how her father goes tree-planting in the summer. She commented on how unusual her drive to tell me everything about herself was, especially since we'd only recently met. Needless to say, we spent most of the night talking. All too soon, I was dropping her off at Christine's house again, up Pass Creek. We decided that indeed it was too soon to part, so we detoured to pay a visit to the creek, where I quickly lost my keys in the current. The next several hours were spent trying to find them, an adventure in itself. We didn't mind.

Then I started to visit Jade exclusively at her house – Christine's place. Christine fit the description of benevolent, teaching me about this Ramtha character and deepening my understanding about the world. Christine was Jade's guardian, but she was also her mentor. In time, she would become mine as well.

I spent weeks with Jade on the deck, reading Rumi and talking until the sky revealed the morning. Eventually I worked myself up and kissed her, and after several more hikes together coupled with a trip to the Kaslo Music Festival with my cousin Zach, the summer drew to a close. I'd fallen in love, and declared it the happiest time of my life.

Yet something very interesting happened the first time I told Jade that I loved her. By then I was familiar with Ramtha's basic teachings and was aware of the fact that he is sometimes referred to as 'The Ram.' Jade and I were alone on a rocky beach, and the water had become too cold to for swimming. I was holding her in my arms and digging tunnels through those voluminous brown eyes. She held her tongue as I confessed my love. Then we heard something to our right. Several meters off stood an enormous male mountain sheep, with thick horns curling around its head: a ram. Jade tried to approach it but I held her back.

Just watch, I said.

With the autumn leaves came college and I enrolled in a university transfer program. Jade and I had our ins and outs, and we divided our time between her home and mine. She was in her final year of high school, and frequently took the bus to come visit me. The late autumn skies dragged snow over the local valley systems and I found time to ski in between classes. Christmas whipped by and before I knew it my first year in college was drawing to a close at the cusp of spring. I had worked for a security company during the winter months, running alarms and conducting patrols around town, so I had some money saved up. I was planning to use it on a trip to Eastern Europe with my brother and sister as we are of Slavic descent, children of the Russian exiles known as *Doukhoboursti*, or Spirit Wrestlers.

However, it seemed that, as my departure to Eastern Europe loomed, Jade and I became more and more unhappy with each other. The space between us grew foreign and turbulent. I remember being fraught with sadness one night, unable to sleep, laying next to her. I placed my head next to Jade's and felt moisture where my left eye met the fabric of the pillow. I thought she was silently weeping, that maybe she felt the same as

I. When she lightly began to snore, I realized that this indeed was not the case and that I'd managed to get drool in my eye.

Before leaving on my great intercontinental adventure, I struck a deal with Christine and said that I would work for her upon my return. Christine works with the mentally challenged, and I thought it would be a good experience. She was so happy when I agreed to work for her in the approaching summer that she hugged me and even kissed my cheek.

The plane ride to Frankfurt was surprisingly short, and it seemed altogether too easy to hop from one continent to another. In fact, it was surreal. Together my brother, sister and I moved through the streets of Prague – snapping pictures of demonesque spires, to the enigmatic walls of the Kremlin, and we even managed to catch a Tchaikovsky performance in St. Petersburg. I was experiencing culture shock when we hit Moscow, and unconsciously turned to Jade for support. Yet this move only deepened my confusion. Things didn't look good for us. Next stop was the clamorous markets of Istanbul, a yacht excursion up the Turkish coast and a nocturnal hike up Mt. Olympus. The mosques of Asia Minor had me in thrall. The architecture was flat-out alien, and the musicality of the call to prayer almost had *me* falling to the floor. It was both intoxicating and frightening.

Yet I couldn't get in touch with Jade.

Not even the Mediterranean could cut her from my reeling thoughts – which would swing from the ruins of ancient empires and right back to her. During the yacht excursion up the Turkish coast we moored in a small town called Seljuk. This is where I finally received word from her via email. Any communication is a good sign, I thought. However the message stated that things would not be the same when I came back home – that our relationship as I knew it would be severed at the quick. This was devastating, even though I had pondered the idea before leaving on my trip. Preparation for that message seemed impossible. While I was reading and re-reading the message, my siblings were taking a nap to avoid the heat. Once the news sunk in, I jettisoned out of the stuffy hostel and began wandering around the baking bricks of the little town, locked in a bona fide stupor. The place was a furnace and I was doing my best to cool down.

The next day we were back on the boat, and an Australian lent me the book *The Power of Now* by Eckhart Tolle. I learned to zone into the moment to get away from my thoughts. Reading that book gave me spiritual grounding, and I salvaged what was left of the trip. After a ferry ride to Italy and a pizza in Rome, it was back to Canada, my home. The day after I arrived back at the local airport, I hiked into the snows of Kokanee Glacier Provincial Park, alone – both to fight my jet lag and to stay the predatory thoughts of lost love. When I came back down from the alpine snows, I was ready to wrap things up with Jade and begin my summer employment with Christine.

I got to know Christine's clients quite well, helping to facilitate a normal life for them. One, a sweet middle-aged native woman, said that she thought I deserved a good, nice girlfriend – one that could make me happy. I thanked her and said who knew what could happen. It was an incredible job, partly because Christine, my boss, would give me life advice and teach me about manifestation. How could I complain? Occasionally I'd run into Jade on the stairwell, as she was still living with Christine. But if I showed up for work with the least bit of sadness in my face, Christine would call it and confront me on it, and I'd feel better. In fact, sometimes I'd wear big aviator sunglasses just so she wouldn't be able to do that, for once in a while I simply wanted to wallow.

Then there was Ramtha. Christine talked about him an awful lot. She asked me if I would like to accompany her on a trip to Ramtha's school, for a Beginner's Retreat. She had a boyfriend named Raymond who had also never been to the school – and neither had Jade. These three people would be my traveling partners, should I choose to go. At this point, I had been working for Christine for about two weeks. I deliberated, hemmed and hawed, but couldn't give her an answer. Once I was alone, though – maybe it was in her laundry room or on the stairwell – I decided that I had relied far too heavily on my head to guide my decisions in this past year of my life. After all, look at what had happened with Jade. Yes, now was the time to listen to my heart. I didn't have much to lose, despite an uncomfortable trip down to the school with the former lover. Christine even said she'd pay me for the work days spent while we were down there learning.

In the end I wasn't going to think about this one, I was just going to do it. I told Christine I was game.

The next few days at work I found myself in front of Christine's TV, watching old intro tapes for Ramtha's school, five hours worth. I took notes – this stuff was good. I registered for the event and prepared myself for this strange school in the States. Little did I know what I was getting myself into.

Typically, after work I'd stop by Zach's place, and we'd go swimming in the creek or talk about physics. Rather, he'd talk about physics and I'd listen. I'd give him my own interpretations on the subject, whatever they were worth, and for some reason I was always extremely glad to see his face before heading home. I just felt really happy around this guy, my cousin. After work, we went for a run in the evening light, and ended up sprinting full tilt down through an overgrown field of knapweed, and I could hardly keep up because I was laughing so hard. I mean it was difficult to breathe. Who would ever have thought that frolicking through a field of purple flowers could be so much fun? I was running a lot back then, partly because it occupied all facets of my attention, and afterwards I was too tired to think about the past.

The eve of our departure to Ramtha's school came a little too quickly. On that day I showed up for work as usual, but something wasn't right with Christine. In the past few days, she'd been telling me to get a new confidant. No thanks. I didn't even know what that was supposed to mean. The only person I could think of was Zach – I wasn't hanging out with a large crowd – and Zach, well he was there for me. But today Christine was insistent, and there was an odd timbre in her voice that I didn't recognize, or necessarily like.

I pocketed my list of duties and errands for the day, and was ready to get at them. We were on the deck, the same deck that Jade and I had spent so many nights on during the previous summer, and Christine cornered me in the morning light – demanding pointedly who really was my confidant, my comrade.

She wasn't going to back down this time.

Well, Zach I suppose. I didn't see the big deal. Christine paused for a moment, and after a while said that I needed to find a new confidant. She looked me directly in the eye and slowly told me that Zach was a person whom I shouldn't trust. I still didn't understand why. Just listen to what I say, she said. Her expression twisted up and Christine turned away. When she next spoke I looked at her face framed by the green of the mountainside, and she was weeping.

Paul I can't stand it any longer! I'm around *their* bliss all night and *your* sorrow all day!

My tongue thickened for a moment. No, I thought. Zach and Jade? That's ridiculous! But Christine didn't have to say another word. I didn't want to believe it but she was clear enough. My boss, mentor, and friend then enveloped me in a sweeping hug. I just sort of stood there in her arms, wrestling with what it all meant. Although she was doing her best to be supportive, Christine was sobbing over my shoulder – this was hard for her too. I didn't know if I was supposed to cry or get angry or shout or what. I felt like a computer that couldn't load anything, the gravity of those words pinning me to the floor. My cousin, my best friend, my confidant who gets me singing every time I visit, has been leading me on in betrayal? This must be why Jade gave me the boot over email when I was in Turkey. And what *about* Jade? This is not the way first loves are supposed to end. It was filthy.

Yet all had gone numb. My insides had turned to liquid and it felt as though I was being held together by my skin. Over at the shed, I was supposed to get the vacuum out and clean Christine's vehicle. But the words on my to do list didn't mean anything. Numb hands, numb eyes. I read the list over, and over, again and couldn't figure it out. I was lost within myself, what I would later understand to be something called 'psychogenic shock,' because I'm a nerd when it comes to words. After a while, Christine hollered to me over at the shed, asking if I was alright. I told her I was.

One of Christine's clients had to go into town, and I got behind the wheel of her vehicle and drove. I'm still surprised that I actually did so, considering the circumstances. I had to think for several moments before I could physically do anything.

Near the end of the day, Christine asked me whether I was still going to Ramtha with her tomorrow. I would have to sit in the same vehicle as Jade – that wellspring of love and betrayal which severed me from the moorings of myself. But there wasn't a chance I was going to back out now. That would be admitting to weakness – in effect, it would be letting her win. I didn't know how I was going to do it, but by rights, I would.

After work on the drive home, I got mad. Like, *real* mad. I had a general idea where the two could be hiding out. Like dirty rats, I thought. There was a swimming hole nearby and I took my chances. An old death-metal CD was kicking around in my truck and I put it on, loud. Speeding along to the music, I felt long tongues of multicolored flame lift off from my skin. I reveled in it. This was the most intense and blinding rage I had ever felt in the entirety of my life and I was going to use it to my advantage. You see, by nature I am not a violent person. Anger was my father's domain, not mine. But this time I envisioned myself stepping up to Zach on the rocks of the creek bed.

I was going to tell him that he'd destroyed me in every way except physically – so he might as well just finish the job. He would stammer and wouldn't know what to say. Then I'd tell him to hit me. I'd call him on. I wanted an excuse to unleash my pain on him in all the force which I was feeling in that moment. If he didn't make a fist, which he probably wouldn't, I'd sock him in the face – once. I'm not sure if I'd meant it to be symbolic or not, but I wanted my knuckles to contact his nose just once because I was convinced that he deserved every square inch of pressure that I could give.

I arrived at the swimming hole, tied my boots tight and lit my tobacco pipe before walking down the trail to the water. When I came around the corner and saw the sun reflecting off the vacant pool, I realized that there was nobody around. So I just sat by the rambling creek and smoked, reflecting. For some reason, in that moment I fancied myself like the water in the creek: able to move around any obstacle, any rock, and still keep going. But the day was far from over – I'd only just gotten off work.

As I drove home, the anger slowly dissipated, retreating with the curves in the road. With a somewhat clearer head, I recalled that Christine had told me not to let Zach and Jade know that I had found out about their affair. This troubled me. If I confronted either of them dead on, they would know that Christine had told me. Christine had said that she certainly didn't want Jade to be her lifelong enemy simply because she had told me what was going on. This complicated things. I called a friend who lived downtown, and we went for a walk down by the riverside. We smoked and I told him of my situation. Together we devised a plan:

I would get Jade to confess to the affair, thereby keeping Christine out of the picture. This would be done by me threatening to assault one of her closest guy friends, Tom, saying that I knew what was going on and that I was on my way to seriously hurt this person. Jade and Tom had been close friend for several years. I must point out here that the object of this scheme was not actually to hurt Tom, but to make Jade think that Tom was in immediate danger, thereby causing Jade to crack and come out with the truth – that she had in fact been sleeping with Zach. If Jade confessed the truth, then she wouldn't know that I had already found out from the lips of Christine. Thus Christine could still maintain a healthy relationship with Jade, and I could freak out on my former lover, releasing this pressure which so desperately needed to find its target.

I had it all figured out by the time I arrived home. My brother and sister were wondering what was up with me, but instead of talking with them I went to the workshop to speak with my dad. I told him everything, including the plan. But when I looked into my old man's eyes and heard his rough sigh of empathy, it was I who cracked. I cried for the first time that day, my father staring at me under the fluorescent lights of the shop.

It reminded me of when I burned my legs in the sixth grade with a jerry can of gasoline. I was sealed up tight like a soldier until I showed my mother the burns. When she uttered that same sigh of compassion, I burst forth in tears.

Now it was my father who held the key, and I wept. He convinced me that my plan was poorly thought out, and that I should wait until I could deal with the issue in a clear state of mind. But this was difficult – I was burning up inside. I needed to confront either Zach or Jade, right now. I needed to have them hear me scream. I wanted them to know what they had done.

That night I hesitantly crawled into bed and picked up my journal. In the beginning I'd let Jade read it, so that we could be honest with each other. Towards the end of our relationship I'd write things down that I didn't want her to see, so this practice stopped before I left for Europe. Now in bed I sat and wrote down the date: July 20th, 2006. In bold letters at the bottom of the page, I drove my pen into the skin of the paper and carved 'I DIED TODAY.' Underneath this heavy statement, I continued to write:

> Love is oblivion. Have you loved? Yes? Have you opened and stared into the eyes of oblivion? Have you died, then? Paul has, he died on July 20, 2006. No one's sure who's taken his place, if anyone, but we're confident that the replacement will bear the burden of oblivion with courage. [Later]...No! No, Paul has not died – a facet of his personality has, but he has not! No – I am yet unbroken.

This last line "I am yet unbroken" would prove to be a major source of strength, my mantra, in the days to come. But as I lay quietly in the dark, sleep wouldn't take me. I was tired but my mind was crackling with a cocktail of virulent emotions. My thoughts were restless, flooding past in waves.

After a while I turned the light back on and grabbed my journal. Below my previous entry I wrote down what I had been thinking in the dark: that the worst prison of all is a glass prison where the convicted, the assailed, and the jailor all are bound. Finally, sleep arrived.

The next day I woke up early and got my possessions in order: I was going to none other than Ramtha's School of Enlightenment. Sleeping bag, journal, discman – I was set. Before driving to Christine's, I paused in the bathroom mirror. This day would be a disaster if I broke. No, I would be a spiritual warrior this day, I said to myself. The mirror had me transfixed. I dug deep and gazed into the centers of the pupils staring back, repeating 'I am yet unbroken' several times. Jade would be near me today, and I would simply withdraw. I would retain this bathroom focus and remain silent – the warrior was all inside.

I arrived at Christine's with my aviator's on. She caught me on the deck and asked how I was. I said I was a fucking warrior, and she smiled. I started to pack the vehicle, which included tying a foam mattress to the Thule box on the roof. This ended up with a knotted mass of cord obstructing the Thule, but that was fine by me – it did the job. Then Jade arrived, and my insides crawled out and under the shed. I turned away and looked through the tint in my sunglasses at the summer sun growing over the valley wall. Jade was giddy with excitement, and I could hear her laugh behind me. She was wearing a hoodie and sweatpants underneath a long grey coat, ready for the road that lay ahead; I was hoping that my face would remain as stiff as the pines which lined it.

I sat in the front passenger seat, with Raymond (a psychiatrist by trade), behind the wheel. We were in Christine's red SUV, a vehicle that shouted RAMTHA in bold letters on the rear license plate. Jade and Christine were effusive with excitement in the back seats. Raymond and I were cool and quiet in the front. I immediately turned on some death-metal in my earphones, as loud as I could stand, hoping to drown out the whole situation. It wasn't my usual taste of music, but the intensity grounded me. So did burying my face in the pages of my journal, rallying for resolve with poems and mantras about spiritual war.

We stopped at a bank on the way out of town, and the girls got out to withdraw some American money. I looked up and found I was alone with Raymond. I pulled out my earbuds and he tried to find some common ground, perhaps more for his own sake than mine.

I heard about what's going on brah. Fuckin' women, eh?

Not bad for a psychiatrist, I thought.

At the border, the officer made Raymond get out of the vehicle to untie my mess of cord. The panjandrum wanted to see inside the Thule and wouldn't let me get out to help Ray undo the knots. No problem here – the less I had to interact, the better.

After a while, Raymond and I switched off and I took the wheel, speeding like Raymond but taking the corners a little easier. Christine liked it and said that she'd rather have me drive. The vehicle maxed out at 140 kilometers per hour on the open freeway, and it was fun. Without my music I started to loosen up and even participated a little in the vehicle banter. We flew through the northern desert and it was my first time seeing the Washington badlands. They were breathtaking.

Eventually we pulled into Olympia, eight hours away from our small community tucked snugly away in the Columbia Mountains. I hadn't yet so much as glanced at Jade. We stayed at Christine's friend's house, also a veteran of the school. Her name was Wendy. She was about Christine's age and when I didn't order anything at the restaurant, she asked why I wasn't eating. I said something stupid, like I'd already ate. Then she asked about my t-shirt. It was from Prague, and had Franz Kafka's name on the front. I was proud of it. I told her that he was my favorite au-thor, saying that his work was enigmatic and cryptic. Wendy replied that I was fairly cryptic myself. I couldn't help it – being quiet and sipping water was about all I could muster right then. So they ate and we left. That night I slept in Wendy's yard, away from everybody. I just wanted to be alone. Our beginner's event would begin the next morning.

My first sight of the school was of the old, mossy brick walls along the side of the high-way. Dense rainforest was contained within. We passed through the gate and unloaded our stuff in the parking field. Then I had my picture taken and received a school ID. I found my seat near one of the camera stations in the centre of the main hall. There was some time to fill before the event started, so I wrote mantras in my journal to keep up my resolve. I even drew a picture of what I thought a spiritual warrior should look like. Maybe it was the Ram himself.

By the end of the event, I would find myself staring at a beautiful young girl in a long grey coat. Her eyes would be glowing with a rich, earthen hue. She would be smiling and I would wonder who this stranger was. Her eyes would lock with mine for a moment, and my heart would be filled with wonder: Jade. All the hardships, disciplines and teachings of the past week came to a dazzling point at that moment, for I hadn't been able to recognize Jade. It was surreal. I knew then that a change had occurred deep within and I had stumbled upon a greater identity. That symbolic moment would stick in my mind for a long time after its experience, for no longer was I that same tattered person who first stepped foot upon the grounds of Ramtha's school. Not at all. Instead I had found the work of a master teacher.

CAROLINA MARTINEZ
Mexico

THE DREAM AND THE PAINTINGS

I t was a typical weekday. I had taken my usual morning shower and I was comb-
ing my hair in front of the mirror trying to get it a little bit drier, unaware that my
life was about to evolve.

As for my personal history, I have to say that since forever, I had always known deep
inside me that there must be and certainly is a greater truth than the one we are generally taught in the normal world; that there is much more to life than just a body, a bunch
of dreams, some to be accomplished, others forgotten, a lot of effort and a big routine,
moments of joy and sadness but just to get to an inevitable moment of death, which
can be postponed but never avoided. I had always known there must be a way in which
everything makes total sense: me, my life, my mission, and God itself, and I've been
searching in and outside of myself, endeavoring to make logic out of everything. I have
always been reflexive, introspective and questioning.

I started the search for a greater and broader truth in my early adolescence. Since
then, I've had several signs throughout my life that, in retrospect I can see have been
nothing more than guidelines that I planned and set for myself that would assure me I
must get to where I am now, to Ramtha.

My request to God for the next step

It was a December morning in 2005. I had just gotten out of the shower, when I found myself one more time talking out loud to myself and to God, as I had done many times before. I knew God always listened, but at that time I was unaware it was from my inside. I was feeling bored and tired of the same typical days, days that were beautiful but just seemed to go by in an instant. Some were packed with wonderful moments but others were just filled with the same old things - moving from here to there, being doubtful, great desperation in knowing there was much more to know and to live but having no clue on how to become it, hearing of Masters and Great Beings but having no idea of how I could be one; having dreams that every now and then became true, watching people out in the world just spending their lives asleep, dormant because of their past experiences and their routine, and living their lives dictated by society, who told what is good and bad and what they were supposed to do and when.

I was wondering about all of these matters and about the significance of life and death and oneself. I looked myself into the mirror, and I talked to God in absolute honesty and surrender and said something like this: "God, I know there is more to this life than this day-to-day world. I have no idea what it is, and I have no idea how to get it, but I do know that I want to know more, I want to know it all, I want to know what is beyond this, what is next. I want to see it all, and I am ready for the next step. I can't imagine what that is, but I am ready, I know I am ready and I absolutely desire it." That's all I said, and I continued with my daily life during the rest of the day.

The phone call and the first time I heard the name Ramtha

About a week later, I received a phone call from an old classmate who was inviting me to register into a Reiki class which she was going to teach. As I had always been interested in healing, I did not hesitate to join the group. I booked and went in for my first Reiki level course around the second week that January, 2006. After my lesson that day and about two weeks later, I went back for the second level, and afterwards I volunteered to give free Reiki therapies once a week. When I went in for the second time to give this therapy, I found that almost everyone who worked there had gone to a so-called Retreat of someone called Ramtha. It was kind of intriguing why everybody was gone, but that was it. This was the first time I heard Ramtha's name. I knew nothing more.

The Dream

Some days went by and then one morning, in those moments between being asleep and awake, I had a dream, a simple dream. I heard a voice, with no face, no nothing, just a deep voice, that said to me calmly: "Come," and I knew it was this Ramtha I'd heard of before; it was a sensation like the one we might have in a dream when we know who is standing next to us but we don't need to even turn around and check the face. In that moment I heard the voice, I just knew who that voice was. When I woke up, I remembered the voice so clearly that for a moment, I could not differentiate between whether it was a dream or if I had really heard it coming from someone in the room, though there appeared to be no one there. The voice kept resounding in my mind…"Come"…so I went.

The manifestation

The next time I went in to give therapy, I asked my Reiki teacher about Ramtha and this school that everyone had attended. The common first response was, "Oh, Ramtha, ok…how do I put it?" and the moment she started talking about Ramtha, I knew I must know even more. So I booked in for a Workshop that was going to be given two weekends from that day, where we were going to watch a Ramtha teaching on Creating Reality, and we were to learn from him the discipline called Consciousness and Energy.

It was Saturday and I attended the first day of the two-day workshop, and for the first time in my life I had found someone that could give a coherent explanation of Who I am, Where I come from, What I am doing here and What's next. Afterwards, many other things came to make sense altogether. Even though I've never been religious, I did believe in a loving God that was somewhere out there. So when I got to know there is no outside God to care and watch over us and our loved ones, I felt a little bit lonely, like when a child finds out there is no Santa Claus - that it was all an illusion. But that feeling was soon gone as I kept learning more about myself, my power, and the great truth I was already discovering.

At the end of the two-day workshop, we watched an introductory video for the Ramtha's School of Enlightenment, which I watched with wide-opened eyes. I felt like a child watching through the toy store window, and I just said to myself, "I must be there." Even when the labyrinth seemed to be a little bit scary, it also looked interesting. I knew I wanted to be there. This was something I've been looking for during my whole life. So I headed towards it.

Going to School

When I got home, I went into RSE's website, checked out the schedule and saw that there was a Beginner's Retreat to be held the next month in Ecuador, and another in Yelm on May 19, 2006, a couple of months later. I decided on Yelm and got started making preparations to attend.

Looking backwards to see it has always been there

I am an artist. I decided to become an artist when I was twenty-two years old, which is only a short time ago. I had always admired many painters, specifically realistic paint-ers. So one day I decided I wanted to paint and I went across the street from my house to the supermarket, where I bought what was available there, a small canvas, a little set of brushes, and some oil paints and when I came back home I started to paint. I have taught myself into this art. Always, before I started to paint, I touched my canvas a lot, making myself one with it and allowing my hands to work by themselves as the music in my studio sounds. I don't usually do a drawing before I get started. Sometimes I have a vague idea and sometimes I see the image I want to paint in the blank canvas and start painting it, directly with brush and paint, and I work on the piece as I get going. As I gained a little bit more practice in painting, which I am still working on, I discovered that I wanted to paint the human figure but show a more spiritual form of it. I started to paint things I wanted to have in my life and I loved to look at them.

About a year after I entered the School, I heard a Ramtha teaching which said something about how, for an artist, paintings are like drawing a card, which one would see and focus upon leading to manifestation. That's why realistic paintings are so wonderful. I started to connect the dots with others of my paintings, in which I had drawn elements that tell me that in my subconscious mind there has been not only the desire for a greater truth but surely I've had either previous experiences with Ramtha's teachings, or maybe had foreseen them in my future. That future is now, as I created it for this incarnation, and in some ways was expressed in my paintings as I held a memory of it. As I look backwards, I can see that this moment and my Teacher have always been there.

The Paintings and their story

When I paint, I sometimes have a vague idea or feeling of what it is I want to paint or show, but other times I just get started. I start with a blank canvas which I bless, I touch, I hug, I make myself one with my canvas. After that, I grab the color I am in the mood for in that moment, I chose the brush for no particular reason I get started.

As I get going the painting starts to come up. Generally, a painting takes days or weeks to be completed. Sometimes I just don't know what it is to be drawn next, and when that happens I take a session or as many as it takes, to sit in front of my painting and just look at it, and allow a figure to appear on my canvas. Just as one can look at the clouds and suddenly see the form of a figure, I see my figures emerging on the canvas. Sometimes I even see a little contour; other moments I just get an idea of what I want to paint next, and I keep going, allowing myself to make changes as the painting evolves.

These are five of the paintings, in which I find elements that are obvious to me, but I will let you judge for yourself.

The centerpiece of my first collection is called in Spanish "El Inicio." The original name was "La Iniciación" but for matters of ease was abbreviated. In English it would be translated as "The Beginning," but the original name would be "The Initiation" (see Fig 1).

The second painting is called "Azul," which in English means "Blue," which pictures two entities looking from the inside of a blue cave into the outside light (see Fig 2).

The third painting, which is called "Danza Luz" in Spanish (that would translate into English as "Dance Light"), was created in 2003 and shows a transparent person, working with their hands, manipulating energy (see Fig 3).

The fourth one is called "Nacimiento," which in English means "Birth," and shows a caped entity who follows a labyrinth coming from an unknown and heading to an unknown into Birth (see Fig 4).

The fifth painting, called "Vientos de Cambio," which in English would be "Winds of Change," was painted in 2001 and shows an entity who has crawled onto a couch surrounded by three flying entities that have come in through an opened window. It shows the flying curtains as the wind enters into the room. The floor is tiles and resembles a grid. (see Fig 5).

Reflection

For this time now, in chronological time, I can count almost two years of being a student at RSE, but to me it seems like I have always been here. It seems as if I have always had this knowledge. Ramtha has been the only one that I know that possesses a total understanding of the human being…way before and beyond it, our feelings and the complexity and yet the simplicity of our mind. I can only say that this school has set fertile ground for me to grow into greatness and to expand my mind beyond all that I've ever known and into the unknown, and that has changed my perspective of many things in life into evolution. There is no little change, there is no little discovery, there is no little manifestation. I have learned to love myself in a way that I had never thought of it. The journey to my Master Teacher I have greatly enjoyed. I now know I belong to the future and have always been this way. So be it!

Fig. 1 "La Iniciación" / "The Beginning"

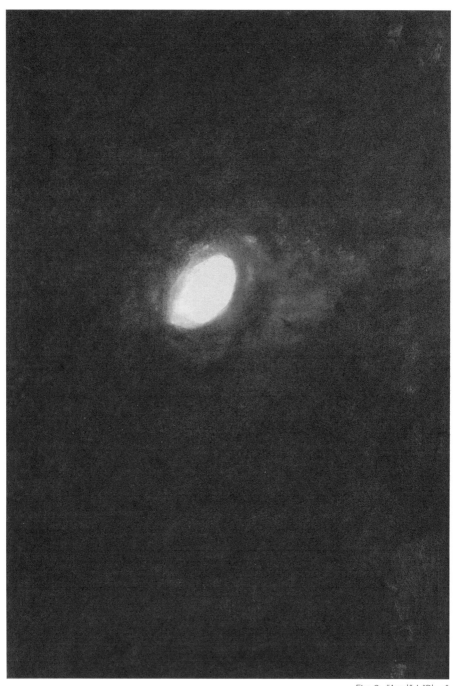

Fig. 2 "Azul" / "Blue"

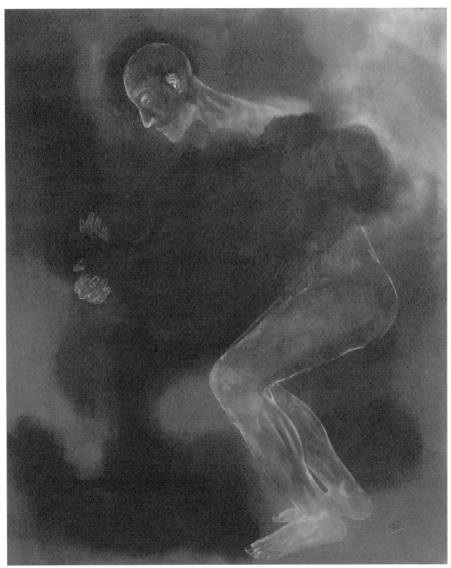

Fig. 3 "Danza Luz" / "Dance Light"

Fig. 4 "Nacimiento" / "Birth"

Fig. 5 "Vientos de Cambio" / "Winds of Change"